Islam

Wiley Blackwell Brief Histories of Religion Series

This series offers brief, accessible, and lively accounts of key topics within theology and religion. Each volume presents both academic and general readers with a selected history of topics which have had a profound effect on religious and cultural life. The word "history" is, therefore, understood in its broadest cultural and social sense. The volumes are based on serious scholarship but they are written engagingly and in terms readily understood by general readers.

Other topics in the series:

Published

Islam

History, Religion, and Politics

Third Edition

Tamara Sonn

WILEY Blackwell

This edition first published 2016
© 2016 John Wiley & Sons, Ltd

Registered Office
John Wiley & Sons, Ltd, The Atrium, Southern Gate, Chichester, West Sussex, PO19 8SQ, UK

Editorial Offices
350 Main Street, Malden, MA 02148-5020, USA
9600 Garsington Road, Oxford, OX4 2DQ, UK
The Atrium, Southern Gate, Chichester, West Sussex, PO19 8SQ, UK

For details of our global editorial offices, for customer services, and for information about how to apply for permission to reuse the copyright material in this book please see our website at www.wiley.com/wiley-blackwell.

Library of Congress Cataloging-in-Publication Data

Sonn, Tamara.
 Islam : history, religion, and politics / Tamara Sonn. – Third edition.
  pages   cm. – (Wiley Blackwell brief histories of religion)
 Includes bibliographical references and index.
 ISBN 978-1-118-97230-4 (paperback)
1. Islam–History. 2. Islam–Essence, genius, nature. I. Title.
 BP50.S65 2016
 297–dc23

                                        2015025659

A catalogue record for this book is available from the British Library.

Cover image: Interior of mosque, Casablanca, Morocco. © Maciej Tomczak/phototramp.com/ Alamy Limited

Set in 10.5/13pt Minion by SPi Global, Pondicherry, India

1   2016

To our loving family.

Contents

Foreword

Since the publication of Tamara Sonn's *A Brief History of Islam* in 2004 the babble of noises around Islam and the violence by and against Muslims has continued to grow exponentially. The daily news cycle invariably has a gruesome Muslim story—a beheading here, a suicide bomber there, a sectarian massacre in one country, and violent demonstrations in another.

The problem is *not* that there is not sufficient material on Islam; the problem is that there is *too* much. We suffer a bombardment of opinions on Islam through round-the-clock information networks, which now include social media with its Twitter, Facebook, etc. We are thus privileged to glimpse the innermost thoughts of just about everyone on the subject of Islam.

That is why we yearn to hear the calm, authoritative voice of the scholar whose task is to study history, its events and actors, the origin and development of ideas, and on the basis of reflection and analysis throw light on contemporary society. Professor Sonn is that voice.

Since her *Brief History of Islam* was published a decade ago, Sonn has consolidated her reputation as a major public intellectual, successfully balancing her scholarship with the need to explain complicated issues in clear and accessible terms. This new volume not only updates her *Brief History* but also adds substantial material to it. There is a new final chapter, "Contemporary Islam," which gives brief but detailed insights into several key Muslim nations including Turkey, Iran, Pakistan, and Indonesia. In addition there is fresh material on the Arab Spring and its consequences for the world. In the violence since the War on Terror began, Sonn points out that well more than a million lives have been lost in the main theaters of war in Afghanistan, Iraq, and Pakistan. The overwhelming numbers of those who have been killed are Muslim.

Professor Samuel Huntington of Harvard University claims in his Clash of Civilizations proposition, which was published just two decades ago, that

Islam and the West are doomed to be locked in a long-running confrontation and that has had a global impact. After 9/11, commentators looking around for an answer to the question, "Why do they hate us?" found it in the idea of the Clash of Civilizations. Huntington's notion, indeed even the phrase, was borrowed from Professor Bernard Lewis at Princeton University. The idea of a perpetual clash between Western and Islamic civilizations is a powerful one and is reflected in history if it is seen from a certain angle. But it is also reductive and simplistic in the extreme. Take an example from the earliest encounter between the West and Islam in which alliances cut across religious lines. Charlemagne, the dominant Christian ruler of Europe, allied with the Caliph in Baghdad against their common enemy, the Muslim ruler of Andalusia. Examples such as this can be found throughout history to challenge the idea of a Clash of Civilizations.

In this environment of hatred and distrust of Islam it should not come as a surprise that current polls consistently show that some half the population in the United States believes that U.S. values and those of Islam are incompatible. In the Muslim world figures reflecting hatred of the West are even higher.

In the midst of the cacophony and confusion around the subject, Sonn restores a sense of perspective and balance. At the end of the book, she reminds us that the Quran extolls the virtues of compassion, kindness, and patience by quoting Surah 2, Verse 177. At a time when so many are so genuinely confused about Islam there can be no greater service than the work of the scholars of integrity who set out to present their conclusions based on scholarship and knowledge all the while holding a steady course despite the turbulence around them. That is why Tamara Sonn's new book *Islam: History, Religion, and Politics* is essential reading for anyone wishing to make sense of the difficult times we live in.

Professor Akbar Ahmed
Ibn Khaldun Chair of Islam Studies
Washington D.C.
April 2015

Preface

As 2010 came to a close, the Arab world erupted into a series of uprisings that came to be known as the Arab Spring. Western observers, accustomed to authoritarian governments like those of Tunisia's Zine El Abidine Ben Ali, Libya's Muammar Qaddafi, and Egypt's Hosni Mubarak, were transfixed. Many commented that the uprisings were completely unpredicted. The eminent journal *Foreign Affairs* titled an entire Summer 2011 issue "Why Middle East Studies Missed the Arab Spring."

But the Arab Spring uprisings were, in fact, just the latest developments in ongoing efforts of formerly colonized peoples to establish good governance, measured in terms of economic development and human rights. Those efforts did not start with the Arab Spring and, as the overthrow of Egypt's first democratically elected leader, Muhammad Morsi, in a military coup in July 2013 demonstrated, they have not ended. Egypt is once again under an authoritarian government, and other Arab Spring uprisings—in Libya, Syria, and Yemen—have resulted in deadly civil wars. As of 2015, only Tunisia appears to have managed a successful transition to democracy. But that victory seems meager because Syria's civil war metastasized, giving rise to the group calling itself the Islamic State (IS, also known as ISIS or ISIL), with its massacres of civilians and gruesome executions of journalists and other captives.

Meanwhile, the chaos of protracted postcolonial struggles in Nigeria and Pakistan has given rise to ever more shocking levels of gang-style violence. In northern Nigeria, the shadowy group known as Boko Haram has kidnapped hundreds of children, most remaining missing as of this writing. Pakistanis, who have long endured spillover from Afghanistan's struggles between foreign and domestic forces, were horrified by an attack in December 2014 that left nearly 150 schoolchildren dead. And in January 2015, Yemen's war with the international terrorist organization al-Qaeda reached all the way to Paris, as two gunmen attacked the offices of satirical magazine *Charlie Hebdo*, killing twelve.

The levels of violence represented in these examples appear unprecedented. What is not so apparent is that the vast majority of the victims of so-called Islamic terrorism are Muslims. And the death tolls of terrorist attacks pale when compared with those in the Global War on Terror itself. The international group Physicians for Social Responsibility, with the Nobel-prize winning International Physicians for the Prevention of Nuclear War and Physicians for Global Survival, published *Body Count: Casualty Figures after 10 Years of the 'War on Terror'* in March 2015. Assessing the death toll in three target countries—Iraq, Afghanistan, and Pakistan—the report notes that the U.S.-led Multinational Force in Iraq reports the deaths of 4,804 of their soldiers in Iraq as of February 2012. In Afghanistan, the North Atlantic Treaty Organization (NATO) and U.S.-led forces report 3,485 deaths. (No death tolls for military personnel are kept for operations in Pakistan because there are officially no NATO or U.S. military personnel involved in fighting there.) The focus of the report, however, is the death toll among Iraqis, Afghans, and Pakistanis. Acknowledging the extreme difficulty of compiling such figures, the authors nonetheless estimate, conservatively, "that the war has, directly or indirectly, killed around 1 million people in Iraq, 200,000 in Afghanistan, and 80,000 in Pakistan, i.e. a total of around 1.3 million."

Headlines convey fleeting and often sanitized images of these horrors. But they cannot provide explanations of the roots of what appears to be the Muslim world's "descent into chaos"—to borrow Pakistani journalist Ahmed Rashid's apt phrase. This revised edition of *A Brief History of Islam* (2004) updates *Islam: A Brief History* (2nd edition, 2010) with developments since the Arab Spring in 2010. It focuses on Muslim majority countries' ongoing efforts to recover from colonization in the context of Cold War and post-Cold War geopolitics. Its goal is to allow readers to discern, despite the "fog of war," the major democratizing trends and recognize that the excruciating paroxysms of violence currently gripping many parts of the Muslim world are a tragic by-product of the ongoing struggle for civil, political, and human rights.

Tamara Sonn
Washington, DC
March 2015

Maps

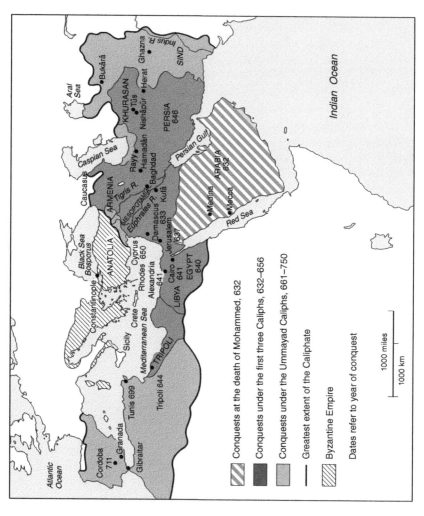

Map 1 Expansion of the Muslim world 632–750.

Source: © Richard C. Martin. Reprinted with permission of the author

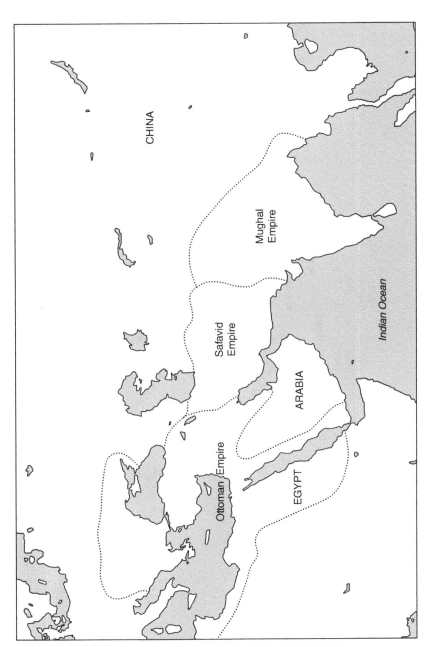

Map 2 The Muslim world in the sixteenth century.

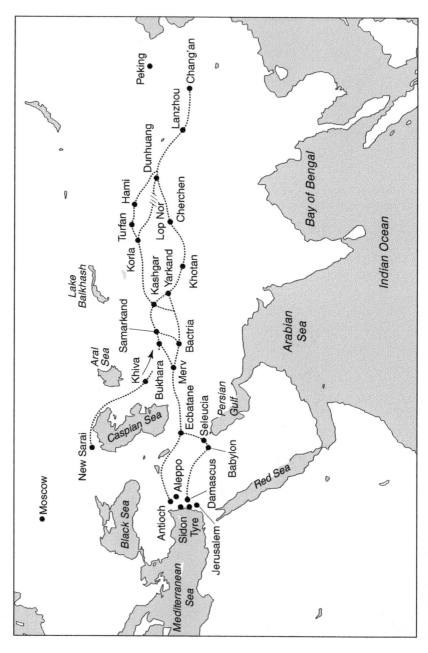

Map 3 The Silk Road.

1

Many Paths to One God: Establishing the Ideals

When Jews speak of their religion, they call it *Judaism* or the *Judaic tradition*. When Christians speak of their religious tradition, they often refer to it as *Judeo-Christianity* because Christianity was an organic outgrowth of Judaism. In the same way, Muslims refer to their religion as part of the Abrahamic or monotheistic tradition because Islam shares the history, basic beliefs, and values of Judaism and Christianity. Muslims consider Jews and Christians to be their spiritual siblings. They are among the *ahl al-kitab*, the "People of the Book" or "People of Scripture." This is the family of monotheists, those who believe in one supreme God, the creator, the sustainer, the benevolent and merciful judge of all humanity. "The Book" is revelation contained in scripture; Muslims believe all revelation came from the only God, who revealed His will to humanity repeatedly, in various times and places to different groups.

The Quran

The Quran ("Koran" is the archaic spelling) is Islamic scripture, the book containing Islamic revelation. It is in Arabic, the language of the prophet through whom it was revealed, Muhammad (d. 632 CE). The term *qur'an* means "recitation," reflecting the belief that the Quran is the word of God

Islam: History, Religion, and Politics, Third Edition. Tamara Sonn.
© 2016 John Wiley & Sons, Ltd. Published 2016 by John Wiley & Sons, Ltd.

(Allah, from the Arabic *al-ilah*: the [one] god), not the word of the prophet who delivered it. Although the Quran was revealed (or "sent down" [*munzal*, in Arabic]) in the seventh century CE, Muslims believe that it is actually timeless. As the word of God, it is co-eternal with God. Like God, it has always existed. It therefore was not created but was revealed word for word in the Arabic language at a particular time, through God's final messenger, Muhammad. The Quran says that its specific words reflect a divine archetype of revelation, which it calls "the preserved tablet" (*al-lawh al-mahfuz*, 85:22). Although anthropomorphic language (using human traits to describe God) is recognized as only symbolic in Islam, still it is not uncommon to hear the Quran described as reflecting the eternal "will" or "mind" of God. However, it is described, the Quran is considered eternal.

The term *qur'an* is sometimes interpreted as "reading," even though Prophet Muhammad is described by the Quran as unlettered or illiterate (7:157, 62:2). Rather than "reading" a message, Prophet Muhammad is described as delivering (or "reciting") a message that God had imprinted on his heart (e.g., 26:194). At one point, the Quran refers to Gabriel (Jibril) as the one "who has brought it [revelation] down upon your heart" (2:97). As a result, traditional interpreters claim that the angel Gabriel was the medium through whom Muhammad received God's revelation.

The Quran uses the term *qur'an* seventy times, sometimes generically referring to "recitation" but usually referring to "revelation." The Quran commonly refers to itself as simply "the Book" (*al-kitab*), a term used hundreds of times to refer to scripture, including the Torah and the Gospels. Muslims therefore frequently refer to the Quran as The Book. They usually use adjectives like "holy," "noble," or "glorious" to show their respect for the Quran. They annually commemorate the beginning of its revelation on the Night of Power (or Destiny [*laylat al-qadr*]), during the last ten days of Ramadan, which is the month when observant Muslims fast from sunrise until sunset.

The Quran consists of 114 chapters, called *suras* (in Arabic, *surah*; pl.: *suwar*). The verses of the chapters are called *ayat* (sing.: *ayah*). The chapters range in length from 3 to 286 verses. The first sura is short, but the remaining suras are arranged from longer to shorter (i.e., in descending order of length), rather than in chronological order.

Chapters of the Quran may be referred to by number, but each also has a name, such as "The Opening" (Sura 1), "Women" (Sura 4), and "Repentance" (Sura 9). These names were ascribed after the Quran was canonized (established in its authoritative form) and typically derive from major references in the chapters. All but one sura (Sura 9) begins with the phrase "In the name of God the Merciful and Compassionate." Twenty-nine suras are also preceded by a letter or brief series of Arabic letters, whose meaning is unclear. Some scholars believe they refer to elements within the sura itself, some believe they refer to early organizational components of the suras or served as mnemonic devices, and some believe these letters have mystical or spiritual meanings. Whatever their significance, these letters are considered to be part of the revelation itself.

People reading the Quran for the first time will notice that it often speaks in the first person ("I" or "We," used interchangeably) and may assume that this usage indicates the voice of Muhammad. But Muslims believe the Quran is revealed in the voice of God. For example, in the verse about the first night of revelation, the Quran says, "Surely We sent it [revelation] down on the Night of Power" (97:1). In this voice, the Quran frequently addresses Muhammad, instructing him to "say" or "tell" people certain things, sometimes in response to specific issues. For example, when people doubted Muhammad's role as prophet, the Quran instructs him: "Say, 'O People, indeed I am a clear warner to you. Those who believe and do good works, for them is forgiveness and generous blessing'" (22:49–50). The Quran also offers advice to Muhammad. When people accused him of being a mere poet or even a fortune-teller, the Quran says, "Do they say that you have forged [the Quran]? Say, 'If I have forged it, my crimes are my own; but I am innocent of what you do'" (11:35). The Quran also offers encouragement to Muhammad when his efforts seem futile: "Have we not opened your heart and relieved you of the burden that was breaking your back?" (94:1–3). At other times, the Quran speaks directly to the people about Muhammad. Concerning the issue of the authenticity of his message, the Quran addresses the community, saying, "The heart [of the Prophet] was not deceived. Will you then dispute with him about what he saw?" (53:11–12). Many of the Quran's verses seem to be in the voice of Muhammad, addressing the community with the word of God and referring to God in the third person. For instance, we are told, "There is no compulsion in religion. Right has been distinguished from wrong. Whoever rejects idols and believes in God has surely grasped the strongest, unbreakable bond. And God hears and knows" (2:256). But such verses are generally embedded in longer passages that begin with the divine command to "tell them" the information thus revealed.

To whom was the Quran addressed? Although its message is meant for all times and places, the Quran's immediate audience was the community of seventh-century Arabia, in which Prophet Muhammad lived. That is why the Quran explains that it is purposely revealed in the Arabic language. Interestingly, and uniquely among monotheistic scriptures, the Quran assumes both males and females among its audience, and frequently addresses the concerns of both. For example, it tells us that God is prepared to forgive and richly reward all good people, both male and female:

> Men who submit [to God] and women who submit [to God],
> Men who believe and women who believe,
> Men who obey and women who obey,
> Men who are honest and women who are honest,
> Men who are steadfast and women who are steadfast,
> Men who are humble and women who are humble,
> Men who give charity and women who give charity,
> Men who fast and women who fast,
> Men who are modest and women who are modest,
> Men and women who remember God often.
>
> (33:35)

Still, the overall audience for the scripture is humanity as a whole. The Quran refers to itself as "guidance for humanity" (*hudan li'l-nas*).

The Quran was revealed through Prophet Muhammad to the community in seventh-century Arabia over a period of twenty-two to twenty-three years, but it was recorded and canonized soon after Muhammad's death. During his lifetime, Muhammad's followers sometimes recorded his pronouncements; some even memorized and transmitted them orally. After his death, and on the deaths of some of those who memorized the Quran (*huffaz*), the Prophet's companions decided to establish a written version of the Quran so that it could be preserved and transmitted accurately to future generations. This process was begun by a close companion of Muhammad, Zayd ibn Thabit (d. 655 CE), who collected written records of Quranic verses soon after the death of the Prophet. The third successor to the Prophet (caliph), Uthman ibn Affan (d. 656 CE), is credited with commissioning Zayd and other respected scholars to establish the authoritative written version of the Quran based on the written and oral records. This was accomplished within twenty years of Muhammad's death. That text became the model from which copies were made and promulgated among various Muslim communities, and other versions are believed to have been destroyed. Because of the existence of various dialects and the lack of vowel markers in early Arabic, slight variations in the reading of the authoritative text were possible. To avoid confusion, markers indicating specific vowel sounds were introduced into the language by the end of ninth century, but seven slightly variant readings (*qira'at*), or methods of recitation, are acceptable.

Copies of the Quran were produced by hand until the modern era. The first printed version was produced in Rome in 1530; a second printed version was produced in Hamburg in 1694. The first critical edition produced in Europe was done by Gustav Flügel in 1834. The numbering of the verses varies slightly between the standard 1925 Egyptian edition favored by many Muslim scholars and the 1834 edition established by Flügel, used by many Western scholars. (Editions from Pakistan and India often follow the Egyptian standard edition, with the exception that they count the opening phrase, "In the name of God, the Merciful, the Compassionate," of each sura as the first verse.) The variations in verse numbering comprise only a few verses and reflect differing interpretations of where certain verses end.

The Quran is considered to be authentic only in Arabic. Even non-Arabic speakers—the vast majority of Muslims—pray in Arabic. Although Arabs comprise less than one-third of the world's Muslim population, the Arabic language still serves as a symbol of unity throughout the Muslim world. Nevertheless, numerous translations of the Quran have been produced. The first Latin translation was done in the twelfth century, commissioned by Peter the Venerable, abbot of the monastery of Cluny in France. It was published in Switzerland in the sixteenth century. Translations (or, more accurately, "interpretations" of the Quran) are now readily available in virtually all written languages and on the Internet. Still, Quranic calligraphy remains not only the highest form of visual art but a spiritual exercise. Beautifully hand-wrought copies of Quranic verses adorn many Muslim homes—in ink on paper, stitched into fabric, or carved into wood, metal or stone. It is also common for Muslims to wear verses of the Quran in lockets or on necklaces. And each year during the pilgrimage season, a special cloth embroidered in gold with Quranic verses is created to drape the Kaaba (the sanctuary in Mecca which is the object of the annual Islamic pilgrimage, the *hajj*).

Many pious Muslims maintain belief in the miraculous power of the words of the Quran itself. Carrying a small replica of Quranic verses is popularly believed to offer protection against illness or accident. Yet by far the most popular way to experience the Quran is by listening to it. The art of Quranic recitation (*tajwid*) is highly developed and extremely demanding. A student must memorize the Quran, in any of the seven pronunciation and intonation patterns (*qira'at*) mentioned previously, understand its meaning (even if one is not an Arabic speaker), and observe a number of rules dealing with spiritual attitudes (such as humility), purity, and posture (such as facing the direction of Mecca, if possible). So important is the experience of hearing the Quran properly and reverently recited that learning Quran recitation is traditionally considered a communal obligation (meaning that not everyone in a given community is required to learn Quran recitation, but enough people must do so to ensure that there are sufficient Quran reciters to serve the community).

Gifted Quran reciters are highly respected throughout the Muslim world. In recent years, a number of women have joined the ranks of popular Quran reciters. But even Muslims who are not able to recite the Quran demonstrate their respect for the Book by making sure they are in a state of spiritual purity when they handle it. As in Orthodox Judaism, blood and other bodily fluids are believed to be agents of impurity in Islam. Therefore, the passing of any bodily fluids requires that Muslims wash before touching a copy of the Quran. Thus, for example, women who are menstruating are traditionally not allowed to touch a copy of the Quran.

Most importantly, the Quran is the focal point of all Islamic belief and practice. It is the miracle of Islam. Unlike Jesus, who according to the Quran performed many miracles, Prophet Muhammad brought no other miracle besides the Quran. And although Muslims are utterly devoted to Prophet Muhammad, frequently express their love for him, and consider him eminently worthy of emulation, Muhammad does not occupy the position in Islam that Jesus occupies in Christianity. The Quran does. The Quran tells us that when people asked Muhammad to demonstrate the authenticity of his prophecy by performing miracles as other prophets had done, he simply and reverently referred to the Quran. The exquisite beauty of its language and wisdom of its sublime message are considered beyond compare and impossible to imitate. This belief is conveyed in the doctrine of the "inimitability" of the Quran (*i'jaz*). Thus, whereas Christians consider Jesus' life as miraculous and the basis of their religion, Muslims consider the Quran to be the cornerstone of Islam. Muslims are required to pray five times daily: at sunrise, midday, afternoon, sunset, evening. At each of these times, verses of the Quran are recited in a specified order and number of repetitions (ranging from twice at morning prayer to four times at evening prayer). Extra prayers may be added individually but, again, they are based on the Quran. The weekly congregational prayer (at midday on Fridays) follows the same pattern, although it includes a sermon (*khutbah*), often based upon a Quranic theme. As well, devout Muslims read the entire Quran during the holy month of fasting, Ramadan. The book is divided into thirty sections for this purpose.

The Quran and Other Scriptures

The Quran contains numerous references to prior monotheistic scriptures, which it identifies as the Torah, the Psalms, and the Gospels. Muslims believe that the Quran reiterates, confirms, and completes these previous scriptures, calling on all people to remember and respect the truths carried in them. Indeed, it assumes people are familiar with those texts. It therefore does not recount their historic narratives. Instead, it uses characters and events familiar to Jews and Christians to make specific moral or theological points. As a result, although references to Adam, Noah, Abraham, Isaac, Ishmael, Jacob, Moses, and Jesus, for example, appear frequently, they are not arranged in chronological order.

The Quran refers to its religion as *al-din*, the monotheistic tradition that began with the covenant between God and humanity marked by the obedience of Abraham. (Interestingly, the term *din*, often translated as "religion," actually means "judgment"; the Quran calls the Last Day, for example, the *yom al-din*, "day of judgment." The term is related to "obligation," "debt," and "law," as it is in Hebrew.) Adam is actually considered the first prophet because through the story of Adam and his wife in the garden— the same story revealed to Jews and Christians—humanity began to learn that God created us with a purpose. Fulfilling that purpose requires obedience to the divine will, and disobedience will bring suffering and punishment. But Abraham is the first major prophet, given the profound impact of his message.

The story of Abraham is familiar to all monotheists. He was an aged Iraqi shepherd who had longed for a child for years. God chose to favor Abraham with a child, but then asked him to demonstrate his obedience by killing his beloved son. At the last minute, God spared the child, but Abraham's willingness to sacrifice his son rather than disobey the command of God sealed the agreement between God and humanity. God promises eternal reward to all who submit to the will of God; "one who submits" to the will of God is a *muslim*. Likewise, God promised punishment for willful disobedience. One of the disagreements between Muslims and Jews concerns the identity of the son Abraham was willing to sacrifice. Although the

Quran does not state it explicitly, Muslims believe that Abraham intended to sacrifice his son Ishmael (Ismail), rather than Isaac (Ishaq), and that Muslims are thus spiritual descendants of Abraham through Ishmael and his mother Hagar (Hajar).

As well, according to Islamic teaching, Abraham's act was personal; its reward was not bequeathed to successive generations. The patriarch serves as a model for others to follow, but each individual must earn his or her own reward from God by likewise submitting to the divine will:

> Those to whom We gave the Book
> and who follow it accurately,
> they believe in it; and whoever disbelieves in it,
>   they are the losers.
> Children of Israel, remember My blessing
> with which I blessed you, and that I
> have preferred you above all others;
> and fear a day when no soul shall substitute
> for another, and no ransom
> will be accepted from it, nor any
> intercession will help it,
>   and they will not be assisted.
> And when his Lord tested Abraham
> with certain words, and he fulfilled them.
> He said, "I make you a leader
> for the people." He said, "And what of my progeny?"
> He said, "My covenant does not extend to oppressors."
>   (2:121–124)

In other words, it is not the group one belongs to that determines salvation; the Quran says that it is demonstrating submission (*islam*) to the will of God through good deeds that brings reward. Nevertheless, Muslims agree that Abraham's willingness to sacrifice his son was of utmost importance; in thus demonstrating his commitment to the will of God he established the foundational covenant between God and those who believe in Him. Jews and Muslims are both descendants of Abraham and heirs to that covenant.

Through another great messenger of God, Moses (Musa), the Torah was revealed. Mentioning the Torah eighteen times, the Quran reminds believers that its guidance continues to be valid. The Quran actually describes itself as "confirming the truth of the Torah that is before me" (3:50) and calls on believers to "bring the Torah now, and recite it" (3:93).

Believers are expected to be honest, charitable, care for the needy, fast, obey dietary regulations, and overall to honor God and respect His creation, just as the Torah instructed.

The last great messenger before Muhammad was Jesus ('Issa). Mentioned twenty-five times in the Quran, Jesus is called the Messiah (although the meaning of that term is not made clear), the son of a virgin, and one who brought great signs from God. His message, the Gospel, is confirmed and described as consistent with the messages of all prophets. Speaking through Muhammad, the Quran says that God is sending the same religion (*din*) that He sent through Noah, Abraham, Moses, and Jesus, saying: "Establish [true] religion [*din*] and do not be divided about it" (42:13). But the Quran does assert that those who believe that Jesus is divine, the son of God, and part of a divine trinity, are mistaken:

> O People of Scripture, do not exaggerate your religion or say anything about God but the truth. The Messiah, Jesus son of Mary, was only a messenger of God, and His word which He sent to Mary, and a spirit from Him. So believe in God and His messenger and do not say "Three" ... God is only one. (4:171)

Still, like the messages of the other prophets, Jesus' message is true, according to the Quran, and the Jews were mistaken to reject it.

Muhammad is presented as the last in the succession of prophets sent by God to reveal the divine will: "And when Moses said to his people, 'O my people, why do you hurt me, though you know I am the messenger of God to you?' ... And when Jesus, son of Mary, said, 'Children of Israel, I am indeed the messenger of God to you, confirming the Torah that is before me, and giving good tidings of a messenger who shall come after me, whose name shall be Ahmad'; then when he brought them clear signs, they said, 'This is sheer sorcery'" (61:5–6). ("Amhad" is a variation on the name Muhammad and refers to Prophet Muhammad in this passage. Muslims believe that the prediction of the coming of Muhammad was deleted from or misinterpreted in Christian scriptures, for example, John 16:6–15.)

Thus, although this monotheistic religion had been accurately revealed before the time of Muhammad, the Quran says that the communities that received those scriptures had become confused about it (42:14). Whether through ignorance or by deliberately distorting the message, many Jews and Christians had fallen into disagreement, each claiming to have the truth. Indeed, the Quran chastises both Jews and Christians for their mutual rejection. "The Jews say the Christians have nothing to stand on, and the

Christians say the Jews have nothing to stand on, while they both recite the same Scripture" (Quran 2:113). It is God who will decide on all people's fate, on the Day of Judgment, when all deeds will be weighed in the scale of justice. Those who have demonstrated their true belief through good deeds "have nothing to fear, nor shall they grieve" (2:112).

The Quran advises that if Jews and Christians understood their scriptures properly, there would be no dispute and, what is more, they would recognize that the Quran truly confirms what had been revealed before. "This is a blessed Scripture We have revealed, confirming that which was before it ... " (6:92). "This Quran narrates to the children of Israel most of what they disagree about. It is a guide and a merciful gift for believers" (27:76–77).

Again, the continuity of the monotheistic tradition is asserted. The Quran also refers to prophets unknown to Jews and Christians. For example, there is a sura named for an Arab messenger, Hud (Sura 11), who warned his community to follow God, but they rejected him. The same community then rejected another messenger, Salih, and they were punished with tragedy. Similarly, the Quran relates the story of the Midianites, who were done away with when they rejected their messenger Shuaib. The point of these stories, like that of the people of Lot, is that people reject the message of God at their own peril. The Quran mentions more than twenty prophets or messengers between Adam and Muhammad and notes that "there is no distinction among prophets" (2:136; 3:84), referring to consistent truth of all their messages.

In fact, the Quran states that every nation has been sent a messenger from God. ("Every nation has its Messenger" [10:47]; see also 16:36: "We sent forth among every nation a Messenger," and cf. 16:63 and 35:24.) The Quran does note that some prophets excel others (2:253), generally assumed to refer to those who left laws or texts, or whose historical impact was greater than that of others. But the message is always essentially the same: God rewards those who do His will and punishes those who do not. The Quran informs its audience that Muhammad's revelation is an integral part of the same tradition:

> He has laid down for you as religion
> what He charged Noah with, and what
> We have revealed to you, and what We
> charged Abraham with, Moses and Jesus:
> Practice the religion, and do not separate
> over it.
>
> (42:13)

The Quran calls on believers to recognize the religion of Abraham, clearly positioning itself as revelation in the same tradition:

> And they say, "Be Jews or Christians and
> you shall be guided." Say: "No, rather
> the religion of Abraham, a true believer;
>   he was no idolater."
> Say: "We believe in God, and
> in what has been revealed to us
> and revealed to Abraham, Ishmael,
> Isaac and Jacob, and the Tribes,
> and what was given to Moses and Jesus
> and the Prophets from their Lord; we
> make no division between any of them, and
>   to Him we surrender."
>   (2:135–136; cf. 26:196–197)

The Quran then confirms that it is the final clarification of the message. Those who accept the message brought by Muhammad are called "the best community brought forth to people, enjoining good and forbidding evil, and believing in God" (3:110). The "People of the Book"—those who have received the previous scriptures—will suffer for rejecting true prophets. "Some of them are believers," the Quran claims, "but most of them are sinful" (3:110). The Quran is the perfect expression of the divine will; no other is necessary. As the Quran puts it in a verse delivered toward the end of Muhammad's career: "Today I have perfected your religion for you, and I have completed my blessing upon you and approved submission [*al-islam*] as your religion. Whoever is forced by hunger to sin … God is forgiving, merciful" (5:3). Therefore, the succession of prophets ends with Muhammad. The Quran calls him the "seal of the prophets" (33:40).

Thus, the Quran reiterates, confirms, and completes Jewish and Christian scriptures. It does not try to establish a new religion but rather to inspire people to new commitment to the one true religion of monotheism. The term *islam* is used only eight times in the Quran, and it is referred to as the true religion. But in the Quran the term means the act of submitting to the divine will, rather than an organized religious group separate from other monotheistic traditions. By contrast, the term *din*, meaning the true religion revealed by the one God at various times throughout human history, is used more than ninety times. Muslims believe that although the Quran corrects some misinterpretations of previous scriptures, overall it focuses on inspiring Jews, Christians, and Muslims to work together toward their shared goal of justice and, in so doing, to achieve eternal reward: "People of the Book, come together in agreement on a word, that we worship only God" (3:64).

Themes of the Quran

Because the Quran teaches that God has sent revelation to all communities, and that revelation includes specific rituals and laws, Muslims do not find it surprising that communities differ in their perceptions and practices. The Quran also says that if God had wanted all people to be the same, He would have made them that way. "For each of you We have established a law and a way. And if God had willed it, He would have made you one people. But [you were made as you are] to test you by what He has given you…." The differences among religions are therefore believed to be part of the divine plan. The Quran invites all people to participate with Muslims in the struggle to do the will of God. In its words, "So compete with one another in good deeds" (5:48).

Solidarity among individuals and communities in doing the will of God is therefore among the themes of the Quran. And the Quran does provide specific regulations for its own community, the Muslims, including purity, prayer, charity, fasting and dietary regulations, and pilgrimage. But the majority of Quranic verses deal with overarching themes and moral guidance, rather than specific regulations. As noted previously, the Quran refers to itself, as well as to the Torah and the Gospels, as "guidance for humanity" (e.g., 3:4). That guidance is expressed through a number of interrelated themes.

The fundamental theme of the Quran is monotheism: *tawhid.* Derived from the Arabic term for "one," tawhid does not appear as such in the Quran (although other forms of the term do), but it conveys the rich complexity of the Quran's insistence on the oneness of God. It entails first of all that there is only one God, the god (*al-ilah*), Allah. None of the deities worshiped by the Meccans is actually divine, the Quran asserts. They can be of little help to human beings. God has no partners. Placing others in His stead or "associating" (*shirk*) partners with God is bound to lead to failure in the human quest for happiness. Further, God is unitary: without parts. The Quran insists, as noted previously, that God is not part of a Trinity, as the Christians believe (see 4:171, 5:73). The notion of *tawhid* goes beyond simple monotheism, however, particularly in the view of modern Islamic thinkers. Just as there is only one God, there is only one creator of all human beings, one provider, protector, guide, and judge of all human beings. All human beings are equal in their utter dependence on God, and their well-being depends on their acknowledging that fact and living accordingly. This acknowledgment is both the will and the law of God. Modern Islamic commentators such as the Egyptian Muhammad Abduh (d. 1905), Muslim Brotherhood ideologue Sayyid Qutb (d. 1966), and revolutionary Iranian leader Ayatollah Khomeini (d. 1989) stress, therefore, that tawhid implies that we must order society in accordance with the will of God. A tawhid-based society is one in which people devote themselves to serving God by contributing to a society that reflects and safeguards the dignity and equality in which all were created. Submission (islam) to that will is the route to our happiness, both in this life and the hereafter.

The Quran presents detailed discussions of the major characteristics of a tawhid-based society, and chief among them is mercy or compassion, another major theme. Although the Quran frequently warns of punishment for those who violate the will of God and describes vividly the scourges of hell, its overriding emphasis is on divine mercy. "The Merciful" (*al-rahman*) is one of the most frequently invoked names of God, equivalent to Allah. As mentioned, all but one sura of the Quran begins by invoking the name of God "the merciful and compassionate." Divine mercy is often paired with divine forgiveness. "God is forgiving and merciful" is a common refrain. At times, especially in the early suras, the Quran sternly warns people that they ignore its message at their own risk: "Woe to the slanderer and backbiter, who collects wealth and counts it continually. He thinks his wealth will bring him eternal life, but no, he will certainly be thrown into hell" (104:1–6). "Have you seen the one who makes a mockery of faith? He is the one who mistreats orphans, and does not encourage feeding the poor. Woe to those who pray but are heedless of their prayer. They are seen [praying] but [then] do not give charity" (107:1–7).

The Quran balances these warnings with sympathy for the weaknesses of human nature: "Indeed, the human being is born impatient. When evil touches him he is anxiety-ridden, and when good things happen to him, grudging" (70:19–21). In this context it offers advice and encouragement: "As for the human being, when God tests him and honors him and blesses him, he says, 'My Lord has favored me.' But when God tests him and restricts his livelihood, he says, 'My Lord has forsaken me.' No; you do not honor orphans or work for the wellbeing of the poor, you take over [others'] inheritance and are overly attached to wealth" (89:15–20).

[W]hen you are aboard ships and they sail with a fair breeze and [those on board] are happy about it, then a violent wind overtakes them and the waves come from every side and they think they are drowning, then call upon God, practicing religion properly [and saying that] if you spare us from this we will be indeed grateful. But when He has rescued them, indeed they begin oppression on earth. O People, your oppression will only hurt yourselves! (10:22–23)

Given this understanding of human nature, the Quran repeatedly reassures people that God is merciful and compassionate. "My mercy encompasses everything" (7:156). "On the day when every soul is confronted with what it has done, good and evil, they will desire a great distance from [evil]. God asks you to beware; God is full of pity for servants. Say: If you love God, follow me; God will love you and forgive you your sins. God is forgiving, merciful" (3:30–31).

Thus, the Quran sets an example for people to emulate in their efforts to establish a just society. Variations on the phrases "be compassionate" or "show mercy" (*rahma*) occur hundreds of times in the Quran. People are told to be kind and cherish their parents (19:14; 19:32), and even to ask forgiveness from God for them if they make mistakes (60:4). Even though the people of Mecca initially rejected Prophet Muhammad and his followers and persecuted and evicted them from their homes, the believers are told that they should show kindness and justice toward those Meccans who did not participate in the aggression. But the Quran places particular emphasis on compassion for the most vulnerable members of society. It mentions orphans often, calling for their care and protection. Their well-being is routinely mentioned as the measure of the piety of both individuals and society. For example, the Quran instructs Muhammad to tell people when they ask about orphans: "Improvement [of their welfare] is great goodness" (2:220).

> Righteous is the one who
> believes in God and the Last Day,
> the angels, Scripture, and the prophets;
> gives wealth, however cherished,
>   to relatives and orphans,
> the needy, travelers, beggars,
>   and for freeing slaves;
> and prays and gives zakat.
> And those who fulfill their promises,
>   ... and are patient in
> misfortune, hardship and peril–

these are the ones who are sincere;
these are the righteous ones.
(2:177)

Interestingly, the Quran's permission for polygyny (multiple wives) is made in the context of concern for orphans. In a sura titled "Women" (Sura 4), people are told to protect the rights of orphans for whom they are responsible—if necessary, by marrying them. In seventh-century Arabia, a society plagued by warfare and poverty, there were many orphans. Female orphans were particularly at risk because this was not a society in which women had economic independence. Unless they inherited wealth women were entirely dependent on men. Because of the brutality of that society toward women, female infanticide was common. People killed their baby girls, fearing they would not be able to provide for them and that they would be subjected to the whims of those who had no respect for women. Out of concern for the protection of women, the Quran forbids female infanticide. It also rebukes men who are ashamed when a daughter, rather than a son, is born. On a practical level, it requires that females be given inheritance shares (4:7) and that the traditional dowry required at weddings be given as a gift to the bride (4:4), rather than to the bride's parents as a "bride price." The Quran also insists that men and women both are entitled to whatever wages they earn. With regard to the orphans in Medinan society, the Quran tells men to treat them fairly, and if they are afraid that orphans are not being treated fairly, that they may protect them by marrying up to four, but only if they can treat them all impartially. If they do not feel they can avoid slighting one of their wives, then they should only marry one (4:3). Although the focus of this verse is compassion for the weak and equity for women, traditional interpreters conclude that it simply allows men to marry four wives at a time. Modern interpreters tend to return to the focus of justice and incorporate the Quran's high ideals for mutually satisfactory spousal relationships when discussing marriage. The Quran says that spouses were created by God to find comfort in one another and to be bound by "love and kindness" (30:21). As a result, many modern interpreters believe the Quran advocates monogamy except under extraordinary circumstances (for example, those in seventh-century Arabia). They believe that the Quran's emphasis on human equality implies that they should work to establish societies in which polygyny is not necessary to protect women.

Similarly, the Quran also acknowledges the institution of slavery but says that moral superiority lies in freeing slaves, as well as in feeding the hungry and orphans (90:13–17). Freeing slaves and feeding the hungry are enjoined as ways of making up for sins (5:89).

Another group for whom the Quran shows special concern is debtors. Charity is to be used to help debtors, and people are supposed to pardon debts owed to them as an act of charity. The Quran is particularly concerned with abolishing usury, which was common in seventh-century Arabia. Pre-Islamic records indicate that interest rates were exorbitant. The Quran therefore forbids usury, stating that usurers "will dwell in fire for eternity" (2:275).

So important is concern for the poor that the Quran warns those who pray but then "are heedless of their prayers," and those who pray but then "mistreat orphans and do not encourage feeding the poor." These people, says the Quran, make a mockery of their faith (107:1–7). Praying and performing other rituals, according to the Quran, are obligatory not because they please God in themselves; they are meant to keep people focused on their reason for existing in the first place and motivated to work toward the fulfillment of God's will in all spheres of life. The Quran says, for example, that the meat that people sacrifice does not reach God; it is for the benefit of believers that rituals are performed: "Their flesh does not reach God nor their blood, but your righteousness reaches God" (22:37). Similarly, sin does not hurt God; it hurts the sinners and their communities: "Muhammad is only a messenger, like those who have passed away before him. When he dies or is killed, will you reject [his message]? Those who do so do not hurt God; God will reward the grateful" (3:144). What is important is not the ritual of prayer or sacrifice itself, but the virtuous life and good deeds it encourages:

> A kind word with forgiveness is better than almsgiving followed by injury. God is absolute and forgiving. O believers, do not make your charity worthless through insult and injury, like the person who gives of his wealth only for show but does not believe in God and the Last Day. (2:263–264)

In the same context, charity is also extremely important in the Quranic perspective. "Surely God rewards the charitable," we are told when the story of Joseph is being recounted (12:88). Charity is often described as a means of making up for offenses. The Quran maintains the biblical ethic of retaliation, a standard means of maintaining order in societies lacking legal enforcement institutions, but it says that forgoing retaliation as an act of charity will help make up for sins (5:45). Charity is also prescribed as a means of self-purification (9:103). All Muslims are required to give charity according to Islamic law. The term used for this kind of charity (*zakah* or *zakat*) actually means "purification." The idea is that wealth is a good thing, as long as it is used for good purposes like helping the needy and "those whose hearts are to be reconciled," and freeing slaves and debtors (9:60).

Overall, the society envisioned by the Quran is characterized by justice: "O Believers, be steadfast [for] God, giving testimony in justice, and do not let a people's hatred cause you to act without justice. Be just, that is nearer to righteousness" (5:8). "Believers, establish justice, being witnesses for God, even if it [works] against yourselves or against your parents or relatives; regardless of whether [those involved are] rich or poor, God has priority for you" (4:135). Thus, the profile of a *muslim* (or *muslima*, the feminine form), "one who submits to the will of God," is integrally linked to the theme of justice. Indeed, the Quran says repeatedly that God has not only called for justice (e.g., 7:29) but that "God loves the just" (5:42, 49:9, 60:8).

A society characterized by justice, wherein the well-being of the entire group is measured in terms of the well-being of its most vulnerable members, is the external manifestation of *islam*. The internal manifestation may be found in a set of virtues that form the Islamic conscience. Muslims are expected to be guided by the will of God in every encounter, every decision, and every action. They are called to live their lives guided by *taqwa*, a term whose common English translation as "fear of God" or "righteousness" does not do it justice. It is a more comprehensive term, indicating the characteristics of a well-formed conscience, an internalized morality, or simply "God-consciousness." The Quran gives guidance on some specific matters, often describing a particular choice as "closer to *taqwa*" or "approximating *taqwa*." For example, in response to questions about divorce before consummation of a marriage, men are told that they should provide support for the divorced bride fairly, in accordance with their means, even if it is not required by the marriage agreement. That is called "closer to *taqwa*" (2:237). Likewise, believers are told that they must never let hatred for a people lead to unjust behavior. "Act justly, that is nearer to *taqwa*" (5:8). In general, people are told to help one another in the effort to achieve taqwa (5:2) and to "conspire for virtue and *taqwa*" (58:9; see Chapter 2, "Spirituality," for further discussion of taqwa). Thus, along with *iman* (belief in God) and *islam* (submission to the will of God), taqwa is one of Islam's quintessential virtues. Belief in God is considered essential for human beings to be able to overcome their innate insecurities and selfishness. It is also considered natural, an inborn instinct to recognize the existence and supremacy of God. Submission to the will of God is believed to be the proper response to recognition of God, indeed the only possible response. True recognition of God inevitably results in taqwa, a conscience guided by God and the best interests of humanity.

Similarly, Muslims are called on to be a "median" or "moderate community" (*ummat al-wasit*), a balance between extremes, "so that you may be witnesses to the people" (2:143). In yet another refrain of the Quran, believers are told that they are the best of communities in that they "enjoin honorable actions and forbid the objectionable" (*amr bi'l-ma'ruf wa nahiy 'an al-munkar*, 3:110; see also 3:104, 3:114, 7:157, 9:67, 9:71, 9:112, 22:41, 31:17).

Through these themes and some specific legislation, the Quran guides humanity. But it does not regulate all human activity. In many cases, it takes the realities of its historic context into consideration, establishes goals, and challenges humanity to achieve them. For example, as indicated previously, the Quran provides a significant amount of legislation concerning the treatment of slaves. It allows the common practice of concubinage, but demands that slave women not be forced into sexual relations (24:33). The Quran acknowledges that slaves do not have the same legal standing as free people; instead, they are treated as minors for whom the owners are responsible. But it recommends that unmarried Muslims marry their slaves (24:32), indicating that it considers slaves and free people morally equal. It also instructs Muslims to allow their slaves to buy their freedom, and even to help them pay for it if possible (24:33). The Quran clearly recognizes that slavery is a source of inequity in society because it frequently recommends freeing slaves, along with feeding and clothing the poor, as part of living a moral life (90:12–18) and a way to make up for offenses (5:89, 58:3). Yet despite its overall emphasis on human dignity and equality, the Quran does not abolish the institution of slavery. As in the days of the Hebrew Bible, slavery was an integral part of the economic system at the time the Quran was revealed; abolition of slavery would have required an overhaul of the entire socioeconomic system. Therefore, instead of abolishing slavery outright, virtually all interpreters agree that the Quran established an ideal toward which society should work: a society in which no one person would be enslaved to another. Therefore, although slavery is permitted in the Quran, it is now banned in Muslim countries.

The principle demonstrated in this example is that there is a distinction between the reality of legal slavery in the Quran, and the moral recommendations concerning slavery. The former is considered a contingent circumstance, able to be changed. The latter reflects the eternal model of human dignity. At the time of the early Muslim community, the immediate emancipation of all slaves would have caused economic chaos, which obviously would not have been conducive to Islamic goals of well-being for all people. But the ideals toward which the community should strive were clearly set forth in this case. Applying the ideals in the modern world requires the abolition of slavery, a goal that has largely been achieved in the Muslim world.

But there is disagreement among Muslims about some other issues in the Quran. For example, in the context of concern for debtors, the Quran allows people to lend money but not to charge usurious interest rates, and when they lend money they must record the amount so that no disagreements will arise. The Quran says that the parties involved in the transaction should get someone to write it down fairly. It specifies that the debtor (or the debtor's guardian, in case the debtor is incapable) is to dictate to the scribe and that he must disclose the full amount of the debt. The Quran then specifies that the transaction must also be witnessed by two men, or by one man and two women in case two men are not available (2:282). All this care is taken to avoid inequity in lending practices. But another question arises concerning the specification that two women's evidence is required to substitute for one man's testimony. Does this verse imply that women will always be unfamiliar with the details of finance and that therefore their testimony on financial issues is always in need of verification? Or does it mean that women's testimony on any issue in general would always need verification? Or does it mean that the testimony of anyone who is uneducated needs corroboration, and that the verse is simply using women as an example, so that the testimony of educated women should actually be considered reliable? Traditional interpreters derive from this verse that women's testimony in court is worth only half that of men. Modern thinkers believe the requirement for two women in place of one man pertains only to circumstances, like those of seventh-century Arabia, in which most women were uneducated and unfamiliar with business transactions. They believe the Quran's essential egalitarianism indicates that the economic skill of women in the Quran's discussion of lending practices is simply an example, not an eternal ideal.

As these examples demonstrate, there is no single formula for achieving justice, but the Quran establishes the standard of human dignity and provides guidance in the struggle to uphold that dignity in ever-changing circumstances. And it informs human beings that the effort to establish justice is the basis on which they will be judged. Those who "believe and do good works," the Quran states repeatedly, will have nothing to fear in the afterlife; they will be richly rewarded. "Believers, bow down and prostrate yourselves in prayer and worship your Lord and do good deeds, and you will prosper. And struggle for God as you should struggle" (22:77–78). This struggle "on the path of God" (*fi sabil Allah*), as the Quran often puts it, is the root meaning of the term *jihad*. Indeed, the Quran presents a challenge to humanity. Using Prophet Muhammad as the model and remembering the forgiveness and mercy of God, people must strive to create a just society. As in the case of previous societies described by the Quran, communities as a whole will be judged in history; God does not allow oppressive societies to flourish indefinitely. But individuals will be judged in the afterlife, based on whether or not they have attempted to contribute to this effort:

> To God belongs whatever is in the heavens and earth. He forgives whom He
>   will and punishes whom He will. God is forgiving, merciful.
> Believers, do not consume usury, doubling and redoubling [the amount].
>   Do your duty to God and you will be successful.
> Protect yourselves from the fire prepared for disbelievers.
> And obey God and the messenger, and you will find mercy.
> And compete with one another for forgiveness from your Lord, and for
>   paradise as great as the heavens and earth, prepared for the righteous.
> Those who [are generous] in [times of] prosperity and adversity, and
>   those who control their anger and who pardon others; God loves
>   those who do good;
> and those who, when they commit an offense or wrong themselves,
>   remember God and beg forgiveness for their sins – and who can forgive
>   sins except God?—and who do not repeat knowingly what they have done;
> these are the ones whose reward from their Lord is forgiveness and
>   gardens with rivers flowing beneath, where they will abide, a great
>   reward for those who work.
> There have been ages before you, so travel the earth and see what was the
>   end of those who disbelieve.
> This is a clear sign for people and guidance and a warning to the righteous.
> Do not give up or grieve, and you will certainly prosper if you are believers ...
> And God will make clear those who believe and blot out the disbelievers.
> Do you think that you will enter heaven without God recognizing those of
>   you who struggle and those who are steadfast?
>
>   (3:129–142)

The Exemplary Life of Muhammad, Prophet of Islam: The Sunna

The Quran thus presents human beings with a formidable challenge. It requires not simply following laws concerning prayer, charity, fasting, pilgrimage, proper diet, and cleanliness. Those rules have been clearly established in revelation and are not subject to change. But the struggle to put the Quran's comprehensive guidance into practice—to be steadfast in faith, honest, sincere, just, merciful, and charitable—requires ongoing effort in diverse and dynamic circumstances. Muslims look to the life of Prophet Muhammad as an inspiring example of how to follow Quranic guidance in all circumstances, no matter how conditions change.

Muhammad was born in poverty in sixth-century Mecca, Arabia, modern-day Saudi Arabia. Most people, including Muhammad's father, worked in the caravan trade for the ruling family of Mecca, the Quraysh. Muhammad's father died before Muhammad was born, and his mother died when he was around six years old. He was taken in by family members, first his grandfather and then his uncle, and entered the caravan trade business as a young man. Even before his call to prophecy, at around age forty, Muhammad achieved success in business and a widespread reputation for honesty and fairness. On accepting the call to prophecy, he devoted himself entirely to the service of God.

At the beginning of his career as a prophet Muhammad had only a small group of followers. They were persecuted by the wealthy rulers of Mecca, who felt threatened by his call for worship of the only God and an end to social injustice. Muhammad and his small community were driven from their homes, forced to live in separate quarters on the outskirts of town, and boycotted. Yet they persevered in their commitment to follow the guidance of God. They were instructed to suffer injustice with dignity. "Call them to the way of your Lord with wisdom and good arguments and reason with them [offering] a better way … If you punish them, do so in the same measure as you were punished. But if you endure patiently, it is better for [you]" (16:125–126).

Despite persecution, Muhammad continued to warn people of the dire consequences of ignoring God's will. He reminded people that God's will is for a just society, one that reflects the equality all people share in the eyes of their Creator. His message was extremely attractive, and he quickly gained a significant following in Mecca and beyond. Muhammad's reputation as a wise and just arbitrator reached Yathrib (some two hundred miles north of

Mecca), a town that had been suffering under intertribal warfare for years. Delegates from Yathrib invited Muhammad to move to their town, promising to abide by his guidance in return for his settling their disputes.

After some hesitation Muhammad accepted the invitation and, with his followers, moved to Yathrib in the year 622 CE. This event begins the Islamic calendar (called the *Hijra* calendar, to commemorate the "emigration" from Mecca to Yathrib) because it marks a profound shift in the fate of the Muslim community. In Medina, the new name of Yathrib (its full name became "City of the Prophet," *madinat al-nabi*, anglicized as Medina), the Muslims became an autonomous community, able to establish the religious practice and social vision revealed by God through Prophet Muhammad. They were able to create a community guided by the Quran's view of human dignity and compassion for the weak.

As the new community of the Prophet grew and its strength increased, so did the Meccans' hostility toward it. When the Meccans tried to destroy the Muslims in Medina by confiscating their properties and attacking their families back in Mecca, the Quran guided the Muslims to fight back rather than suffer patiently:

> And fight in the way of God with those who fight you, but do not be aggressors; God does not love the aggressors. And slay them wherever you find them, and expel them from where they expelled you; persecution is more grievous than slaying … But if they [cease hostilities], surely God is all forgiving, all compassionate. Fight them until there is no affliction and religion is God's. Then if they [cease hostilities], there shall be no aggression except for the oppressors. (2: 190–193)

This is an example of the kind of guidance given by the Quran that is geared toward specific circumstances. In the first instance of oppression, the community is advised to endure with patience; in the second, it is given permission to fight in self-defense. Scholars of Quranic interpretation (*tafsir*) study the circumstances of revelation to determine the applicability of verses such as these. There are several approaches to determining appropriate applications of Quranic verses. The majority of traditional *mufassirun* (scholars of *tafsir*) believe that later verses abrogate earlier verses, so that the verses revealed in Medina, after the Hijra, become the standard guidance. (This is called the theory of abrogation, *naskh*.) According to this approach, then, Muslims must fight when they are attacked or have been evicted from their homes, rather than suffer in patience as they were told to do in Mecca. Other scholars, however, believe that the advice given in Quranic verses is geared toward the circumstances in which it was revealed. According to this approach, if Muslims are weak and outnumbered, as they were in Mecca, they should not attempt to fight, but if they are strong and able, as they were in Medina, retaliation against attacks is required. In either case, it is necessary to know the "circumstances of revelation" (*asbab al-nuzul*), as they are known in Quranic studies. For those who believe that later verses abrogate earlier verses, the circumstances of revelation provide the data necessary to determine the historic order of revelation of the verses because, as noted previously, Quranic verses are not arranged in chronological order. For those who believe that Quranic guidance is geared to specific circumstances, the *asbab al-nuzul* provide data that allow believers to identify the historic conditions that were being addressed in various verses.

Not all Quranic guidance is dependent on circumstances, of course. The verses that give specific legislation such as the requirement for prayer, charity, fasting, pilgrimage, and dietary laws, as well as prohibitions on murder, theft, usury, prostitution, gambling, and the like, are considered eternal; there are no foreseeable circumstances in which requirements for worship will be abrogated or violations of human dignity be sanctioned. However, as we have seen, the majority of Quranic verses are more general, presenting a consistent and coherent vision for a just society, based on divine providence and mercy, and encouraging people to struggle to establish such a society.

The task of fully submitting to the will of God is thus all-consuming. It requires constant effort, but not because any single individual is expected to take more responsibility than she or he can manage. The Quran often counsels that God does not require from people anything beyond their strength (2:286, 6:152, 7:42, 23:62). People will be judged on their intentions: "God … will hold you responsible for what your hearts have earned" (2:225). Nor is any one group expected to be successful in the struggle to establish a just society in a given time or place. But believers are expected to work toward that goal, by following the guidance given in the Quran and the model established by Prophet Muhammad in Medina as a guide. Thus, Muhammad's role extends beyond the task of delivering revelation. His life is also a model for humanity of how to live every moment and make every choice in accordance with God's will. The way he lived his life is described by the Quran as the best example of Islam: "Indeed in the messenger of God is a good example for those who look to God and the Last Day and remember

God often" (33:21). Together, the Quran and the example (called the *Sunna*) set by Prophet Muhammad comprise the guidance Muslims need in their collective responsibility to establish justice.

The Early Muslim Community and the Pillars of Islam

The community established by Prophet Muhammad in the seventh century was resoundingly successful in its effort to create a society characterized by justice, peace, and harmony. The decades of internal strife that had plagued Medina ceased. On his arrival in Medina, the Prophet struck an agreement between the various tribes there and his community of Meccans. This agreement is recorded in history as the Constitution of Medina. According to the provisions of the agreement, all religious communities in Medina form a single community, "separate from other people."[1] They are to be mutually supportive, particularly in case of attack. Reflecting the Quran's teaching, Jews and Muslims are expected to maintain their own religious practices; disputes are to be referred to Prophet Muhammad and God. There were no Christian tribes in Medina (although there were some individual converts), but later on Christians and other religious groups were accorded religious freedom, based on the Quran's prohibition of compulsion in matters of religion (2:256) and on the precedent established in the Constitution of Medina. Before the establishment of the Islamic community in Medina, tribes had been the dominant form of social organization. Tribes were extended families, under the leadership of dominant males, and each was an autonomous unit. Although occasionally alliances would be formed through marriage, there was no effective precedent in the region for a social organization that included peoples of varying families and religious traditions cooperating in the pursuit of shared ideals.

The peace and prosperity of this community comprising various tribes with differing religions living in harmony quickly attracted the attention of its neighbors. There had been some internal dissent. On three occasions local tribes were believed to have violated the constitution by fighting with Muslims or conspiring with outsiders against the Medinan community. They were therefore expelled (in the first two cases), or executed (in the third case). Because all three of these tribes were Jewish, some people think that the community in Medina turned against Jews. In fact, some verses from the Quran referring to incidents such as these caution the Muslims against trusting Jews and Christians.

(For example, "O you who believe, do not take Jews and Christians for friends. They are friends of one another," 5:51.) However, other Jewish tribes continued to live in peace in Medina. Furthermore, the majority of verses of the Quran, as noted previously, endorse pluralism. The following verse is typical of the Quran's acceptance of Jews and Christians (among others): "Surely, those who have believed, and the Jews and the Sabians and the Christians, whoever believes in God and the last day and does good deeds need have no fear nor shall they grieve" (5:69). Most commentators therefore agree that the verses criticizing other religions are directed at specific beliefs or actions, not against the groups as a whole.

Indeed, the model of intertribal harmony established at Medina seems to have been attractive to the surrounding communities. During the lifetime of the Prophet, most tribes of the Arabian peninsula accepted Islam and pledged their allegiance to the Prophet, making Muhammad the most powerful leader in the region. Within eight years of the Hijra, and after several battles, the Meccans also recognized the authority of the Prophet. The event was dramatic. In 628 it was revealed to Muhammad that he would pray in Mecca (48:27). He therefore set out with about one thousand unarmed pilgrims who also wanted to pray in Mecca. They were stopped outside the city at Hudaybiyyah by the Meccans. To preserve peace, the Prophet negotiated a ten-year truce, agreeing to postpone the pilgrimage for a year. But two years later the truce was violated and Muhammad marched on Mecca. He was met by the leader of Mecca's leading tribe, the Quraysh, who accepted Islam and negotiated peace. Granting amnesty to the city that had persecuted his community, Muhammad entered the city peacefully, and rededicated the Kaaba, the ancient shrine at the center of Mecca. According to the Quran, the Kaaba was originally built by Abraham and his son Ishmael to honor the one God, but it had since been taken over by local tribes, who had filled it with symbols and relics of their polytheistic religions. Local tribes made annual pilgrimages to Mecca, in combination with the city's annual trade fair and cultural events. When Prophet Muhammad returned to the Kaaba, he cleared the idols from it and made it the focus of pilgrimage for Muslims.

The pilgrimage (*hajj*) is known as the fifth pillar or basic practice of Islam. The first pillar is the *shahadah*, the pledging of commitment to God and the teachings of His prophet, Muhammad. "I bear witness that there is no god (*ilah*) but the God (*al-ilah*/Allah) and Muhammad is the messenger of God." Anyone who sincerely commits to live according to this pledge is considered a Muslim.

The second pillar is prayer (*salat*). Muslims pray five times daily (at sunrise, midday, afternoon, sunset, and nighttime). The prayers consist of recitations of verses of the Quran performed in a series of submissive postures (including bowing low from a kneeling position, so that the forehead touches the ground), and are meant to keep Muslims focused on the will of God in all aspects of life. Many people perform their prayers in mosques (*masajid*, "places of prostration"), although prayers may be performed anywhere that has been swept clean (symbolizing entering a state of purity). The prayer rug, a small carpet usually with a directional indicator to be pointed toward Mecca (the proper direction of prayer), is often used for this purpose. Some people substitute a piece of cloth or cardboard if they have no rug. Believers are instructed simply to precede prayer by washing (or symbolically washing, if no water is available), to prepare themselves spiritually to focus entirely on God. On Fridays the midday prayer should be performed communally in the mosque. At that time, the prayer leader (*imam*) often offers a sermon (*khutbah*).

The third pillar is *zakat* (also spelled *zakah*), or charity. As noted, all Muslims are required to be charitable; zakat requires all adult Muslims to give a share of their wealth annually for the support of the poor and to further the cause of Islam.

The fourth pillar is fasting (*sawm* or *siyyam*). All healthy Muslims (i.e., neither the very young nor the very old, nor those who are sick, pregnant, or nursing) are expected to fast from sunrise until sunset during the ninth month of the Islamic calendar (Ramadan). This is a spiritual time, during which Muslims pray regularly and read the Quran, and focus on the equality of all people in their utter dependence on God. At the end of the month of fasting comes one of Islam's two major holidays, the one that celebrates the breaking of the fast (*Eid al-Fitr*). Families and communities celebrate this feast for three days, sharing joyous meals and giving gifts to the children.

As noted, the hajj is the fifth pillar. Muslims are obligated to make the pilgrimage at least once in their lifetime if they are physically and financially able, during the month designated as "the month of pilgrimage" (*dhu al-hijja*). During that time pilgrims dress in simple clothes, removing any indicators of social rank, and together perform ceremonies designed to remind them of the founding of the Kaaba and their reliance on (submission to) God. The pilgrimage culminates in the feast of the sacrifice (*Eid al-Adha*), the other major holiday. Sheep are slaughtered, symbolizing Abraham's sacrifice; the meat is then consumed and any excess is given to the poor.

The five pillars (*arkan*) are the basic practices of Islam. They structured Islamic life in Medina, as they continue to do today. The pillars are simple practices designed to remind believers constantly of their commitment to the divine will. They also focus attention on the core values of Islam: the equality of all human beings in the eyes of God and the responsibility of all believers to contribute to the well-being of society. Around these practices and core values, the early Muslim community was built and prospered. Following the rededication of the Kaaba in 630, Prophet Muhammad received overtures from tribes throughout the Arabian peninsula, accepting Islam and becoming part of the community, or pledging alliance with the Prophet. The Christian tribes among the bedouin (desert-dwelling nomadic herders) and Jewish tribes, many from the desert oases, generally kept their religious identities, as in Medina, while the polytheistic tribes generally became Muslim. By the time of the Prophet's death, the Islamic community based in Medina was the most vibrant moral, social, and political force in the Arabian peninsula.

The Successors ("Caliphs")

When Prophet Muhammad died after a brief illness in 632, his followers were distraught. Abu Bakr, one of his closest companions, declared to them, "If anyone worships Muhammad, [know that] Muhammad is dead. But if anyone worships God, [know that] God is alive and does not die." His goal was to refocus attention on the message, rather than on the Messenger. Muslims maintain the deepest respect for Muhammad and continue to be inspired by his example. But he was a man, a servant of God, as Abu Bakr reminded the community on this sad occasion when he repeated the Quranic verse, "Muhammad is only a messenger; messengers have died before him. When he dies will you turn your back on him? Whoever turns back does no harm to God but God will reward the grateful" (3:144). The believers were comforted and inspired by this; they were to maintain their commitment to the will of God, taking individual responsibility for their actions. But what about the community as a whole? Who would lead them?

A number of possibilities were suggested. Some of the nomadic tribes around Medina felt that their allegiance had been to Prophet Muhammad. For them his death meant the end of their affiliation; they indicated their withdrawal from the alliance by ending their zakat payments to Medina. Some believed that in the absence of Muhammad's central leadership, the tribes and communities—including Mecca—should revert to local leadership. Others believed that the Prophet had designated his cousin and son-in-law, Ali, as his political heir and that leadership of the community should remain within the Prophet's family. These would be called the "partisans of Ali, *shi'at* Ali, or simply Shia or Shii. (The development of Shii thought will be discussed further in Chapter 3.) But the majority believed that the Prophet had not discussed political systems or specified a successor to take over after his death. Abu Bakr was among these. He and other close companions of the Prophet were convinced that leadership should be chosen by tribal representatives, as was common in Arabia. They would be called the Sunnis. They believed, further, that Muslims had to remain a single community— not just morally unified through commitment to monotheism and the message of Prophet Muhammad, but politically unified as well. Their opinion prevailed. The companions of the Prophet pledged allegiance to Abu Bakr as leader of the community, referring to him as the Prophet's representative (*khalifah* or "caliph"). (He preferred the title "leader of the believers," *amir al-mu'minin*.) He was first among equals, leading through consultation (*shura*) with other elders in the community, just as the Prophet had done, and in accordance with the Quranic directive: "So pardon them and ask forgiveness for them and consult with them on the conduct of affairs" (3:159).

Abu Bakr then led the community in a momentous decision: to bring the tribes that had seceded back into the community by force, if necessary. The Quran stipulates that "there is no compulsion in religion" (2:256). It reinforces that position elsewhere. For example, when discussing preaching to the People of the Book, Muhammad is instructed:

> If they argue with you, say: My followers and I have surrendered ourselves to God. And say to those who have received Scripture and to the illiterate: "Have you surrendered [to God]?" If they surrender [to God], then they are rightly guided, and if they turn away, then it is your duty only to preach. (3:20)

This verse, in fact, guides Muslim attitudes toward proselytizing. Nevertheless, the decision was made to enforce the political unity of the believers militarily. The seceders were declared apostates, and the campaigns against them are still known as the wars of apostasy (*riddah*). The decision to enforce unity among believers had a significant effect on the development of Islam. It established a policy that resulted in one of the most extraordinary political expansions in history. By the time Abu Bakr died in 634, almost all the tribes of the Arabian peninsula had been brought into the Islamic political orbit. Under Abu Bakr's successors, Umar and Uthman, the Islamic army set out to rid Syria and Mesopotamia (Iraq) of the hated Byzantine and Sasanian empires. (Further implications of the decision to enforce political unity will be discussed in Chapter 4.)

At that time the Middle East was in the final throes of devastating competition between the eastern Roman Empire (the Christian Byzantines) and the Sasanian Persian Empire (Zoroastrian). The Byzantines had occupied coastal Syria, which at that time included parts of the present states of Syria, Lebanon, Jordan, Israel, the Palestinian territories, and Egypt. The Sasanians of Persia (called Iran since the 1930s) controlled most of present-day Iraq. After decades of debilitating wars, both empires were weakened internally. Arab tribes on the frontiers of the empires readily accepted the leadership of the Muslims. The formerly great Roman and Persian armies were defeated with little trouble.

The Byzantines had long persecuted their Jewish subjects, as well as those Christians who rejected Orthodoxy. For these groups Muslim rule was especially welcome. Those who accepted Islam were taught the basics of the religion by Quran reciters. But Christians and Jews were free to retain their religious identity. In addition, the taxes imposed by the Muslims were generally lighter than those of the older empires, and unlike many conquering armies, the Arab Muslims were not allowed to take control of the conquered lands for personal use. Thus, Jerusalem was liberated from Roman rule in 636, Mosul was taken from the Persians in 641, and the Romans were defeated in Alexandria by 646. The last Sasanian ruler was killed in 651, the Roman fleet was destroyed by Muslim sea power in 655, and the Muslim state headquartered in Medina became the most powerful in the region.

Early Communal Disputes

The phenomenal expansion of Islamic sovereignty was a result of the early decision by the Prophet's successors that Islamic unity must be assured through political unity. But political unity proved virtually impossible to maintain as Islamic sovereignty continued to spread. Efforts to enforce that unity engendered conflicts that called into question the very nature of the Islamic community. A recurring theme in the early conflicts was the tribal nature of Arab culture. In pre-Islamic times, tribes were the basic unit of social organization, and each tribe had its own values, sources of authority, organization, rituals, and beliefs—all of which would later be identified as aspects of religion. This is the context for understanding the gravity with which the question of apostasy was treated in early Islam. To change one's religion was not simply a matter of spiritual persuasion as we see it today. Because religious loyalty and political loyalty were often linked, to change one's religion was tantamount to changing one's political loyalty, a potentially treasonous act. Christianity had attempted to supersede this religio-political identity. Jesus' command "to render unto Caesar the things that are Caesar's, and unto God the things that are God's" (Matt. 22:21) could allow people to follow their religious conscience without it calling into question their political loyalty. People could be Christian in the Roman Empire without being considered subversives. But the equation of religious and political loyalty was reimposed when Christianity was declared the official religion of the Roman Empire. The Quran's teaching of religious freedom was a return to the ideal espoused by Jesus. It was a reassertion of the independence of religious and ethnic identity. This ethic was institutionalized in the Constitution of Medina, when Prophet Muhammad included Jews and Muslims in the same political community. Again stressing the struggle against tribalism, the Prophet said in his final speech that Arabs have no superiority over non-Arabs.

Nevertheless, the tribal tendency to equate religious and ethnic national identity was so well entrenched that it reemerged soon after the Prophet's death. Umar, the second caliph, determined that only Islam would be allowed in the Arabian peninsula, the Quran's teaching and the Prophet's example of religious tolerance notwithstanding. Under his administration, Jews and Christians were expelled, so that all Arabs (meaning those who lived in the Arabian peninsula; later on, the term *Arab* would apply to all Arabic speakers) were Muslim; thus, religious and ethnic identity were rejoined. Umar's successor, Uthman, reasserted a tribal tendency that challenged even other Arab Muslims. He headed an administration staffed almost exclusively by members of his own Meccan clan, the Umayyads, resulting in numerous protests. Umar's policy concerning land taxation also resulted in protests. It stipulated that revenues from conquered land would be sent to Medina for the benefit of the central administration, the conquering Arab soldiers and their families. Non-Muslim Arabs felt that their land taxes should be used locally. Policies such as these seemed to violate Islamic norms of justice and equality, and resentment mounted. Umar was murdered by a Christian Persian slave in 644. Uthman continued

Umar's policies, resulting in more discontent. Minor rebellions broke out in towns established solely for Arab Muslim conquerors in Egypt (al-Fustat) and Iraq (Kufah). In 656, rebellious Muslims from Egypt marched to Medina and assassinated Uthman.

Those participating in the growing discontent found a champion in Ali, the Prophet's companion, cousin, and son-in-law. Following Uthman's death, Ali was chosen by majority opinion within the community to be the next "leader of the believers." He was well respected and, as noted previously, had been a contender for the office since the death of Prophet Muhammad, but he was not as senior as Abu Bakr, Umar, and Uthman. His Shii supporters believed that he should have succeeded Prophet Muhammad as leader of the Muslim community, and that the first three successors (Abu Bakr, Umar, and Uthman) were actually usurpers. But not all Ali's supporters believed that his legitimacy rested on the Prophet's designation. Many supported him because of his piety, wisdom, and courage, particularly in this time of civil strife. These included a group later identified as the Kharijis (or Kharijites, "the Seceders"), who believed that Uthman's nepotism (staffing his administration with members of his own family) was such a serious violation of Islamic principles that he was no longer eligible even to be called a Muslim, let alone a caliph. But Ali also had enemies. Chief among them were Aishah, widow of the Prophet and daughter of the first caliph Abu Bakr; and Muawiyah, the governor of Damascus appointed by Uthman. Aishah, who held personal grudges against Ali, led a rebellion against him near Basra (in Iraq, near Kufah, where Ali had established his headquarters) in 656. Ali's troops easily defeated her troops (which she personally led). Muawiyah challenged Ali to find and punish the assassins of his kinsman Caliph Uthman. When he did not, Muawiyah led an army against him (657). On the verge of defeat, Muawiyah's troops asked for arbitration, which Ali granted. The arbitration allowed Muawiyah to maintain his post in Damascus. Unfortunately, this effort at reconciliation cost Ali the support of the Kharijis. In 661 Ali was assassinated by one of them, leaving the caliphate to the Umayyad family in Damascus. (For further discussion of the Kharijis, see Chapter 4.)

Conclusion

The violent end of three of the first four caliphs reflects the turmoil that gripped the Muslim community after the death of Prophet Muhammad. The community had the Quran and his example (the Sunna) to guide them, but still they were left with an enormous challenge. As noted previously, the Quran is not a law book but a guide and source of moral inspiration. It reaffirms the covenant accepted by Abraham, the "trust" that human beings accepted at creation, the agreement that God offers eternal reward to those who take up the struggle to recreate in society the equality all human beings share in the eyes of God. But there are no formulae for ensuring that justice is always done. That is the part human beings have to figure out, each community and every generation, in an endless variety of circumstances. They must evaluate the circumstances in light of moral guidance, and then determine what actions and institutions are most conducive to justice in those specific circumstances. And they must do it in cooperation with others because no one can create justice alone. The Quran describes its guidance as clear, and it is; there is no doubt about what the goals of a just society are. But it is difficult to figure out how to achieve those goals "on the ground"—as anyone who is engaged in social activism knows.

Early Muslims were faced with the enormous challenge not only of institutionalizing justice in their own communities but also sharing those ideals and institutions with others who had suffered injustice just as they had. It is certainly to their credit that they relieved the region of the heavy burden of Roman and Persian imperialism. That conflicts would arise over the practical matters of governance is not surprising. It is natural that, among tribal people, some would believe leadership should stay within their own community, whereas people outside that community would reject that model of leadership. It is just as natural that, among moralizing people, many would believe that leadership should be based on piety, and many would rebel against rulers deemed unjust. In reality, the early years of Islam reflect both the benefits and the difficulties encountered in the transition from a community whose security is based on tribal bonds of mutual and unquestioned loyalty to a community committed to justice on a global scale. This is a struggle that continues to this day. Like people of many other faiths, Muslims continue to explore the implications of working for justice in a pluralist society. Is salvation reserved only for Baptists, or Catholics, or Jews, or Muslims? Must we separate religious beliefs from political convictions to be able to live peacefully with people of other faiths? Indeed, can we separate the two? Does accepting the legitimacy of other faiths require abandoning one's own, or a "willing suspension of disbelief"? These are questions that confront all religions today. They are the same kinds of questions that the early Muslims struggled with.

The fact that there was conflict reflects the complexity of the problems faced and the depth of commitment on the part of the participants. In the context of Islamic history, it does not detract from the valiance of their efforts. Although Shii Muslims continue to believe Ali was the first legitimate successor to the Prophet, the majority of Muslims, the Sunnis, believe the first four caliphs were "rightly guided" (*al-rashidun*). They look to this period as one in which the Quran's moral challenge dominated Islamic life. The Muslim community, with all its conflicts and failings, extended every effort "in the way of God" (*fi sabil Allah*). Even today, traditionalist Muslims look to this community as an example of truly Islamic life and accept some of the precedents established during this period (such as the death penalty for apostasy). Reform-minded Muslims, on the other hand, respect the efforts of this early community, while rejecting some of its precedents, and look to the Quran and Sunna for guidance in facing the challenges of modern life.

Whether Sunni or Shii, traditionalist or reformist, all Muslims consider this period the time during which Islamic ideals were established. Although the Shiis do not accept Abu Bakr, Umar, and Uthman as legitimate leaders of the community, and modern-day reformers reject some of their specific judgments, all Muslims believe this community took up the challenge of the *khalifah*. This term, appropriated in the political sphere to mean "successor" of the Prophet, actually has a much broader meaning in the Quran, where it is used twice. In a famous passage that encapsulates much of Islamic teaching, the Quran says that God created humanity to be His *khalifah* (2:30). Clearly the meaning here is "steward" or "deputy." Human beings were put here to be responsible for maintaining the equality in which all were created. Elsewhere, the Quran describes God addressing King David as his *khalifah* who, as such, must judge in all things with honor and justice (38:26). Despite its weaknesses and conflicts, the early Muslim community accepted the challenge of stewardship and struggled to enjoin good and prevent evil. It is that legacy that has continued to inspire Muslims throughout the ages.

Note

1. W. Montgomery Watt, *Muhammad at Medina* (Oxford: Clarendon Press, 1956), 221–225.

2

The Pursuit of Knowledge in the Service of God and Humanity: The Golden Age

The conflicts that gripped the Muslim community during the caliphate of Ali interrupted the spread of Islamic sovereignty. But following his death and the establishment of the seat of Islamic government in Damascus in 661, expansion resumed with continued success. After replacing Roman rule in Egypt, Muslim forces pushed across North Africa. Joined by Berber (indigenous North African) converts, the Arabs crossed the straits from Africa to Andalusia (in modern-day Spain), ascending the mountain to which their leader Tariq gave his name ("Gibraltar" comes from the Arabic *jabal tariq*, Tariq's Mountain or Mount Tariq). Within just one century of Prophet Muhammad's death, Muslims had established Islamic sovereignty throughout much of Spain, which remained Islamic until the *Reconquista* in 1492. The Muslims' advance into Europe was stopped in Gaul (France) by Charles Martel at the battle of Tours in 732.

In the east, Islamic rule was established throughout former Sasanian lands, all the way to the Indus River and the border of China by the early eighth century. Islam continued its eastward spread through the fourteenth century, when traders and itinerant preachers traveled to China, South Asia, and Southeast Asia, establishing roots for the current Islamic countries of Indonesia and Malaysia. The Indian subcontinent was ruled by Muslims from the thirteenth century until the British took control in 1857. It was, indeed, a phenomenal expansion. And with it came the development of a

Islam: History, Religion, and Politics, Third Edition. Tamara Sonn.
© 2016 John Wiley & Sons, Ltd. Published 2016 by John Wiley & Sons, Ltd.

highly sophisticated culture. Marked by openness and creativity, it was inspired by the Quran and Prophet Muhammad's example and still serves as a model of what many believe a truly Islamic society can achieve.

Institutions

As noted in previously, many subjects of the Byzantine (eastern Roman) and the Sasanian Persian empires generally welcomed Muslim rule because it allowed respite from religious persecution and resulted in overall lower taxes. This reflected the rationale for the expansion of Islamic rule; Muslims sincerely believed that Islam was divinely ordained to bring peace and relief from oppression for all humanity. Thus, when Muslims approached a new community, they offered the protection of Islam. Those who chose not to accept Islam as their religion were offered treaties; they could pay a tribute in return for the right to retain religious freedom and internal autonomy. Those who refused either to accept Islam or to live in peace with Muslims through treaty agreements were forced to submit by means of military action.

This method of conquest resulted in a division of the world into three parts: *dar al-Islam*, *dar al-'ahd* (or *sulh*), and *dar al-harb*. Dar al-Islam refers to those territories in which Islamic law prevails. Dar al-'ahd (region of covenant) and dar al-sulh (region of truce) were both regions whose leaders had agreed to pay the Muslim leaders a tribute and to protect the rights of any Muslims or Muslim allies who lived there, but who otherwise maintained their autonomy, including their own legal systems. Dar al-harb was a region whose leaders had made no such agreement and where, therefore, Muslims and their allies were neither guaranteed the right to live by Islamic law nor were protected by it. For this reason it was called "region of warfare." This does not mean that such regions were automatically subject to attack by Muslims because *harb* is not legitimate warfare in Islam. When warfare is sanctioned in Islam, it is called *jihad*, which is struggle "in the way of God" that is carried out through military means and according to strict rules of engagement. This is the only kind of warfare allowed under Islamic law. Referring to a region as *dar al-harb* reflects the perception that the region itself was warlike and Muslims were not safe there.

Through this system, the Muslim world—regions where Muslims made up the vast majority—was transformed into the Islamic world, which was a world dominated by Muslim institutions but including significant non-Muslim populations. Such an enormous and complex world required administration beyond the simple model established by the Prophet and his earliest successors. That model had been relatively informal and based on direct interaction of community members and leaders. In the expanded Islamic empire, more sophisticated administrative systems became necessary.

A system of taxation was the first order of business. In general, the Muslim conquerors allowed local authorities to collect taxes according to their established customs. Because some of the newly acquired territories had been variously administered according to Roman law, Persian law, and other regional systems, the system of taxation under Muslim rule became quite complex. Iraq, for example, was conquered through military victory, with the help of local Arab tribes, over the drained Sasanian forces. The native Arabs were left in control of taxation and followed the Sasanian tradition, which included both a land tax and a poll tax (a tax based on the number of people living there). But the poll tax varied according to the degree of wealth among the populace, except for the aristocracy, who were exempt from the poll tax. In Syria, where Islamic dominance was achieved largely by treaty, tax collection was left to the discretion of the native administrators. They followed in basic outline the fiscal system of the previous Roman overlords, which was even more complex than the Persian system.[1] The central treasury therefore had to be sophisticated to keep track of all these differing systems of taxation.

Law

Of far greater importance than taxation, however, was the institutionalization of law because it regulated Islamic practice overall. In this area, too, the Muslim practice of leaving in place systems that had dominated a region prior to the coming of Islam was evident. In accordance with Islamic principles and the Prophet's practice, religious freedom was the norm throughout Islamic realms. The right accorded to Jews in the Constitution of Medina to maintain their religious and legal systems was extended to Christians and later to Zoroastrians, Hindus, and Buddhists. But what about those who chose to become Muslim? The inclusion of vast new populations in the community of Muslims meant that an expanded legal system had to be developed. According to tradition, Prophet Muhammad stipulated that local customs were to be tolerated as long as they did not interfere with Islamic principles. But someone had to determine what was or was not in accordance with Islamic principles. Muslims had to develop a legal system that would be flexible enough to function effectively throughout Islam's expansive and diverse realms but rigorous enough to maintain a distinctive Islamic identity.

In the days of the first caliphs, when the system was still relatively informal and modeled on the practice of the Prophet, Muslims were simply expected to follow Islamic practice, including regular prayer, charity, fasting, and pilgrimage. Regarding other issues of governance and in matters of conflict, the Quran had stipulated that Muslims were to "obey God and the Messenger and those among you in authority" (4:59). But beyond that, the Quran had specified no particular form of government. Muhammad's early successors, therefore—as his "representatives" (caliphs) and "leaders of the believers"—attempted to follow the Prophet's example by living lives of piety and arbitrating disputes when they arose. But with the expansion of Islamic sovereignty this informal practice proved insufficient and was gradually transformed into a legal system that could function independent of the head of state.

The first major transition in Islamic governance came with the assumption of power by the Umayyads, descendants of a powerful Meccan family. Although some people had argued that Ali should be appointed successor to the Prophet because of his family relationship with him, hereditary leadership was not a pattern common in Arab society. But after the Umayyad Muawiyah was recognized as caliph, his family kept control of that office until a revolution ousted them in 750. During the Umayyads' reign, a distinction between specifically religious and the coercive/executive levels of political authority developed. Damascus became the political or administrative capital of the empire, whereas Mecca remained the religious/legislative center. But still there was no theory on which the government was based. As noted, the caliphs left in place whatever systems had prevailed before the Muslim conquest. For other legal issues, the Umayyads introduced into their administration a new office, that of judges (sing. *qadi*). These were political appointees with varied administrative responsibilities, including police and treasury work, but generally charged with settling disputes in accordance with local custom and Islamic principles. They were allowed a great deal of latitude, exercising their own judgment about what was permissible in view of Islamic principles and administrative necessities.

However, it soon became apparent, to some people at least, that Umayyad leadership no longer was the model of wisdom and piety that Islamic leadership ideally symbolized. This recognition gave rise to opposition groups, including scholars who objected that Umayyad policies violated Islamic principles. In the process of discussing which actions and policies were Islamic and which were not, scholars actually developed the formal theories of Islamic law that became the core of Islamic life.[2] When Christianity became politically institutionalized in Rome in the fourth century, it devised a way to determine who was really a Christian by developing a "creed," a list of beliefs. Whoever accepted the beliefs of Christianity was a Christian and therefore a full citizen; those who rejected Christian beliefs were non-Christian and considered a threat to the Christian community. That is why the major discipline in Christianity is theology, a discussion of beliefs. In Islam, on the other hand, just as in Judaism, the emphasis is not so much on beliefs as on actions. Belief is important; correct behavior is assumed to be based on correct belief. But the critical point of religious identity is based on the discipline that deals with practice, and that is law. This does not mean that Islam became legalistic, however; like Judaic law, Islamic law is not simply a code of injunctions enforceable in a courtroom. As modern Islamic scholar Fazlur Rahman put it, Islamic law is "an endless discussion on the duties of a Muslim rather than a neatly formulated code or codes."[3] Law was therefore central to Islamic life in terms of daily life and religious practice, as well as state administration.

By the mid-eighth century there was a discernible body of scholars who were popularly regarded as having the authority to identify and interpret the sources of Islamic law. They fell into schools of thought that generally developed according to regional practice. In Medina, for example, a school of Islamic legal thought developed based on local practice and in view of the interpretations of scripture and reports (*ahadith*; sing. *hadith*) from the local people about what the Prophet said or did (his normative or exemplary practice or "Sunna"). This body of ideas about practice was expressed in the work of Malik ibn Anas (d. 796) and is known as the Maliki school of law. Another center, with different local customs and different hadith reports, grew up in Kufa (in Iraq): the school of Abu Hanifa (d. 767), largely developed by his students Abu Yusuf (d. 798) and al-Shaybani (d. 804), and known as the Hanafi school. The development of these schools was essentially democratic; decisions about what was proper practice, in accordance with the Quran and the Prophet's example, were based on local consensus (*ijma'*). In cases where there were no apparently applicable precedents in the Quran or Sunna, legal scholars used their discretion to determine the implications of revelation for the question at hand. They practiced *ijtihad*, the name given to this interpretive work.

The Umayyads lost control of the caliphate when they were overthrown by the Abbasid family in 750 CE. As members of the opposition to the Umayyads, the legal scholars (*fuqaha'*) were naturally favored by the Abbasids. The new ruling family appointed these scholars as judges, rather than simply calling on loyal functionaries, as the Umayyads had done. This represented a significant step in the formalization of Islamic law. As legal historian N. J. Coulson put it, "The legal scholars were publicly recognized as the architects of an Islamic scheme of state and society which the Abbasids had pledged themselves to build, and under this political sponsorship the schools of law developed rapidly."[4] The scholars began to identify weaknesses in the system and the need for greater rigor in legal thought. Thus, a third school of Islamic law developed around the idea that legal reasoning should be consistent throughout the Islamic world. This was not an argument for uniform practice or judgments, only for agreement on the sources of Islamic law and the ways to achieve sound legal rulings in cases for which no precedent could be found. It was an argument for procedural continuity, reflecting a growing awareness that, regardless of the shifting political winds, the core of Islamic unity was law. The school that emerged from this movement was named for its energetic founder, Muhammad ibn Idris al-Shafii (d. 820). It is called the Shafii school of legal thought.

Al-Shafii had traveled to the major cities in the Muslim world and noticed significant variations in legal reasoning. He set out to achieve consistency in legal procedures by articulating clearly the roots of Islamic law and their rank in terms of priority. For al-Shafii, as for all other Muslims, the first source is the Quran. In cases for which the Quran offers no specific judgment, the next source of guidance is the practice of Prophet Muhammad, the Sunna. But at the time of al-Shafii, the process by which the Sunna was communicated was still largely informal based on the opinions of educated people about the Prophet's principles or ways of making decisions. Al-Shafii attempted to formalize the Sunna by equating it with credible hadith reports of what the Prophet said or did in specific circumstances. As a result, the concept of the Sunna was eventually restricted to specific examples of the Prophet's behavior. These could concern personal matters with no significant legal implications, such as how to clean one's teeth or whether or not to shave, as well as matters with important legal significance, such as how to conduct business or deal with poverty. In either case, these precedents became models to be imitated. And once they achieved such an important place in Islamic administration, the process of collecting, verifying, and codifying hadith reports began in earnest. By the ninth century, there were two collections of reports that were considered "sound" (*sahih*, meaning that the people who reported them had been scrutinized and found trustworthy, that the content of the report was in keeping with Quranic teaching, etc.) and therefore, authoritative. Those were the collections of two individuals—Bukhari and Muslim. Four other collections were considered valuable sources of insight concerning the Prophet or the Quran but not as authoritative as the collections of Bukhari and Muslim. (The Shiis also have hadith collections, verified by virtue of transmission through Ali and his descendants.)

The third source of law for al-Shafii was the consensus of the community. The Prophet is reported to have asserted that his community would never agree on an error, and group consensus has therefore always been important in Islam. But al-Shafii concluded that only the consensus of the entire Islamic community should be considered authoritative, not just consensus within the various regions. And by the time he was working, given the extent the Islamic community had reached, full consensus was virtually impossible to attain. Therefore, al-Shafii believed it was preferable to follow precedent as much as possible. The third source of Islamic law, then, became judgments that had been reached by consensus of previous generations about the meaning and application of the Quran. Independent reasoning (ijtihad), the fourth source of Islamic law, could be practiced only as a final resort, and it too was circumscribed. The intellectual effort to determine the implications of the Quran and Sunna was to be carried out through syllogistic reasoning, or reasoning by analogy (*qiyas*), rather than the more informal ijtihad based on personal opinion (*ra'y*).

Al-Shafii's school of jurisprudence remained only one of several within the Islamic system. A fourth school of thought was developed by one of his students, Ahmad ibn Hanbal (d. 855). Called the Hanbali school of legal thought, it places even greater emphasis on precedent than the Shafii school, although it also allows greater freedom in the use of ijtihad. Shii Muslims would develop a school of legal reasoning as well, known as the Jafari school. Nonetheless, al-Shafii came to be known as the "architect of Islamic law" because his work consolidated Islamic legal thought into a recognizable discipline at the core of Islamic life.[5] From his time on, a Muslim was officially defined as one who follows Islamic law.[6]

The systematization of legal administration gave the Islamic world a basic structure that has endured to this day. The Maliki, Hanafi, Shafii, Hanbali, and Jafari schools of legal thought still characterize the Islamic landscape worldwide. Each tends to predominate in a specific region: Maliki law in North and West Africa; Hanafi in areas formerly under Ottoman control and India; Shafii in Indonesia, Malaysia, and the Philippines; Hanbali in Saudi Arabia and Qatar; and Jafari in Shii regions such as Iran. But the schools of thought differ relatively little and are, in fact, mutually acceptable. For example, all Muslims accept the five-part division of actions into those considered required (such as the five pillars), those recommended (such as giving charity above and beyond the required zakat), those considered neutral (such as smoking, according to most Muslims), those that are discouraged (such as divorce), and those that are forbidden (such as consuming intoxicants, eating pork, and gambling). Actions in the first category are believed to be rewarded, and willful failure to perform them is punishable. Actions that fall into the second category are rewarded, but failure to perform them will not bring punishment. Actions considered to be neutral bring neither reward nor punishment. Those who avoid discouraged actions will benefit from their abstinence, and those who perform forbidden (*haram*) actions will be punished.

The classic formulations of Islamic law, accepted by all schools of thought, reflect the Quranic ethic of punishment by retaliation (*qisas*) for physical offenses, from assault to homicide. The person who strikes a physical blow is subject to whatever offense he has committed. As the Quran says, "A life for a life, an eye for an eye, and a nose for a nose, and an ear for an ear, and a tooth for a tooth, and for [other] injuries, fair retaliation" (5:45). The victim or the victim's family may choose to accept compensation (*diyah*) instead, and this is encouraged by the Quran. (The foregoing verse continues: "And whoever waives the right to this in charity, it will be an atonement [for sins].") There is another class of crime for which Islamic law has established specified mandatory punishments (*hadd*; pl. *hudud*), provided the perpetrator acted in full control of his senses and with full knowledge of his offenses, and that strict rules of evidence can be met. These *hudud* punishments include capital punishment for apostasy, highway robbery, what we now call terrorism (i.e., crimes against random victims), and illicit sex between married people; amputation of the hand for theft; and whipping for illicit sex between unmarried people or legal minors, or for drinking. (See Chapter 5 for further discussion of terrorism.) The rules of evidence required for these crimes are indeed strict. For example, conviction of adultery requires substantiation by four adult male eyewitnesses. Although such punishments seem harsh, they are considered primarily deterrent and, in fact, have proven to be effective in that regard. Most Muslims also believe that the hudud punishments are applicable only in conditions where high social standards have been met. They are not applicable in conditions of widespread ignorance, poverty, or social instability. Throughout history there are few reports of the punishments actually being administered.

In traditional Islamic law, the courts are used to decide any issues other than physical injury or death, and those requiring hudud punishments. These include detailed laws concerning transactions (sales, rentals, loans, gifts to nonprofit organizations [*waqf*; pl. *awqaf*], etc.), family law (such as marriage, divorce, guardianship, custody), and laws of inheritance. In the traditional Islamic court, the judge (*qadi*) is given significant latitude. He may ask for an authoritative opinion (*fatwa*) from a professional legal scholar (*mufti*) but is not required to do so. Individuals may seek legal representation but in general are expected to state their case personally. The judge decides whether the plaintiff or the defendant bears the burden of proof, on which the prosecutor must produce two witnesses (for most cases). If the evidence is unconvincing, the defendant is given the opportunity to swear innocence by a sacred oath. If the defendant refuses to offer such an oath, the case is decided in favor of the plaintiff.

In the modern era, traditional Islamic civil and criminal law was largely replaced by European legal codes during the period of colonization. Only matters considered private in European culture—those concerning family law—were left to Islamic courts. This has led to an interesting dynamic. Because of the centrality of law to Islamic society, there was a strong sense that the Europeans were stripping Islamic society of its identity. As a result, there was a tendency to safeguard traditional Islamic legal codes whenever possible. We will discuss in greater detail in Chapters 4 and 5 the tension this tendency has created in the modern era between reformers and traditionalists. Despite such tensions, however, Islamic law continues to represent the unifying element of diverse Islamic societies. Throughout the numerous political upheavals that have marked Islamic history, Islamic law has provided a sense of unity and allowed the Muslim community to remain cohesive. Scholars, far more than rulers, are considered the symbols of Islamic unity.

A good illustration of this phenomenon is found in the adventures of Ibn Battutah, the fourteenth-century legal scholar and world traveler, Islam's precursor to Marco Polo. From his home in Tangier, Ibn Battutah traveled throughout the Muslim world, including all of North Africa, the Arab, Turkish, and Persian Middle East, the Maldive Islands, Sri Lanka, Bengal, and as far as China. His diary, still available, records that as a legal scholar he was welcomed in town after town all along his route and given fine hospitality and respectful audiences. In the modern era, instant communications have made such international travel and personal contact unnecessary. Yet it is still the religio-legal scholars who have the potential to appeal well beyond their ethnic, national, and sectarian origins. As we will see in Chapters 4 and 5, scholars, more than politicians, have influenced events in the Islamic world from North Africa to Southeast Asia.

Political Structure

There is no characteristic political system in Islam. A government is not marked as Islamic based on the nature of its executive authority. Throughout history Muslims have devised numerous political systems, from simple tribal groups led by elders (sheikhs); to empires ruled by caliphs, sultans, or shahs (kings); to constitutional democracies and military dictatorships. What is required for political legitimacy in Islam is that whatever executive or administrative system exists, the law of the land must be based on Islamic sources. This was explicitly articulated in the eleventh century by Shafii scholar al-Mawardi (d. 1058). In a work titled *Al-Ahkam al-Sultaniyya* (*The Rules of Government*), he explains that the duties of political leaders fall into three categories: defense, treasury, and executive.[7] He is to defend the community from attack (article 3), maintain frontier defenses (article 5), and wage war against those who refuse to either become Muslim or enter into treaty with Muslims (article 6). Regarding fiduciary responsibility, he is to collect both the alms payments (zakat) required of all Muslims and the legitimate spoils of wars (article 7). He must fairly determine and pay salaries from the treasury (article 8) and make sure those he appoints manage the treasury honestly (article 9). But most importantly, the ruler must make sure that the established principles of religion are safeguarded (article 1) and that legal judgments and penalties are enforced (articles 2 and 4). In other words, the ruler's authority is strictly executive and coercive. This position was reinforced by the great fourteenth-century Hanbali scholar Ibn Taymiyya (d. 1328), who said that the form of government can vary from time to time and place to place, depending on custom and circumstance. But legal authority—articulating and adjudicating the law—not only remains distinct from executive administration but is also of primary importance: the ruler can be any of a number of kinds, but as long as he makes sure an Islamic legal system is maintained, the government is legitimate.

In the medieval period, as the wealth of the Islamic empire grew, the office of the ruler became increasingly absolute in matters that concerned him. In fact, the Abbasids (who were called caliphs) adopted the pre-Islamic Persian model of kingship in which the monarch was considered "the shadow of God on earth." However, the matters that concerned the caliph were not generally those that concerned the population at large. It is ironic that, despite the caliph's absolute power, classical Islamic government allowed for unprecedented freedom among the populace. Other than collecting taxes, the government did not interfere in the daily affairs of society. People were born, educated, married; they made their living and bequeathed their wealth; they engaged in trade and other kinds of business—all without interference from the central government. Virtually all of daily life was under the purview of Islamic law, articulated and administered by legal scholars who operated for the most part independent of the central government.

It is often said that in Islam there is no distinction between politics and religion. This claim is misleading, however. It is true that Islam does not distinguish between political and religious values. The values that guide political or public life are the same as those that guide personal or private life. But in terms of administrative structure, Islamic law was quite separate from the executive branch. The executive branch had the authority to appoint judges, of course, but the judges were trained in institutions that were autonomous. In a system that bears striking similarities to our modern separation of powers, Muslim legal scholars maintained their autonomy through sources of income independent of government control. Their independence was maintained through a system of charitable foundations, called *awqaf* (singular: *waqf*) that have throughout history been at the core of Islamic civil society. A waqf is a kind of trust fund, a gift or bequest of property, or the proceeds from a business to benefit society. People could give money or various business funds to establish something as small as a local fountain or as large as a hospital. Mosques are common beneficiaries of waqf trusts, and such endowments often include the education and support of legal scholars. These endowments had to be legally registered and were bound by the law of perpetuity; they could not revert to private use but had to continue to be used for charitable purposes as specified in their original charters. Waqf endowments were administered privately, by someone designated as the trustee at the time of endowment. There have been notorious cases of misuse of waqf funds, and government confiscation of waqf properties to control civil society. Theoretically, however, waqf endowments remain independent funds. As such, waqf funds allow for the independence of the institutions that trained legal scholars, the arbiters of political legitimacy in the classic Islamic model.

It should be noted, too, that ordinary citizens always had the right to appeal to the caliph if they felt that justice had not been served by the Shariah courts. Special courts, called *mazalim* courts, were maintained for this purpose. Staffed by representatives of the central government, the officials of these courts had full discretionary power. People could come and appeal the decision of a local official or court, or lodge a criminal complaint, and the mazalim judge could make any decision he felt suitable, without being held accountable to standard Islamic law as established by the legal scholars.

Cultural Achievements

During the Middle Ages, Islam's unique system of religious freedom and administrative flexibility allowed for remarkable stability and growth. It also produced a period of peace and prosperity in which the sciences and arts were brought to new levels of perfection. The Islamic world from Spain to India—with its plurality of cultures, ethnicities, and religious communities—produced an unprecedented cultural efflorescence. At its root was an openness to diverse heritages and intellectual influences. The environment produced was one in which learning was both a cherished value and a collective pursuit. Muslim scholars who discovered long-forgotten Greek texts in Egyptian libraries worked with Christian scholars who could translate them into their native Syriac and then into Arabic. Combining them with the intellectual heritage of Persia and India, these scholars built a magnificent cultural edifice that included the most advanced science and arts of the age. As Dennis Overbye has characterized it:

> Commanded by the [Quran] to seek knowledge and read nature for signs of the Creator, and inspired by a treasure trove of ancient Greek learning, Muslims created a society that in the Middle Ages was the scientific center of the world. The Arabic language was synonymous with learning and science for 500 years, a golden age that can count among its credits the precursors to modern universities, algebra, the names of the stars and even the notion of science as an empirical inquiry.[8]

The Abbasid court of Harun al-Rashid (d. 809), immortalized in the stories of the *Thousand and One Nights*, is best known in the West for its splendor. The royal palace, surrounded by beautiful gardens, was so huge that its upkeep required hundreds of servants. It reputedly had thousands of finely woven carpets and curtains of spun gold. The queen's table was set only with dishes of gold and silver, inlaid with precious stones. The king's audience chamber was known as the Hall of the Tree, named after the decorative artificial tree that was its centerpiece; it was handmade of gold and silver and had mechanical golden birds chirping in its branches. Baghdad was undoubtedly the center of the civilized world. It received envoys from around the globe, including the court of Charlemagne, Harun al-Rashid's contemporary. (Harun also sent envoys to Charlemagne. In response to a request from Charlemagne, Harun sent as a gift to the court at Aachen a white elephant. Its name was Abu Abbas, meaning "Father of Abbas," in honor of the Abbasid caliphate. The elephant survived for eight years in the harsh European climate.) The wealth of Harun's court was based not only on taxes collected from the Abbasids' enormous holdings, but from trade in prized goods from Africa, India, China, Central Asia, Russia, and beyond. Coins minted there have been found as far north as Germany, Sweden, and Finland. Medieval Islamic Spain was at least as sophisticated as Baghdad. In the tenth century Cordoba, the capital of Umayyad Spain, was known throughout Europe as a great city. Under Muslim rule, its population had nearly quadrupled to 100,000, roughly equivalent to the population of Constantinople at the time. Its streets were illuminated by thousands of state-maintained lanterns; it had hundreds of fountains and baths supplied by aqueducts. It enjoyed great prosperity based on an agricultural revolution that included the introduction of new irrigation techniques and crops. Oranges (the name comes from the Arabic *naranj*) and lemons (from the Arabic *laimon*), artichokes (from the Arabic *ardi shoki*), cotton (from the Arabic *qutun*), and sugar cane (from the Arabic *sukkar*) are among the many crops introduced to Europe at this time. The city also had public libraries. The court library alone had more than 400,000 books. (The largest library in Europe at the time, in a Swiss monastery, held approximately 600 books.)

Indeed, although its political power would inevitably fade, intellectual achievements are the lasting legacy of the Islamic empire. Even before the time of Harun al-Rashid, translation of classical texts had begun. These were texts that had lain in oblivion in Egyptian libraries after the decline of classical Greece and Rome and included the medical works of Galen and

Hippocrates and Ptolemy's and Euclid's work on mathematics and astronomy. The value of the texts was immediately recognized in the Islamic world, and the work of translation was considered so important that a family of Christian translators, Hunayn b. Ishaq (d. 873) and his son and nephew, achieved widespread fame for their work. They improved on previous translations and expanded the works available in Arabic to include those of Aristotle and Plato. According to legend, Harun's successor al-Mamun placed so much value on learning that he paid Hunayn with the weight of the books he translated in gold.

Based on these translations, scholars in the Muslim world developed an intellectual culture unrivaled in the West since the days of classical Greece. Among the earliest areas to develop was the rational analysis of revealed truths. By adapting Greek rationalism to revelation, they developed Islamic philosophy. In doing so, their works became both sources for European knowledge of classical Greek learning, and models for developing Christian and Judaic philosophies. Al-Farabi (Alpharabius, in Latin; d. 950), for example, from Turkic central Asia, composed commentaries on Plato and Aristotle, as well as a highly original description of the ideal state. For him, that was "The Virtuous City" (*al-madinat al-fadilah*), headed by a morally and intellectually enlightened leader for the benefit of its inhabitants. The two most influential philosophers in the Muslim world were Ibn Sina (Avicenna, in Latin; d. 1037) and Ibn Rushd (Averroes, in Latin; d. 1198). Ibn Sina, from Bukhara (in modern Uzbekistan) was perhaps the most broad-ranging intellect of the medieval Islamic world. He wrote on art, astronomy, geometry, and medicine, among other topics. But his most lasting influence—even to the modern age—is in philosophy. His rational clarification of Islamic teaching was heavily influenced by his reading of Plato and Aristotle and established the model for medieval philosophical theology. Ibn Rushd of Cordoba (Spain) interpreted Aristotelian thought more accurately than had Ibn Sina and became early medieval Europe's most important source of knowledge of Aristotle.

The Muslim philosophers' work was controversial both in the Muslim world and beyond. Rational articulation of religious principles given in revelation, if kept within the limits of revelation, was acceptable to traditional scholars. That is what we call theology (called *kalam*, in Arabic; see Chapter 4 for a further discussion of Islamic theology). But philosophy had no theoretical limits to its rational inquiry. In cases in which the results of rational inquiry seemed to conflict with revelation, philosophers generally concluded that revelation should be understood as metaphor for deeper truths inaccessible to the untrained mind. Such conclusions were unacceptable to religious scholars. This controversy prompted one of the most interesting philosophical exchanges of the medieval world: theologian al-Ghazali's critique of philosophers for "incoherence" (*Tahafut al-falasifa* [*The Incoherence of the Philosophers*]), and philosopher Ibn Rushd's response (*Tahafut al-tahafut* [*The Incoherence of Incoherence*]).

Al-Ghazali (d. 1111) was a Persian scholar of law, philosophy, and theology, but he experienced a spiritual crisis at the height of his intellectual career and turned to mysticism. There he found spiritual sustenance and became convinced that the practices of Sufism (see discussion in this chapter) were the only source of the kind of certainty necessary to sustain a life of faith. That is what motivated him to write his diatribe against philosophers' attempts to find certainty through reason. He attempted to show that logical analysis was inherently incapable of dealing with religious truth and inevitably led to self-contradiction. Among his arguments was that if logic were capable of bringing certainty on metaphysical issues, then

Figure 1 Raphael's School of Athens showing Ibn Rushd with Aristotle. Source: © akg-images/Album/Oronoz

everyone would agree on them, just as everyone agrees on the conclusions of logic regarding mathematics, for example. But, in fact, philosophers disagree all the time about these issues. Al-Ghazali attacked a number of specific philosophical arguments, but he was most concerned with proofs for the existence of God because they entailed the claim that the universe is eternal, rather than created in time. Some philosophers had made use of Aristotle's argument about the need for a "prime mover"—a force to originate all motion, change, and causality in the universe—to prove that there must be a God, an "unmoved mover." The Prime Mover, as God, was eternal and perfect, and that means that the Prime Mover is also changeless because change implies going from a state of incompleteness (or "potentiality," in philosophical language) to completeness ("actuality," in philosophical language). Therefore, the universe must also be eternal, or else one would have to claim that God changed (or moved) when He decided at some point to create the world. Because this conclusion contradicts the revealed truth of creation, al-Ghazali tried to demonstrate its fallacy. He said the problem was that the philosophers had failed to distinguish between the originator of the action and the action itself. He concluded that God willed from all eternity that the world and everything in it would eventually be created. But that does not mean that the created things themselves are eternal. In response, Ibn Rushd pointed out that al-Ghazali had failed to distinguish between willing something and actually doing it. One can decide to do something long before one does it, but it will not be done until the person who made the decision adds action to decision, bringing us right back to where we started: either the world is eternal or God is not perfect. Neither side was convinced by the other's arguments, and the theologians and philosophers parted ways.

In Europe Ibn Rushd inspired a school of thought known as Latin Averroism that vied with Thomas Aquinas' scholastic theology, which itself was based on the understanding of Aristotle that he had derived from the Muslim philosophers. This controversy prompted Aquinas to pen one of his more famous works, *Summa contra Gentiles*, attempting to refute the beliefs of the "heathen" Muslims. It also landed Ibn Rushd/Averroes in Dante's hell, although in the first circle, the least uncomfortable realm. Dante respected Ibn Rushd for doing philosophy, but in Dante's Christian world, a Muslim could not escape eternal punishment. (Dante placed Muhammad at the depths of the eighth—out of nine—circles.)

Jewish thinkers in the Muslim world also attempted to rationalize revealed religion by means of classical Hellenic philosophy. Working with texts that typically were translated from Greek into Syriac into Arabic and then into Hebrew, Jewish thinkers followed the same patterns as their Muslim compatriots. Ben Gabirol's (d. ca. 1058) *Yanbu' al-Hayah* (*The Fount of Life*) was an important source of Platonic thought in Islamic Spain as well as in Europe. The great Mosheh ben Maymon of Cordoba (d. 1204; Maimonides, in Latin; Musa ibn Maymon, in Arabic) was both a distinguished philosopher and physician, highly placed in the royal court. He was the personal physician to Salah al-Din (Saladdin, of Crusades fame; see Chapter 3).

Although highly respected in the Islamic world as in Europe, philosophy was relatively marginal to the daily life of medieval society. Of more obvious benefit were the practical sciences on which medieval Islam's advanced civilization was based. And of the practical sciences, the most prized was medicine. Al-Ghazali even counted the study of medicine as a communal religious duty, a kind of duty incumbent on a sufficient number of Muslims to meet the needs of the community. Medical expertise was so highly valued that, according to tradition, it was first revealed by God (through the prophet Idris/Enoch). Scholars in the Muslim world developed the most advanced medical research of the age. The Abbasids were particularly interested in supporting medical research. Harun al-Rashid established the first hospital in Baghdad under the guidance of Christian scholars trained at Gundaishapur Hospital, a research institute established in sixth-century Persia (Iran). By the end of the ninth century several other hospitals had been established in Cairo, Mecca, and Medina as well, and mobile medical units had been established for rural areas. These hospitals treated males and females, had outpatient facilities, and offered services for the poor. Many of the hospitals had mental wards, libraries, and classrooms. By the early tenth century, standard exams were needed to practice medicine in Baghdad, a city with nearly nine hundred registered physicians. The Mansuri hospital in Cairo, built in the thirteenth century, is still in use today for the treatment of the blind. It had a policy of turning away no one, regardless of gender, religion, or financial means, and was equipped with specialty wards, a pharmacy, lecture rooms, a library, and a chapel as well as a mosque. By the fourteenth century, a number of hospitals had been established in Islamic India as well. As in the Arab world, medical treatment was free, supported by waqf endowments and government patronage.

The famous Persian medical researcher al-Razi (d. 925) worked at an institute in Baghdad that had twenty-four doctors, each with a different specialization. His *Kitab al-Asrar* (*Book of Secrets*), translated into Latin in the twelfth century (*De spiritibus et corporibus*), was a foundational text on alchemy, the forerunner to modern chemistry. His compilations of medical knowledge were likewise translated into Latin and remained standard sources in Europe as late as the sixteenth century. Even more influential was the philosopher–physician Ibn Sina. Not only were his commentaries on Aristotle a primary source for Latin scholars, but his fourteen-volume compendium of Greek and Islamic medical knowledge—*al-Qanun fi'l-Tibb*, one of the first books to be printed in Arabic (1593)—was an authoritative text for European scholars. Completed in 1025, it was unsurpassed by Western scholars for six hundred years.

Diseases of the eye were common in the Middle Eastern and North African climate of intense sun, sand, and dust. As a result, ophthalmology was among the medical specialties in which Islamic scholars made significant advances. The oldest existing systematic treatment of the subject is that of Ibn Masawayh from the ninth century. Trained as a mathematician, Ibn al-Haytham (b. 965) was inspired by Ptolemy's work on optics and made significant contributions to the understanding of vision. He developed a theory of vision incorporating Aristotelian ideas of matter and form with careful observations of anatomical experiments. In the process, he advanced the development of scientific method. His *Kitab al-Mandhir* (*Book of Optics*) includes as well important descriptions of reflection and refraction.

Also associated with practical needs were technical developments, including those in the field of optics. Technicians produced magnifying and refracting lenses that aided in both microscopic and macroscopic viewing. Navigational instruments such as the astrolabe and sextant were perfected and produced in abundance. But perhaps the most universally useful technological development was the introduction of the use of paper, in the late 700s, replacing parchment (the skin of sheep or goats) as the preferred writing surface. The use of paper was introduced in the eastern Islamic empire from China. It spread quickly westward. In Islamic Spain writing paper was produced locally. It was via Spain that the use of paper was introduced to Europe, although its use was limited until the Europeans developed movable type.

Mathematics was a basic field in the medieval Muslim world and another area in which Muslim scholars excelled, again for practical purposes. Accurate calculations were essential for efficient navigation, and the numerical system dominant in the ancient world simply did not allow the kind of accuracy these calculations demanded. Perhaps the most important contribution made in this area was Arabic numerals, replacing the letters used in the Greek and Roman letter-based systems. These numbers—which in Arabic are called *hindi* because they were originally Indian—were adapted for use, along with the zero (*sifr*, in Arabic; in English, cipher), in advanced calculations by al-Khwarizmi (d. ca. 850) in the ninth century. Translated into Latin in the twelfth century, al-Khwarizmi's work was the source of the West's knowledge of algebra (*al-jabr*, which he developed in his book *Hisab al-Jabr wa'l-Muqabalah* [*Calculation of Integration and Equation*]). Al-Khwarizmi's work was also the source of the term *algorithm*, a Latin transliteration of al-Khawarizmi's name. Around the same time, al-Battani (d. 929) developed trigonometry. Like other mathematicians in the Islamic world, al-Battani studied the classical texts, verifying and refining their work. In al-Battani's case, he corrected some of Ptolemy's calculations of the lunar and planetary orbits.

Al-Biruni (d. 1050) was a prolific scholar and scientist, working in the eastern cultural center of Ghaznah (in modern Afghanistan). Knowledgeable in Persian, Arabic, Hebrew, Turkish, Syriac, and Sanskrit, al-Biruni wrote treatises on mathematics, astronomy, and ancient calendars, among other things. He supported the theory of the rotation of earth, conceived to be a sphere, against those who argued that the world was flat. He also accurately calculated the longitudes and latitudes of the earth. At the other end of the Islamic empire, the Spanish mathematician and astronomer al-Zarqali (d. ca. 1087) made numerous profound discoveries concerning the movement of the stars and perfected the astrolabe in the process. Both al-Battani and al-Zarqali were quoted by Copernicus in *De revolutionibus orbium coelestium*. The science of astronomy was so highly developed in the Islamic world that permanent observatories were established. The ruins of what is probably the oldest observatory in the world are still visible in Maragheh, in northwestern Iran. Built in 1259, it attracted scholars from as far away as China and included an extensive library. The contributions of astronomers from medieval Islam were also immortalized in the names they gave to various stars, such as Altair (*al-ta'ir* [the flyer]) and Betelgeuse (*bayt al-Jawzi* [the home of Jawzi], the Arabic name for Orion), as well as technical terms like zenith (*as-samt*) and nadir (*nadhir*).

The translations of classical Hellenic, Persian, and Indian texts in the intellectually charged atmosphere of medieval Islam became the basis of the Muslim world's great cultural flowering in the Middle Ages. They were the basis of Europe's, as well, and were transmitted there via Syria, Sicily, and, especially, Spain. A school was established in eleventh-century Toledo specifically for translating Arabic texts into Latin, the language of learning throughout Europe. There scholars came from as far away as England and

Scotland to discover the learning of the Islamic empire and transmit it to Europe. The first translation of the Quran was produced at this school by Robert of Chester and Herman the Dalmatian at the request of Peter the Venerable, the abbot of Cluny in France. It was also in Toledo that the classics of Hellenic learning were translated from Arabic into Latin. The debt of Europe to the medieval Islamic scholars is impossible to measure. As historian Philip Hitti put it, "Had the researches of Aristotle, Galen and Ptolemy been lost to posterity the world would have been as poor as if they had never been produced."[9]

Preserving, developing, and passing on classical studies was not the only contribution of the medieval Muslim world to global culture. Islamic scholars also produced wholly original works, laying the foundations for academic disciplines that were not developed in the Western world until the modern era. The work of Ibn Khaldun (d. 1406) is a case in point. His *Muqaddimah* (*Introduction* [to the History of the Arabs, Persians, and Berbers]) is often cited as the first work of historiography and forerunner to the modern disciplines of anthropology, sociology, economics, and political science. In the *Muqaddimah*, Ibn Khaldun outlines patterns of social and political development, observing along the way patterns in history and economics. That is why historian Arnold Toynbee declared the *Muqaddimah* to be "the greatest work of its kind that has ever yet been created by any mind."[10] Ibn Khaldun was quoted more than once by US President Ronald Reagan, in fact, on the relationship between tax cuts and inflation.[11] He clearly predicted the observations of Marx concerning the impact of historical conditions on the development of ideologies. To understand social, political, and historical developments, he said, we must understand how the people in question make their living, their level of education, their religious beliefs and customs, whether they live in rural or urban conditions, and how they govern themselves. His insistence that individual events be understood in terms of their causes because nothing occurs in a vacuum, became an essential principle of modern historiography. Ibn Khaldun was also an advocate of critical thinking. He rebuked scholars who simply transmit received wisdom without examining it in light of new information and those who write with political bias, "smearing the reputation of others" for the sake of "selfish interests and rivalries, or swayed by vendors of tyranny and dishonesty."[12] Ibn Khaldun was fond of quoting Prophet Muhammad's assertion that "scholars are the heirs of the prophets," and perhaps no individual scholar or sentiment better captures the vibrant intellectual spirit of the medieval Muslim world than this brilliant and multifaceted scholar.

Spirituality and the Mystical Tradition: Sufism

There was another side to medieval Islam, besides the sophisticated bureaucracies and highly public, creative scholarship. The inward, personal side of Islam was also developing into a deeply spiritual tradition known as *Sufism*. For all the great achievements of Islamic rulers and scholars, Islam remains essentially a personal commitment. Law deals with the external manifestation of believers' personal commitment. But *islam*—submitting to the divine will—is more than a matter of mere obedience. Muslims believe that sincere belief will be manifested outwardly in righteous actions. But the core motivation for those actions is still internal. Pious actions reflect a kind of turning of the will that is at once passive and active. It is a giving of oneself to the divine will, but in so doing, it is also undertaking a commitment to do the things necessary to fulfill the divine will. This unique combination of acceptance and commitment—this *islam*—is expressed in the Quran as the virtue *taqwa*. The Quran calls for faith, hope, and charity (*iman, amal, sadaqa*)—the virtues most commonly discussed in Christianity—in terms that are directly parallel to their English meanings. But taqwa is not easy to translate. As discussed in Chapter 1, its common translation, "fear of God," is misleading. The term comes from a root that has to do with protection, preservation, or security. The Quran never defines the term, in the sense of limiting it to some specific action or actions. Instead, it gives examples of the kinds of actions that stem from a well-formed conscience. For example, the Quran tells people not to allow other people's unjust actions to lead them to unfair behavior. "So long as [the polytheists] stay true to you, stay true to them. Indeed, God loves those with taqwa" (9:7).

Taqwa does involve virtuous behavior, but it is not just an external thing. It also involves intentions. It is the internalization of God's will. Taqwa is the willing choice to allow one's conscience to be guided by God, expressed externally through goodness and charity. That willing submission to God will inevitably express itself through righteous behavior—and the combination of a well-formed conscience and honorable actions will preserve the believer from real danger—the danger of eternal punishment.

But how does one develop such virtue? Scholars and lawyers can help guide understanding and actions. But making God's will your own requires spiritual practice. This inward, spiritual aspect of Islamic practice, Sufism (Arabic, *tasawwuf*), is often called "interior Islam." It can also be described as mature Islam. Whereas a child is motivated to do good and avoid evil based on the promise of reward and the threat of punishment, a mature believer experiences personal gratification through virtuous deeds and finds evil deeds personally repugnant. Sufi teachings and practice grew in Islam as a way to help people develop this ability to take joy in virtue.

Sufism has its roots in the earliest centuries of Islam. During the lifetime of Prophet Muhammad, the community benefited not only from religious and political leadership but also from his personal example. Muhammad lived a life fully motivated by the desire to do the will of God. He was a prophet, of course, but he was also a man and distinguished between those two aspects of his life. He cautioned people that there was a difference between those of his choices that were inspired by God and those that were simply based on his best judgment. On matters of revelation, the words he spoke were not his own; they had the unquestioned authority of their divine origin. But on everyday matters, he sought the advice of his community when needed, as guided by the Quran (see 3:159 e.g.), and displayed great humility. For example, when people asked him questions about planting their crops, he advised them that he knew no more about it than they did. This principle of consultation (*shura*) established a basis for democratic governance in Islam according to many modern interpreters. But even so, the Quran says that Muhammad set the best example of Islamic behavior. His personal choices, the way he conducted his life, and the way he treated people all served as examples that inspired his community to piety. But his death left a void in this regard. True, reports of Muhammad's actions in various circumstances circulated in the community and were eventually recorded to provide guidance for people. But reports are different from the personal, lived examples of piety. As the scholars and other officials established the details of Islamic legal and governmental institutions, the challenge of providing living examples of spiritual development was often taken up by individuals—some scholarly, some not—who simply gained a reputation in the community for their ability to inspire and guide others on the path to piety.

There were exemplars of the simple, pious lifestyle among Prophet Muhammad's companions and in the generation that succeeded him. Hasan of Basra (d. 728) is often mentioned in this regard. Known for his ascetic lifestyle, he is said to have worn the same wool cloak every day and still, when he died, it was sparkling clean. Indeed, the name *Sufi*—the term used to describe a Muslim who seeks in-depth spiritual development—comes from the term for wool (*suf*), as a symbol of simplicity and humility. The habitual use of prayer beads as a way to "remember God always"—a Sufi refrain—is also attributed to Hasan. As well, Hasan's lack of regard for the affairs of this world and focus on the path to eternal life inspired many. But among the most effective ways to inspire piety was through telling stories about the Prophet and his family. Some preachers became extremely popular for their ability to move audiences with uplifting stories of the Prophet's virtue, wisdom, and extraordinary devotion to prayer, attracting audiences of spiritual seekers from far and wide. Gradually, it became common for people to gather for extra devotional practices, "remembrance" (*dhikr*) of God through recitation of verses of the Quran, and discussions of religious themes in groups called "circles" (*halaqat*).

From informal beginnings such as the halaqat, Sufism developed into a diverse global phenomenon, with a number of distinct expressions. One was a distinctive intellectual tradition because religious scholars were drawn to the path of spirituality. Harith bin Asad of Basra (d. 857), for example, was given the name al-Muhasibi, "the introspective one," for his emphasis on examination of conscience to ensure that one's motives for all actions are pure and honorable. This introspection, he taught, would yield ever deeper spirituality and habitual virtue. Scholars like al-Muhasibi, who worked in Baghdad, attracted many students, forming early schools of thought. Al-Muhasibi is known as the founder of the Baghdad school of Sufi thought, known for such luminaries as Junayd of Baghdad (d. 910) and Ali al-Hujwiri (d. 1077), whose tomb in Lahore is a popular shrine even today. Al-Hujwiri's *Kashf al-Mahjub* (*The Unveiling of the Veiled*, or *Revelation of the Mystery*) is among the first systematic treatments of the developing Sufi tradition and remains an important source of our understanding of early Sufis' lives and ideas.

The notion of progressive levels of spiritual development was soon formalized into a set of steps or "stations" of practice (*maqamat*) and accompanying psychological "states" (*ahwal*). The steps are derived from the Quran's encouragement to practice repentance, self-control and moderation, patience, gratitude, and trust in God. Ideally, these steps take the spiritual seeker to a condition of joyful, continuous awareness of the Divine Presence. As Sufi thought developed, some scholars began to identify the final stage of the spiritual journey as a kind of absorption or extinction (*fana'*) of the self in the overwhelming experience of Divine Presence. The Egyptian Dhu'l-Nun (d. 859) and the Persian Bayezid (or Abu Yazid, in Arabic) al-Bistami (d. 874) are associated with this stage of the formalization of the Sufi way. Reflecting the experience of absorption or annihilation of the ego, al-Bistami is said to have proclaimed, "Glory to me; how great is my majesty!" Al-Kharraz (d. 899) of the Baghdad school put it another way. For him, the goal was "survival" or "subsistence" (*baqa'*) in God. Perhaps the most renowned expression of this experience was that of the tenth-century Persian al-Hallaj (d. 922): "I am the Truth." Unfortunately for him, this claim was considered the height of blasphemy. Claiming to be "the Truth" (*al-haqq*) is equivalent to saying, "I am God" because "the Truth" is one of the divine names. Al-Hallaj was famously executed by dismemberment culminating in decapitation, then burned, and his ashes thrown into the Tigris River.

In response to such exuberant expressions of mystical rapture, other scholars encouraged moderation. The Persian Abu Nasr al-Sarraj (d. 987) and his contemporary Abu Bakr al-Kalabadhi (d. ca. 995) each wrote books describing Sufi practices of their day, and both cautioned against those who only pretended to have achieved special awareness of the inner meanings of things; these "charlatans" could lead innocent believers away from the path of true piety. Both books are valuable resources for understanding the early development of Sufi thought and practice, and show that Sufism was gaining popularity and spreading geographically. Al-Kalabadhi wrote in Bukhara (in modern Uzbekistan). But their works also indicate that the development of Sufism was not without conflict. Among the reasons for concern is that the highest state of spiritual awareness is sometimes described as allowing a special kind of knowledge (*ma'rifa*), a kind of direct intuition of Ultimate Reality (or the nature of things, or even of God). This special knowledge is described as going beyond mere belief in matters of faith, and beyond even the rational understanding of things for which traditional religious scholars are known; ma'rifa provides immediate understanding and brings with it absolute certainty that this understanding is of divine origin. That kind of certainty leaves little room for argument—for example, from religious scholars who might understand things differently. It may even allow for the possibility of bypassing Shariah. For these reasons, scholarly Sufis like al-Kalabadhi not only cautioned moderation in Sufi practice, but also sought to demonstrate that Sufism is consistent with mainstream Islamic belief and practice.

Al-Sarraj's and al-Kalabadhi's work was followed by others' efforts to "mainstream" Sufism, including al-Qushayri (d. 1072). Al-Qushayri's *al-Risala* (*Epistle*) presents the biographies of dozens of the most influential Sufis and a manual of their belief and practice, specifically to demonstrate Sufis' respect for the Shariah.[13] But the scholar most commonly associated with integrating Sufi belief and practice into mainstream Islam is Abu Hamid al-Ghazali. In his magnum opus, *Ihya' 'Ulum al-Din* (*Revival of the*

Religious Sciences), al-Ghazali describes the various religious sciences as they relate to worship and daily life. These are *fiqh* (jurisprudence or legal studies) and *kalam* (rational study of revealed truths; theology), and he says they are absolutely essential for all religious seekers, including Sufis. These fields of study provide the foundation for all correct belief and practice. But, he says, they do not necessarily lead to the kind of deep piety identified as "closeness to God." The ultimate goal of correct belief and practice is to overcome the human tendencies that keep one from closeness to God, such as anger, greed, and lust. These negative traits must be replaced with the positive traits described previously: repentance, moderation, patience, gratitude, and trust in God. The ultimate goal, then, is not a special kind of knowledge, as some Sufis had claimed, but rather the interiorization of virtue for the purpose of salvation. For al-Ghazali, the Sufi way was directed toward deeper awareness of and motivation to follow the revealed will of God. Al-Ghazali's autobiography, *al-Munqidh min al-Dalal* (*The Deliverance from Error*), demonstrated that he spoke from experience. He was a trained legal scholar of the Shafii school and had studied both theology and philosophy in depth. But these intellectual pursuits left him unfulfilled. Sufism allowed him to move beyond mere obedience and imitation to the "life of the heart" where true faith is found.

Other scholars took a more philosophical approach, attempting to give a rational explanation for the mystical experience of absorption into Ultimate Reality. Among them was Shihab al-Din al-Suhrawardi (d. 1191). Al-Suhrawardi described existence in terms of light; all individual existents ("creatures" in ordinary language) are like rays, emanating from the One, Pure "Light of Lights," God. The further from this Source a being was, the paler its manifestation or share of Light. The goal of spiritual development was to move ever closer to the Source, gradually expanding one's participation in Light/Existence, and eventually losing all individuality by being absorbed into or reunited with the Source. For this reason, al-Suhrawardi is called a philosopher of illumination (*hikmat al-ishraq*). His teachings were judged by orthodox scholars to blur the distinction between God and creatures. He was therefore put to death, and so is often called *al-Maqtul*, "the Killed." But his Illuminationist thought was later taken up by the Persian Mulla Sadra (d. 1636), who remains one of Iran's most influential philosophers.

Among the best known of the Sufis who gave philosophical expression to Sufism is the renowned Spanish mystic Ibn al-Arabi (d. 1240). Ibn Arabi claimed famously that although it may appear that the world is full of endlessly diverse and discrete existents, in fact, all existence is One. This is the doctrine of the "oneness of being" or "unity of existence." Ibn Arabi explained this unity of existence by using a Neoplatonic theory of "emanation," common in his day and still accepted by some mystical thinkers. According to this theory, God is Ultimate Existence or undifferentiated Absolute Reality. From that undifferentiated Absolute Reality is generated lower existents in a kind of cascade of descending degrees of perfection. This process of generation or emanation begins with divine awareness of its own perfect attributes: Truth, Beauty, Love, and so on. These Divine Attributes or Names of God then become externalized in the phenomena of nature: the celestial spheres, earth, human beings, the lower animals, and nature. Thus, all existence is an effect or manifestation of the Divine, a "theophany." But what has thus been externalized can likewise be internalized—in effect, reabsorbed into the Oneness of Ultimate Reality. And this, again, is the goal of the religious seeker, for Ibn Arabi. Using the terms *fana'* and *baqa'*, Ibn Arabi explains that human beings may, through careful practice and contemplation, ascend the levels of existence to be reunified with their source.

Ibn Arabi describes the experience of being reabsorbed into Ultimate Existence poetically: For example:

My Beloved, joy of my eyes
You are me as Myself,
there where I am My companion at every moment—
May God be glorified—
You are my essence.
Hand in hand let us enter together into the presence
of the only Beloved.
Let there be no more distinction between us
Becoming One in Reality.
Oh, how wonderful a thought
and what subtle blending:
 The transparency of the glass, the purity of its contents
become identical, causing confusion:
Is it the glass or is it the wine that we see?
All life in the universe vanishes.
Moons are eclipsed, the sun disintegrates,
the stars explode.
We are thus thrice annihilated,
similar to annihilation itself.
And we attain to the three degrees of Permanency
following the example of Permanency itself.[14]

Indeed, poetry became a far more popular means of expressing the mystical sense of the undifferentiated oneness of all existence than philosophy. A characteristic expression was that of the great Persian poet Jami (d. 1492):

> Neighbor and associate and companion—
>> Everything is He.
> In the beggar's coarse frock and in the king's silk—
>> Everything is He.
> In the crowd of separation and in the loneliness
>> of collectedness—
>>> By God, everything is He, and by God, everything is He.[15]

Like al-Suhrawardi, mystic poets often use the metaphor of light to describe the perception of the oneness of Being, as in this excerpt from Farid al-Din Attar's (d. 1220) *Mantiq al-Tair* (*Speech of Birds*):

> Who in your Fraction of Myself behold
> Myself within the Mirror Myself hold
> To see Myself in, and each part of Me
>> That sees himself, though drown'd, shall ever see.
> Come you lost Atoms to your Centre draw,
> And be the Eternal Mirror that you saw:
> Rays that have wander'd into Darkness wide
> Return, and back into your Sun subside.[16]

Water, as well, was a common metaphor for the ebbing and flowing of undifferentiated Being, as in this excerpt from the same poem by Farid al-Din Attar:

> As Water lifted from the Deep, again
> Falls back in individual Drops of Rain
> Then melts into the Universal Main.
>> All you have been, and seen, and done, and thought
> Not You but I, have seen and been and wrought:
> I was the Sin that from Myself rebell'd:
> I the Remorse that toward Myself compelled ... [17]

Similarly, the incomparable Jalal al-Din Rumi (d. 1273) uses water to symbolize Being, and the inevitable return of raindrops to the sea as a metaphor for the creature's quest to return to the source of creation:

> Happy was I
> In the pearl's heart to lie;

> Till, lashed by life's hurricane,
> Like a tossed wave I ran.
> The secret of the sea
> I uttered thunderously;
> >   Like a spent cloud on the shore
> I slept, and stirred no more.[18]

The individual seeker's desire to return to the Source of All Being is often described in terms of profound longing, as if the perception of individuality is a burden. The liberation of the Sufi from what twentieth-century existentialist Gabriel Marcel would call the "the wound I bear within me which is my ego" was clearly a cherished goal of many Sufi seekers. But, as noted, claims of the oneness of all Being seemed to blur the distinction between the Creator and creatures, and thus would be seriously challenged, even by other Sufis. (See Chapter 4 for further discussion of critiques of Sufism.) But not all Sufism was expressed in this kind of ecstatic "God-intoxication," as it was sometimes called. Parallel to the development of the Sufi intellectual tradition, and arguably far more influential, was the development of popular Sufism. This took the form of various methods or "ways"—*tariqas*, sometimes translated as "orders"—toward spiritual development, each attributed to a specific acclaimed Sufi master. The search for spiritual development is clearly a personal one, but as the example of al-Hallaj demonstrates, it is one best pursued with guidance lest one become delusional. The recognition of this need developed into a regularized pattern whereby the spiritual seeker would submit to the tutelage of one who had already demonstrated success in the Sufi way. The student (the *murid*, *darwish*, or *faqir*) affiliates with a guide—*pir* (in Persian, *sheikh*; in Arabic, *murshid* or *muqaddam*)—to receive careful instruction in the steps along the spiritual path. As al-Ghazali explained:

> The disciple must of necessity have recourse to a director to guide him aright. For the way of the Faith is obscure, but the Devil's ways are many and patient, and he who has no Shaykh to guide him will be led by the Devil into his ways. Wherefore, the disciple must cling to his Shaykh as a blind man on the edge of a river clings to his leader, confiding himself to him entirely, opposing him in no matter whatsoever, and binding himself to follow him absolutely. Let him know that the advantage he gains from the error of his Shaykh, if he should err, is greater than the advantage he gains from his own rightness, if he should be right.[19]

Some of the great Sufi guides were recognized as saints or "friends" of God (sing. *wali Allah*). These were people who had gained reputations for extraordinary piety that was often recognized as a kind of spiritual power. They subsisted in such intense awareness of the Divine that they seemed to have supernatural gifts. Being in their presence was transformative. They seemed to be able to read people's souls and know their innermost thoughts. Some seemed to evince the spiritual energy that kept the world spinning as it should. As early as the ninth century, Sufis developed the notion that every generation has such a spiritual "axis" or "pole" (*qutb*), although they are not always recognized as such. The reputations of the great saints of Sufism spread quickly, often enhanced by graphic stories about their spiritual powers. Not every great Sufi was a qutb, but the spiritual gifts of many were often described in miraculous terms. Their closeness to God, their sainthood, was evidenced by their spiritual power or "blessing" (*barakah* or *karamah*). Many Sufis believed that this blessing allowed such saints not only to read people's minds, but also often to know the future, bi-locate, withstand extraordinary physical duress, cure illnesses, and prescribe remedies for various afflictions. As well, this spiritual power was often believed to survive the saint's death, so that the tombs of saints became important pilgrimage sites for people seeking spiritual favors and even intercession with God.

But most important was the reputation of the saints' ability to guide people on the path to spiritual development. There were—and continue to be—many routes to spiritual development, with varying emphases on such practices as asceticism, contemplation, and prayer. Some stress solitude, whereas others encourage social interaction. Some involve living in extreme simplicity; some incorporate rhythmic chanting, music, or dance. Sufi "ways" range from "rustic" to "ecstatic," but most fall between those two extremes. One of the oldest identifiable tariqas is the Qadiri, named after Abd al-Qadir al-Gilani (d. 1166). As a youth al-Gilani showed such intelligence and devotion that he was sent to Baghdad to study and quickly became an expert in philosophy and law. But he also became known for his inspiring sermons advising Muslims how to go beyond mere obedience to fully spiritual religious practice. Instead of focusing on self-denial, as some teachers did, al-Gilani stressed simple piety, charity, honesty, and sincerity. His own life was a model of the kind of spiritual search that leads people to the spiritual path. The story is told of his trip to Baghdad as a young student. His mother had sewn his money into the lining of his clothes so that he would not lose it on the trip. But on the way to Baghdad his caravan was waylaid by robbers. The thieves demanded that everyone give them their money and jewels, but they overlooked the ragged-looking boy. When he realized what was happening, al-Gilani told the robbers that he had some money, too. The criminals were so moved by the boy's honesty and sincerity that they converted on the spot and went on to live virtuous lives.

As with many spiritual leaders, stories about the power of al-Gilani's piety spread quickly. The Qadiri tariqa and its offshoots spread throughout the Middle East, westward across North Africa and eastward to China and South Asia. Unlike some orders that devised their own sets of rules, Qadiris were advised to simply follow Islamic legal codes and internalize them through spiritual practice. The Qadiri order was also relatively informal; unlike some orders that required strict initiation rites and distinctive rituals, the Qadiris remained flexible so that local customs in various regions could be accommodated. Sometimes local customs or practices came to dominate a tariqa's practice in a particular region so that they generated a sub-tariqa with a unique identity. This was the case, for example, with the Muridis, established in the late nineteenth century in Senegal and Gambia. Although the order was strongly influenced by the Qadiris, its founder Ahmadu Bamba stamped it with its own characteristics. Still, the Qadiri tariqa remains among the most widespread orders in the world today. Al-Gilani's tomb in Baghdad is still a popular pilgrimage site.

Another example of a localized order is the Badawi or Ahmadi, named for Ahmad al-Badawi (d. 1276), especially popular in rural Egypt. The miraculous works of its founding saint achieved such notoriety that his birthday is celebrated annually across Egypt. However, its other festivals are connected with the seasons of the Nile River and are timed in accordance with the pre-Islamic solar calendar of the Copts rather than the lunar calendar of Islam.

Similar to the Qadiri order in its simplicity, the Shadhili order began in Egypt under the inspiration of Abu'l-Hasan Ali al-Shadhili (d. 1258). The Shadhilis focus on carrying out their daily responsibilities in a state of prayerful gratitude to God. In fact, they emphasize spiritual wakefulness so strongly that they introduced the use of coffee to stay awake during long prayer sessions. The Shadhili order's popularity has spread across North Africa and Sudan.

In contrast to this kind of sobriety is another early order from Iraq, the Rifai, named for Ahmad al-Rifai (d. 1182). The Rifais' *dhikr* sessions are so loud that they are known as the "Howling Dervishes." Their loud chant, combined with intense, rhythmic head-shaking, is meant to induce a state of ecstasy that leaves them impervious to physical pain. This condition may then be demonstrated by skin piercings and other similar forms of self-inflicted torture.

The Rifai order, with its extravagant dhikr practices, spread westward into Egypt, northward into Turkey, and eastward into Asia. As noted, the Qadiri tariqa also spread far and wide, including eastward into Central Asia and the Indian subcontinent. The Suhrawardis, named after Abu Najib al-Suhrawardi (d. 1168) of Persia and developed by his nephew Umar Suhrawardi (d. ca. 1235), is another early order that became prominent in South Asia. The Suhrawardis are a "sober" order, stressing the Sunni Shariah, regular prayer, and active community involvement.

Some orders are associated more extensively with Turkey, such as the Bektashi. The Bektashi originated perhaps as early as the thirteenth century in Central Asia. They spread westward into Turkey and the Balkans, as well as into South Asia. Their orientation is far more eclectic than that of the Suhrawardis, involving both Shii elements such as veneration of the descendants of Prophet Muhammad and Ali, and Christian elements, such as the use of bread and wine in some rituals and the full participation of women in all ceremonies. They are also known for their highly developed tradition of poetry. The Naqshbandi, named for Baha al-Din al-Naqshband (d. ca. 1390), originated in Bukhara (in modern Uzbekistan) and are quite the opposite: they are a notably "sober" order. Rejecting music, chanting, and dance, they stress instead "silent dhikr." Rather than encouraging self-deprivation to control carnal desires, the Naqshbandi focus on spiritual education through mindful simplicity, concentrating on God, and cultivating a sense of solitude even in a crowd. Nevertheless, the Naqshbandis also produced some great mystical poets, including Jami, cited previously.

The Naqshbandis spread widely, including into South Asia, the home of the majority of the world's Muslim population. But one order in particular is associated primarily with South Asia, the Chishti tariqa. Named for Mu'in al-Din Chishti, who died in northern India in 1236, the order may well have begun far earlier in what is now Afghanistan. Among the most beloved of Sufi saints, Mu'in al-Din is known as Gharib Nawaz, "Friend of the Poor." He taught his followers to cultivate three virtues, attributed to al-Bistami: "a generosity like that of the ocean, a mildness like that of the sun, and a modesty like that of the earth."[20] The order itself reflected these virtues. Its lack of discrimination made its community centers extremely welcoming, especially in the environment of India's hierarchical caste system. Mu'in al-Din's teaching would later be summarized in the phrase *sulh-i kul,* "peace with all," by the Mughal emperor Akbar (d. 1605; see Chapter 3). Another enormously attractive aspect of popular devotion often associated with Chishtis is *qawwali* music. Still today, popular qawwali performers attract thousands to their highly evocative and often lively performances of songs of praise. Mu'in al-Din's tomb at Ajmer remains a popular pilgrimage site.

Other orders are perhaps better known in the West, such as the Mevlevis or "Whirling Dervishes." The Mevlevis incorporate a rhythmic spinning into their prayer recitals. The spinning motion makes their full white robes fan out in a dramatic display. That spectacle, accompanied by music, has earned the Mevlevis invitations to demonstrate their ritual around the world, including at Carnegie Hall. The founder of their order, Jalal al-Din Rumi, cited previously, is also well-known in the West. His exquisite poetry is among the bestselling poetry in the United States today.

Among the most enduring themes of Sufism, and the basis of its universal appeal, is the emphasis on love. That was the theme of Sufism's first saint, a young woman from Iraq named Rabia (d. 801). According to legend, she

Figure 2   Mevlevis or "Whirling Dervishes".
Source: © Ian Berry/Magnum Photos

was born into poverty and sold into slavery. But her piety so inspired her owners that she was freed, so that she could inspire others to lives of utter devotion and absolute, selfless love of God. Numerous verses, attributed to her and passed down through the ages, still have the ability to inspire. She confesses to God, for example, that she has two kinds of love for Him. She does nothing but think of God all day, but she says that is a selfish kind of love because it brings her so much happiness. The love that God deserves, she says, is one that strips away all separation between herself and God, so that she is no longer even aware of herself. Elsewhere, Rabia asks God to let her burn in hell if her devotion is motivated by fear of hell and keep her out of heaven if she is only motivated by hope of reward. Her goal—like that of other Sufis—is to love God without external motivation:

> My peace, brothers, is in my aloneness
> Because my Beloved is alone with me there—always.
> I've found nothing to equal His love,
> That Love which harrows the sands of my desert.
> If I die of Desire, and He is still unsatisfied—
> That sorrow has no end.
> To abandon all He has made
> To hold in my hand
> Proof that He loves me—
> That is the name of my quest.[21]

The teaching of the scholars is important, but it is only a first step toward spiritual awareness, in the Sufi view. As Rabia puts it, "The real work is in the Heart."[22] Even the sober al-Sarraj (d. 987) proclaimed: "Love is a fire that has been lit within the breasts and hearts of the lovers. It burns and turns to ashes everything but God."

But it is Rumi who is best known for expressions of ecstatic love. His poetry beautifully expresses the yearning for spiritual freedom that characterizes much of Sufism. It is a desire to be released from the bonds of selfishness, desire, and greed to be completely absorbed in divine goodness and beauty. Like Rabia, Rumi encourages people to go beyond the externals of religious practice and seek deeper personal awareness:

> For years, copying other people, I tried to know myself.
> From within, I couldn't decide what to do.
> Unable to see, I heard my name being called.
> Then I walked outside.

The key to spiritual awareness, says Rumi, will not be found in books:

> Today, like every other day, we wake up empty
> and frightened. Don't open the door to the study
> and begin reading. Take down a musical instrument.
> Let the beauty we love be what we do.
>   There are hundreds of ways to kneel and kiss the ground.[23]

Instead, true happiness is to be found in the intoxicating love of God:

> God has given us a dark wine so potent that,
> drinking it, we leave the two worlds.
>   God has put into the form of hashish a power
> to deliver the taster from self-consciousness.
> God has made sleep so
> that it erases every thought.
> God make Majnun love Layla so much that
> just her dog would cause confusion in him.
> There are thousands of wines
> that can take over our minds.
> Don't think all ecstasies
> are the same!
> Jesus was lost in his love for God.
> His donkey was drunk with barley.
> Drink from the presence of saints,
> not from those other jars.
> Every object, every being,
> is a jar full of delight.
> Be a connoisseur,
> and taste with caution.[24]

So popular is spiritual poetry that even today, for example, Muhammad Iqbal (d. 1938; see Chapter 4), although he was a profound philosopher and is the "Father of Pakistan," is most beloved for his poetry. And he begins his masterpiece, the *Javid Name*, with a tribute to Rumi:

> Tumultuous love, indifferent to the city—
> for in the city's clangour its flame dies—
> seeks solitude in desert and mountain-range
> or on the shore of an unbounded sea.

> I, who saw among my friends none to confide in,
> rested a moment on the shore of the sea:
> the sea, and the hour of the setting sun—
>   the blue water was a liquid ruby in the gloaming.
> Sunset gives to the blind man the joy of sight,
> sunset gives to evening the hue of dawn.
> I held conversation with my heart;
> I had many desires, many requests—
> a thing of the moment, unsharing immortality,
> a thing living, unsharing life itself,
> thirsty, and yet far from the rim or the fountain,
> involuntarily I chanted this song.[25]

Conclusion

The extraordinary accomplishments of the medieval Muslim world stand as a tribute to the dynamism and creativity in the service of God and humanity that many see as the true spirit of Islam. Many Muslims see them as a reflection of the Quran's unique commitment to intellectual endeavor. The Quran commands even Prophet Muhammad to seek knowledge (20:114). But as Ibn Khaldun observed, no empire lasts forever. Muslims soon faced the challenges of epidemic disease, internal conflict, and external attacks that would eventually shake the empire to its core. But the law, science, and spirituality developed in the medieval world would survive and serve as a foundation for reorganization and renewed growth in the Muslim world, until it was ultimately subdued by European colonization.

Notes

1. See al-Baladhuri, *Futuh al-Buldan*, ed. DeGoeje (Leyden: E. J. Brill, 1866), trans. Phillip K. Hitti as *The Origins of the Islamic State* (New York: Columbia University Press, 1916), 110–112; Daniel C. Dennet, Jr., *Conversion and the Poll Tax* (Cambridge, MA: Harvard University Press, 1950), 12ff.; C. Cahen, "Djizya," in John L. Esposito, ed., *Encyclopedia of Islam*, 2nd ed. (New York: Oxford University Press, 2009), 2:559; H. Lammens, *Études sur le regne du Calife Omaiyade Mo'awia Ier* (Beirut: Imprimerie Catholique, 1930), 226.

2. See N. J. Coulson, *A History of Islamic Law* (Edinburgh: Edinburgh University Press, 1964), chs. 2 and 3, on which this account is based.
3. Fazlur Rahman, *Islam and Modernity: Transformation of an Intellectual Tradition* (Chicago: University of Chicago Press, 1982), 32.
4. Coulson, *A History of Islamic Law*, 37.
5. For a discussion of this claim, see Wael B. Hallaq, "Was al-Shafi'i the Master Architect of Islamic Jurisprudence?" *International Journal of Middle East Studies*, 25 no. 4 (Nov. 1993), 587–605.
6. "He who holds what the Muslim community holds shall be regarded as following the community, and he who holds differently shall be regarded as opposing the community he was ordered to follow." Trans. in Majid Khadduri, *Islamic Jurisprudence: Shafi'i's Risala* (Baltimore: Johns Hopkins University Press, 1961), 287.
7. Trans. Bernard Lewis in *Politics and War*, vol. 1 *of Islam* (New York: Harper Torchbooks, 1974), 171–179.
8. Dennis Overbye, "How Islam Won, and Lost, the Lead in Science," *New York Times*, Oct. 30, 2001, retrieved July 1, 2015, from http://www.nytimes.com/2001/10/30/science/how-islam-won-and-lost-the-lead-in-science.html?pagewanted=1
9. Philip K. Hitti, *History of the Arabs: From the Earliest Times to the Present* (New York: Palgrave Macmillan, 2002), 363.
10. Cited in E. B. Fryde, "History," *The New Encyclopedia Britannica* (Chicago, 1991), 20:566.
11. See, for example, Ronald Reagan, *Public Papers of the Presidents of the United States: 1981* (Washington: United States Government Printing Office, 1982), 745, 871.
12. Ibn Khaldun, *The Muqaddimah: An Introduction to History*, trans. Franz Rosenthal, ed. and abridged N. J. Dawood (Princeton, NJ: Princeton University Press, 1974), 11, 13, 23.
13. See Jawid A. Mojaddedi, "Legitimizing Sufism in al-Qushayri's 'Risala,'" *Studia Islamica*, 20 (2000), 37–50.
14. http://ibnarabisociety.org/.
15. Annemarie Schimmel, *Mystical Dimensions of Islam* (Chapel Hill: University of North Carolina Press, 1975), 283.
16. Quoted in A. J. Arberry, *Sufism: An Account of the Mystics of Iszlam* (London: Mandal Books/Unwin Paperbacks, 1979), 109.
17. Arberry, *Sufism*.
18. Arberry, *Sufism*, 117.
19. Quoted from H. A. R. Gibb, *Muhammedanism* (Oxford: Oxford University Press, 1961), 150–151.
20. See Schimmel, *Mystical Dimensions of Islam*, 345–346.
21. Schimmel, *Mystical Dimensions of Islam*, 24.

22. See Charles Upton, *Doorkeeper of the Heart: Versions of Rabi`a* (Putney, VT: Threshold Books, 1988), 23, 27, 43.
23. John Moyne and Coleman Barks, *Open Secret: Versions of Rumi* (Putney, VT: Threshold Books, 1984), 77, 82.
24. Mathnawi IV, 2683–2696, in Coleman Barks et al., *The Essential Rumi* (San Francisco: HarperCollins, 1995).
25. http://www.allamaiqbal.com/.

3

Division and Reorganization

The Crusades and Other Disasters

Among the catastrophes that struck the Muslim world in the late Middle Ages was the Black Death. That was the name given to the bubonic plague, a gruesome, deadly disease that swept Europe in the mid-fourteenth century, killing up to two-thirds of the population in some places. In England alone it reduced the population by half. But the plague hit the Muslim world equally hard. From the Black Sea, trading ships spread it throughout the Mediterranean, including Islamic North Africa and Spain, killing more than half the population in some cities.

Unfortunately, the plague was not the only disaster to hit the medieval Muslim world. It was also besieged by European invaders who believed they were fighting a holy war for Christianity. By the tenth century, Europe had become mired in corruption and conflict. Much of it stemmed from the competition for supreme power between the Holy Roman emperors and the popes. This was not a struggle between secular and sacred or earthly and heavenly authority; the competitors did not believe they were in the process of dividing up spheres of influence (even though that is how it turned out in the long run). Both the emperors and the popes were struggling for overall authority on earth, sanctioned by heaven. At the end of the eleventh century, Pope Urban II was determined to reassert church leadership, not just in the

Islam: History, Religion, and Politics, Third Edition. Tamara Sonn.
© 2016 John Wiley & Sons, Ltd. Published 2016 by John Wiley & Sons, Ltd.

spiritual realm but also in the earthly one. A request from the Byzantine emperor in Constantinople (in modern Turkey) for assistance in his struggle against the growing power of the Muslims in the Middle East provided the perfect opportunity. The chance for Rome to help Constantinople had the added bonus of demonstrating that the pope was leader of both Western and Eastern Christians. Pope Urban II therefore called a church council and challenged his Christian warriors to rise to the occasion.

Christians were already prone to be suspicious of Muslims. They had heard that they were "infidels," and followers of a "false prophet." St. John of Damascus (d. 749) had described Islam as a heresy derived from Christian sources.[1] Eulogius, the bishop of Cordova during the ninth century, when Cordova was the capital of Islamic Spain, did not help matters. He claimed that when Muhammad died Muslims expected angels to come and take him to heaven. Instead, he said, dogs consumed his body and therefore Muslims conduct an annual slaughter of dogs. Clearly, fear of Muslims was growing in Christian Europe. By the end of the tenth century, the story of a minor battle between Charlemagne and the Basques at Roncesvalles in the eighth century had been transformed into one of France's earliest epics, the "Song of Roland." In this telling of the story, Charlemagne's enemies were not the Basques but the Muslims of Spain. The Muslims, so the story goes, had colluded with a disgruntled French soldier and killed one of France's noblest knights. The poem was the source of another version of the story of Muhammad's death, this one with pigs consuming the Prophet's body. This story was used to explain the Muslim prohibition of the consumption of pork. Other interpretations explain that Muhammad was killed by the pigs while he was drunk; that, Christian audiences were told, was why Muslims also prohibit drinking.[2]

According to the increasing rumors in Europe about Muslims, not only were they infidels, but they were also ruthless killers determined to take over the world. They had already taken over most of Spain, along with parts of southern France and Sicily, not to mention the formerly Christian Byzantine lands in the Middle East—including the "Holy Land." Such stories prepared the ground for the papal call to arms issued in 1095. Pope Urban II is reported to have contributed to the hysteria about Muslims as he tried to encourage his faithful at the Council of Clermont to join in his holy war. His exaggerated stories of hideous torture of Christians, including brutal circumcisions, aroused fear and hatred, of course. But vengeance was hardly a Christian virtue, and killing was still considered a mortal sin. It was a violation of both a sacred commandment and the example set by Jesus. Since the fourth century, when Christianity had become politicized under the emperor Constantine, Christians had been called on to serve as soldiers, but they still had to do penance if they killed someone. But with the Crusades came the transformation of Christianity from a pacifist religion to one that fully condoned war under certain circumstances. Pope Urban II told his flock that killing people in wars declared just by the church was not a sin. It was virtuous, in fact, and any sincere fighter who died in the process became a martyr. All punishment due in the afterlife for sins committed in the here and now would be waived; the martyr was assured immediate entry into heaven.

Thus, it became both a Christian duty and a quick route to "present and eternal glory"[3] to join in the holy war against Muslims, and many Europeans enthusiastically responded to the papal call. Rich and poor, professional and amateur, European Christians joined the call to retake the Holy Land. Wave after wave, they went into Muslim lands, killing Jews and Christians as well as the Muslims who were their main target. The first army of Crusaders captured Antioch and Jerusalem, killing all their inhabitants. They then established their own "Crusader states" in Jerusalem, Tripoli, Antioch, and Edessa. The Second Crusade, called by Pope Eugenius III in 1144, failed in its effort to take Damascus. Eventually, Salah al-Din ("Saladin," d. 1193) succeeded in organizing the Muslims sufficiently to fight back against the European invaders. An Iraqi Kurd who served the Muslim ruling family in Syria and Egypt, he led the campaign to recapture Jerusalem in 1187. The Europeans continued their invasions periodically over the next two centuries. But their last stronghold in the area, Tripoli, was retaken by Muslims in 1289. The ruins of Crusader castles remain in the Middle East, as does the chilling effect of the term "crusade." It recalls the brutality of the Christians and the utter contempt they showed for anyone who did not share their European Christian identity.

To this day, the treachery of the European invaders is recalled with horror. When the Muslims conquered Jerusalem, taking it from the Byzantines in 638, Caliph Umar guaranteed the security of its Christian inhabitants, their property, and churches. When the European Christians took Jerusalem in 1099, according to their own accounts, their leaders promised security to those who surrendered. But except for a few men who had barricaded themselves in a tower, the Christian soldiers slaughtered all the inhabitants, men, women, and children, Muslim and Jewish. Then the Europeans disemboweled the corpses to get at the gold coins they believed the Muslims had "gulped down their loathsome throats."[4] In Jerusalem's al-Aqsa mosque alone, according to Muslim sources, the Crusaders killed "more than 70,000 people, among them a large number of Imams and Muslim scholars, devout and ascetic men who had left their homelands to live lives of pious seclusion in the Holy Place."[5]

The plight of the victims of the European Crusaders was known throughout the Arab Muslim world. One of the historians at the time, Ibn al-Athir (d. 1234), quotes the lament of an Iraqi poet of the era:

> We have mingled blood with flowing tears, and there is not room left in us for pity.
> To shed tears is a man's worst weapon when the swords stir up the embers of war.
> Sons of Islam, behind you are battles in which heads rolled at your feet.
> Dare you slumber in the blessed shade of safety, where life is as soft as an orchard flower?
> How can the eye sleep between the lids at a time of disasters that would waken any sleeper?[6]

Despite the sympathy for the Crusaders' victims, and the strong desire to rescue them, Muslims are proud to recall the valor and restraint shown by Salah al-Din as he rescued Jerusalem, in contrast with the Crusaders' butchery. It took nearly a century for the Muslims to regain Jerusalem, but eventually the European leaders surrendered the city and asked for general amnesty for all its inhabitants. Otherwise, they said, they would kill all their wives, children, prisoners, and animals, and destroy the Islamic holy places. Salah al-Din granted them amnesty and allowed them to be ransomed by their people. Even though the Christian leader of Jerusalem looted both the Christian and Islamic holy sites, Salah al-Din let him go and had him escorted to Tyre. The Muslims were horrified that the ancient holy site, al-Aqsa mosque, had been used by the Christians as a storeroom and latrine, yet Salah al-Din did not rescind his amnesty. He simply ordered the shrines to be cleansed and restored to their original use.

In fact, Salah al-Din was not always so magnanimous. There is a horrific eyewitness account of the treatment received by two groups of religious warriors—the Templars and the Hospitallers, who had terrorized Muslims for years. Salah al-Din had some two hundred of them beheaded, and the onlooker who gives us the gory report claims that the soldiers who carried out the executions received great praise. This was a violation of Islamic norms, which forbid killing prisoners of war. Obviously, Salah al-Din believed that even as prisoners these soldiers were a threat to the survival of the community; he treated the other captive knights with dignity and allowed them to be ransomed later. But most Muslims are unaware of this deviation from Salah al-Din's standard policies. To this day, in recognition of his nobility in victory at Jerusalem, Salah al-Din is eulogized as a model of Islamic virtue: "just, benign, merciful, quick to help the weak against the strong." He was generous, courageous, steadfast, humane, and forgiving.[7] Salah al-Din's valor and nobility had saved Islam from the Western invaders. Their subsequent campaigns, and there were many, were ultimately failures.

A third disaster then struck at the heart of the Muslim world. No sooner had the European invaders been vanquished than the Muslims were attacked from the other direction. Beginning in 1220, waves of Turkic tribesmen, called Mongols, came riding in from central Asia, conquering everything in their path. Led by Genghis Khan, these nomads had no regard for settled, urban life. But they did depend on some of the products of the civilized populations of Islam's great trading cities along the Silk Road, and these became desirable targets for the mighty Mongols.

The Silk Road, made famous by Marco Polo in the thirteenth century, was the ancient trade route established in Greek and Roman times across the Middle East to China. It stretched from the Mediterranean to the Great Wall, crossing Syria, Persia, Afghanistan, Pakistan, India, and central Asia. Along the route, travelers had to contend with treacherous deserts and mountains, including the highest in the world: the Himalayas, the Hindu Kush, and Karakorum; excruciating heat and subzero temperatures; and bandits of every variety. Yet trade along the route thrived until sea travel was developed enough to make it more efficient than land travel over great distances. The silk traded by the Chinese gave the route its name, but it was not the only commodity of value for the thousands who engaged in Silk Road commerce. Precious metals, ivory, oils, skins, ceramics, glass, and spices were some of the other desired products. As well, explorers, missionaries, and conquerors used the route on their adventures. Afghanistan and Pakistan were at the crossroads of the various trails that made up the Silk Road. Alexander the Great traveled to this region in the fourth century BCE. Still today, some residents of modern Afghanistan and Pakistan claim to be descendants of Alexander's troops. Buddhists from India came into Pakistan and Afghanistan in the first century CE, establishing their religion and leaving monuments, including the magnificent sculptures at Bamiyan that were destroyed by the Taliban in 2000. Nestorian Christians fled eastward from Roman authorities who had declared them heretical, in the fifth century, and two centuries later, Muslim traders and teachers along the Silk Road brought Islam as far as China, where it remains a significant presence today.

For centuries the Silk Road was the most important bridge between the East and West. Along its route were some of the most magnificent cities of the ancient world. Bukhara, for example, in present-day Uzbekistan, was established at the site of an oasis by the first century CE. Built around a central fortress, the city provided both protection from the dangers of the road and a trading site. Its inhabitants' gold embroidery and metalwork were valuable commodities in the East–West trade. In the early eighth century it was conquered by Arab Muslims and became a regional capital known for his beautiful mosques and many schools. One of the two leading hadith collectors, in fact, Abu Abd-Allah Muhammad ibn Ismail (d. 870), was from there, which is why most people know him only as al-Bukhari. But Bukhara was attacked and destroyed by the Mongols under Genghis Khan in 1220 and twice thereafter in the next century. Ibn Battuta, the Islamic Marco Polo, visited the city in the 1330s and said, "Its mosques, colleges, and bazaars are in ruins. … There is not one person in it today who possesses any religious learning or who shows any concern for acquiring it."[8] Samarkand, also in present-day Uzbekistan, was another ancient city of central Asia. Originally called Maracanda, Samarkand was established at the crossroads of the India and China routes on the Silk Road. Alexander the Great captured it in 329. When it was conquered by Muslims in 711, the city was renamed Samarkand and remained an important and prosperous regional center. Bukhara and Samarkand were considered among the most beautiful cities in the Muslim world, but like Bukhara, Samarkand was also destroyed by Genghis Khan in 1221.

Under Genghis Khan's successors, the Mongols continued their advance through the Muslim world. In 1258 they reached Baghdad and burned it to the ground. Unlike other Islamic centers like Mecca, Jerusalem, and Damascus, Baghdad was not an ancient city. It was a planned city, established on banks of the Tigris River on the site of a Persian village in 762, as the Abbasid capital. Its architects set up Baghdad around the caliph's palace and a great mosque, with three concentric walls surrounding it and four roads leading out from the center to the four corners of the empire. Markets and suburbs were built outside the walls. Nicknamed Madinat al-Salam (City of Peace), Baghdad quickly became the center of the empire's economic and cultural life. It was described in the *Thousand and One Nights* as one of the world's treasures. Ships from around the Indian Ocean and as far away as China visited its harbor. The city had known conflict in the years following the reign of Harun al-Rashid, but it was still thriving when Hulegu Khan, Genghis' grandson, and his troops descended on it.

Some of the cities destroyed by the Mongols did recover. In Baghdad, the old Abbasid palace survives, as does the Mustansiriyyah, a school of higher Islamic learning built in 1234, but the city did not regain its greatness until the modern era. Timur Lang, or Timur the Lame (Tamerlane, d. 1405), inherited the conquests of the Mongols. A Muslim born of Turkic parents near Samarkand, he took it upon himself to make Samarkand the most splendid capital of a reconstituted Mongol empire. He brought in experts to build great mosques and schools. His buildings were typically large, with domes and arched doorways and decorated with marble and mosaics, many with gold and precious stones. They are still among the greatest architectural monuments of the Islamic world.

The Mongol invasions traditionally mark the end of the political unity of Islam. It was also, for all practical purposes, the end of the Abbasid caliphate. While Baghdad burned, the Abbasid caliph packed up and moved to Cairo. His successors continued to be recognized as Islamic leaders, if in name only, until the last one (al-Mutawakkil III) was taken by Ottoman conquerors to Istanbul in 1517. However, many areas of the Muslim world reorganized eventually and went on to great power and prestige. We will examine the rise of three of them: the Ottoman Turkish and Arab world, Safavid Persia, and Mughal India.

The Decline of the Abbasids and Rise of the Ottomans

Egypt had already become autonomous. It was always difficult for the Muslim leaders to control Egypt from their capitals in Medina, Damascus, and Baghdad. Rebellions in Egypt had marred the reign of the third caliph, Uthman, and there were sporadic uprisings against taxation and religious discrimination thereafter. By the ninth century, the caliphs had begun to grant tax revenues to people they appointed as administrators to this rich region. They also chose people with no tribal ties in the area—primarily Turks who had been purchased as slaves—as administrators for these "tax farms" in an effort to maintain loyalty to the central government alone. These Turkish administrators soon established themselves firmly enough to become autonomous, too, including setting up their own slave army. The architect of this autonomy was a governor named Ibn Tulun. Through careful management of agriculture and taxation, his administration grew rich and powerful, and was even able to take control of Syria from the caliph. He also built the famous Mosque of Ibn Tulun, which still stands in

Cairo. The Abbasids were able to briefly regain control of Egypt in the early tenth century, but in 969 the Shii Fatimid dynasty, headquartered in Tunisia, conquered Egypt and ruled it until 1171.

The Fatimids were a formidable force. They were from a branch of Shii Islam (see discussion in this chapter). Their name comes from that of Prophet Muhammad's daughter Fatima because they believe that only Muhammad's descendants through the marriage of his cousin Ali to his daughter Fatima were legitimate *imams* (in Shii usage, "rulers"). The Fatimids therefore considered themselves not just independent of the Sunni Abbasid caliph, but also the rightful holders of his position. From their original base in Yemen, they were able to establish sovereignty all across North Africa, as well as in Sicily, Syria, and western Arabia. They were fiercely committed to their cause and gained the loyalty of many Muslims discontent with Abbasid rule. They quickly became wealthy and powerful. It was the Fatimids who established the city of Cairo in 969 and built it into a splendid center of military, including naval, power. Cairo was also a magnificent cultural center: the Fatimids established al-Azhar University there, which was the first university in the Western world and is still thriving. But the Fatimids had their own problems with the question of succession. A group broke away from the rest of the Fatimids in 1094: its members believed that the legitimate successor, Nizar, had been unfairly passed over in favor of his younger brother. Known by Islamic historians as the Nizaris, this group plunged the regime into civil war. The group is known by European historians as the Assassins, because they fought the crusaders so fiercely. (The name Assassins comes from the Nizaris' alleged use of hashish to prepare themselves for battle; they were called the *Hashishin*, "those who use hashish.")

The Fatimids were in power in Egypt when the crusaders first descended on Jerusalem. Many people believed that the Fatimids' lack of cooperation with Baghdad weakened the overall Muslim effort against the Europeans. They were the ones that Salah al-Din overthrew to return Egypt to the Sunni fold so that he could create a unified front against the Crusaders. But Salah al-Din also established an independent dynasty in Egypt, the Ayyubids (1171–1250). With the powerful army he established in Egypt, he was able not only to defeat the Crusaders and gain control of Jerusalem and the Holy Land but also to gain control over Syria, Iraq, Yemen, and western Arabia (Hijaz). Despite the stability and prosperity his victories brought to Egypt, power struggles developed. Like the Abbasids before them, the Ayyubids sought to maintain a loyal army by staffing it with slaves (*mamluks* from the

Arabic term for slave), mainly Turkish. The idea was that, as foreigners, these slaves would have no local loyalties that could develop into rival power structures. But by the end of the ninth century, mamluk soldiers had gained control of the Abbasid caliphate. Abbasids remained caliphs, but mamluks were the real rulers (sultans), and even they did not control the entire Muslim world. The caliph was acknowledged as the spiritual leader of the Muslim world but Egypt was autonomous. By the mid-thirteenth century, Ayyubid mamluks became Mamluks—in effect, a dynasty in its own right, in control of the Egyptian empire that Salah al-Din had established.

Not all Mamluk sultans placed their sons on the throne, but all were from a particular branch of former slave soldiers. And to ensure that they were recognized as legitimate rulers, the Mamluks invited the Abbasid caliph, who had been deposed by the Mongols from his palace in Baghdad (1258), to take up residence in Cairo. By this time, there were no pretensions of combined religio-political rule. The caliph had no earthly power whatever. He was a symbol of Islamic unity and gave legitimacy to the political rulers.

Making use of their own military, the Mamluks were effective rulers for the first half of their two-and-a-half-century reign. They became heroes by defeating the Sixth Crusade and repulsed an early Mongol invasion (1260). But they were not able to fully protect their lands. By the fourteenth century, the plague had hit Egypt and decimated its population. What is more, the Europeans came back, this time not as warriors but as traders. Portuguese traders developed safe and efficient sea trade routes around the Indian Ocean, bypassing the overland routes that had been a significant source of revenue for the Mamluks. And the Mongols came back, too. After they had taken over the Abbasid capital in Baghdad, they established a number of regimes throughout Central and South Asia and the Middle East (Southwest Asia).

By that time, the Mongols had become Muslims themselves, at least in name. The famous Timur Lang (Tamerlane), who would rebuild Samarkand and make it his splendid capital, tried to unify all the Mongols. He subdued the local *khans* (rulers) in Central Asia, the Crimea, Persia (which at that time included what is now western Afghanistan), and Mesopotamia (Iraq), and raided as far as Delhi in India. He was brutal beyond belief. Stories are told of entire cities' populations being massacred. His troops gained a reputation for being expert riders and archers who built towers of the skulls of their thousands of victims. But he was also successful, amassing the great wealth he used to rebuild and beautify Samarkand, for example. Inevitably, he turned again toward the Arab world. In 1401 he defeated Egypt's Mamluk army and took control of Syria and Iraq. Damascus was taken and Baghdad was once again destroyed.

By the time Timur died (in 1405, on his way to China), Mamluk power was on the wane. The Mamluks continued to rule Egypt, but they never recovered the country's economic prosperity or military might. Another of the autonomous forces during Abbasid times with whom the Mongols tangled were the Seljuks (also spelled Seljuqs), a dynasty named for the leader of one of the nomadic Turkic tribes from Central Asia. They began as border guards for a semi-autonomous Persian family (the Samanids; see discussion in this chapter) in the ninth and tenth centuries. By the mid-eleventh century they were in control of Baghdad, ruling in the name of the Abbasid caliph.

The Ottomans were another Turkic dynasty. Like the Seljuks for whom they originally worked, they had begun as border warriors, guarding the northwest frontier against invasions and launching their own attacks against the Byzantine forces in the name of Islam. The power struggle between the Seljuks and Mongols weakened the Seljuks sufficiently to allow the Ottomans to firmly establish their power in Anatolia (present-day Turkey) in the thirteenth century. Their armies became a magnet for men seeking employment, both Muslims looking for work as *mujahiddin* (warriors in the struggle to spread Islam) and Christians looking for work as mercenaries. By the fourteenth century they had established a regular cavalry and an infantry, called the "new troops" or *Janissaries*, consisting mainly of converted Christian conscripts from the Balkans. By the end of that century, the Ottoman chief Bayezid had managed to establish sovereignty in the Balkans. The name of the Ottomans came to symbolize hope for a reunified Islamic empire; the nominal Abbasid caliph in Cairo began to call the Ottomans sultans of Islam, rather than the Mamluks under whose protection they were living.

By this time, the ferocious Timur Lang felt the challenge. Although he was busy expanding his sovereignty from Central Asia toward India, he decided to stop the advancing Ottoman powers. The two most powerful forces in the Islamic world at the time were competing for dominance. It was Timur's forces that triumphed in battle at Ankara in 1402. But the result was not reunification of the empire. Timur's power would continue to be felt in the eastern regions, whereas the Ottomans continued their consolidation of power in the west.

The Europeans also began to worry about Ottoman expansion and even organized a new Crusade (1444) to try to drive the Ottomans back across the Dardanelles (the straits that separate Europe from Asia at Gallipoli). But it failed, largely because of the loyalty of the Serbian Christian rulers to the Ottoman sultan. In 1453, under Mehmed (Muhammad) II, "the Conqueror" (r. 1451–1481), the Ottomans put an end to the Byzantine empire, capturing Constantinople. It became the new Ottoman capital, and later became known as Istanbul.

By the turn of the sixteenth century, Ottoman forces had subdued rival Muslim rulers in the region and expanded Ottoman sovereignty further in the Balkans, including Serbia, Bosnia, and Albania, as well as Crimea, and were well on their way to establishing naval superiority in the eastern Mediterranean. The idea of a reunified Islamic world may have been out of the question, but reunifying former Byzantine lands under the banner of the Ottoman sultan was not. The Ottomans simply had to oust their Seljuk cousins from Syria and Egypt. That was accomplished by Sultan Selim I (r. 1512–1520), who was just the man for the job. He had killed his own brothers and nephews and four of his own five sons to make sure no one interfered with his hold on the throne. By 1517 his forces had swept away the remaining impediments to Ottoman dominance in the Arab world, including the conquest of Syria and Egypt. The Ottomans then claimed that the last Abbasid caliph had transferred the rights to the caliphate to them.

The way was thus clear for Selim's hand-picked (i.e., only surviving) successor, Suleiman, to become "the Lawgiver" (r. 1520–1566). Suleiman's predecessors had established a stable administration. The practice of granting land in return for service, which was the source of weakness in so many administrations of the time, was replaced with uniform taxation throughout Ottoman domains, thus avoiding another traditional source of discontent. Islamic law was guaranteed as the law of the land, but it was only part of the law. In a move that would have significant consequences in the modern era, the Ottomans devised a legal system whereby their legitimacy was maintained. The Ottomans enforced Islamic law, but at the same time they retained the right to issue their own laws for matters not yet developed in Islamic courts. Islamic law, identified as Shariah, was in force side by side with Ottoman law, called *Kanun* (Arabic: *qanun*). The application of Islamic law was effectively limited to ritual and personal matters (e.g., the proper ways to cleanse oneself, pray, give charity, fast, and perform pilgrimage, and the correct procedures for marriage, divorce, and inheritance), which were the most highly developed aspects of Islamic law at the time. That left the Ottoman bureaucracy considerable leeway in developing law for administrative, commercial, and other areas of vital concern to the government. Non-Muslim religious communities—Jews and Christians—were given autonomy, precluding dissent on grounds of religious discrimination.

The stability achieved during this period of Ottoman history allowed for enormous prosperity. Ottoman wealth can perhaps best be measured in its artistic achievements, chief among which are its architectural monuments. Ottoman architecture reached its high point during the reign of Suleiman, a generous patron of the arts. His chief architect was Joseph Sinan (d. 1588), a Greek Christian citizen drafted into service in his early twenties, who designed hundreds of mosques, palaces, schools, public baths, and poor-houses, in addition to bridges, fountains, and granaries. Many of his works are still counted among the most spectacular in the world. Two of the most famous are the great mosques of Suleiman (Suleymaniyya) in Istanbul and Selim in Edirne (Selimiyya). Sinan's buildings are supremely light and elegant. Their enormous central domes and walls are pierced with dozens of windows, and their walls are covered in light colors, inlaid with beautiful tile and mosaic designs. The mosque of Selim is probably Sinan's greatest achievement. It went beyond his previous technique of achieving lightness and spaciousness through minimal internal supports, to designing a building without any internal supports whatsoever. It is not only a monument to architectural beauty; it is an engineering masterpiece.

The stability and prosperity of Ottoman administration also allowed for further expansion. From their base in Egypt, the Ottomans expanded their authority over the numerous autonomous regimes in North Africa (the Maghreb). By the end of Suleiman's reign their empire included Libya and Algeria; Tunisia would be included soon afterward. To the Europeans, Suleiman came to be known as "the Magnificent," as he continued Ottoman expansion in their direction. Belgrade fell to Ottoman forces in 1521, and twenty years later, so did Hungary. By 1529 Suleiman's army was besieging Vienna. Although Suleiman's westward expansion was stopped at Vienna, the Ottomans were powerful enough to take advantage of Europe's divided politics. The sixteenth century was a time when Catholics were battling Protestants, and ruling families were competing for control of the disinte-grating Holy Roman Empire. The Habsburgs, still holding the title of Holy Roman emperors, reigned supreme in Austria, the Netherlands, Luxembourg, Burgundy, and Spain. France, naturally, felt surrounded, and was therefore happy to support Suleiman's efforts in the East, hoping it would weaken the Habsburgs. It was this combination of circumstances that allowed Suleiman's forces to take Belgrade in 1521.

Figure 3   The mosque of Selim complex (1557) in Istanbul.
Source: © Chris Hellier/Corbis

The Habsburgs and Ottomans continued to compete for Hungary for another twenty years, and Europe continued to fear the Ottoman expansion right through the seventeenth century, when the last attempt to take Vienna was turned back. By that time, the Ottoman Empire was well into its declining years, although it would survive until the end of World War I, and with it, the caliphate. The last person to be named caliph, Abdulmecid II, died in exile in Paris in 1924; the office of caliphate was officially abolished in 1924. Despite the caliphal title and the greatness achieved by the

Ottomans, the Muslim world never again achieved political unity. From their stronghold in Anatolia, the Ottoman Turks consolidated control only over the Arab world. The Persian world was organized independently.

Persia: The Safavid Empire

While Ottoman expansion was halted in Europe at Vienna, its eastward push was stopped in Persia, which would establish the second great Islamic empire of the middle period. It is arguable that if Suleiman had concentrated all his efforts in the Islamic world instead of pushing into Europe, Islamic political reunification might have been possible. But as it was, Suleiman ended up fighting on two fronts. In the east, he pushed beyond Syria, taking Iraq and parts of Azerbaijan. There he ran up against the expanding power of the Persian shah (king) Esmail and his son Tahmasp I.

After the destruction of Baghdad (1258), various Mongol dynasties established their regimes in the region and competed for control the area after the death of the last Il Khanid, Abu Said in 1335. Not surprisingly, it was Timur Lang who came out on top, taking Khurasan and eastern Persia by 1385. From there he continued to consolidate his holdings in the region, as we saw previously. Although the warrior Seljuks were able to gain dominance in Baghdad and Syria, giving way eventually to the warrior Ottomans, in Persia it was the descendants of a religious order, the Safavids, who were able to oust the Mongols. This would give a different character to Persian history from that of the Turks and Turkish-dominated Arabs.

The Safavids were a Sufi order that originated in Turkic Azerbaijan in the fourteenth century. Identifiable by their red turbans (which is why they were known as Kizilbash, or "Red Heads"), the Safavids attracted followers from throughout Iran as well as its surrounding territories (Syria, eastern Anatolia, the Caucasus, and beyond). As their influence grew, their ideology also developed. During the fifteenth century, they highlighted their distinction from their primarily Sunni neighbors by identifying themselves as a specifically Shii order. Basing their legitimacy on the main branch of Shii Islam, they became more and more powerful and gradually overcame other local rulers. By the turn of the sixteenth century, they had evicted the Mongols from northern Iran and declared themselves sovereign.

As Safavid influence spread northwestward into eastern Anatolia, the Ottomans decided they had to stop them. As champions of Sunni orthodoxy, the Ottomans considered the Shii and Sufi Safavids to be heretics.

Several serious clashes between the Ottomans and Safavids took place in the early sixteenth century. The Ottomans took the challenge so seriously that when their own Sultan Bayezid (r. 1482–1512) began to be attracted to Sufi mysticism they deposed him. The ferocious Selim I then took up the struggle against the Shii Safavids. The Safavids were no match for his artillery-equipped troops. Still using archers, the Safavids were defeated in 1514 and sent back into their central Persian strongholds. But the Ottomans, also engaged in Europe, were unable to gain further victories against the Safavids. In a treaty signed at Amsaya (1555), Suleiman agreed to leave Azerbaijan and the Caucasus to Persia and allow Persian pilgrims access to the holy cities of Mecca and Medina and to Shii pilgrimage sites in Iraq.

The western Muslim world thus achieved equilibrium, delineated between the Sunni Ottomans (1517–1922) and the Shii Safavids (1502–1722). Shii Islam, now represented in a state, was free to develop its unique character. As noted in Chapter 1, Sunni and Shii Islam differ little on essential doctrinal issues. The main difference between the two branches of Islam is in their respective theories of government and its relationship to prophecy. In Sunni Islam, the death of Prophet Muhammad marked the end of prophecy and the beginning of human beings' responsibility to find ways to implement the Quran's demand for justice, inspired by the Prophet's example, in ever-changing circumstances. In Shii Islam, the death of the Prophet marked the end of prophecy but not the end of prophetic guidance. According to Shii thought, divinely inspired guidance continues through the family of Prophet Muhammad. His descendants were therefore the only legitimate successors to the Prophet's earthly leadership. His descendants were not themselves prophets, but their interpretations of scripture were authoritative. By contrast, in Sunni Islam, legal scholars were charged with the responsibility of interpreting scripture for application in daily life, and the profession of scholarship was open to anyone willing to undertake the requisite training. As it happens, Shiis did not always agree on which descendant of the Prophet should rule. Shiism split during the seventh century over this issue; there had been other disputes prior to this, and there were other minor splits later on. But the major branch of Shii thought (the Twelvers, *Ithnaàshari* Shiis) believes that the line of Prophet Muhammad's descendants eligible for community leadership ended by the ninth century. The last imam (identified as Muhammad al-Muntazar, by the Twelver Shiis) will return before the end of the world as the *Mahdi*, "guided one." The Mahdi will then lead humanity in creating a just society before the end of time and final judgment. Until that time, the last imam exists in a hidden or spiritual form (often called "occultation" or *al-ghaibah* in Arabic) and continues to offer guidance to the community through the legal scholars. Until the Mahdi returns, Shii Muslims are instructed to cooperate with their governments and follow the guidance of the scholars.

In the absence of the imam, Sunni and Shii theories of government, therefore, are not terribly different. Shii Islam, however, particularly Twelver Shiism, did develop an ethos or overall character different from that of the dominant Sunnis. This character stems primarily from the fact that the Shii were persecuted by the early Sunnis. The Prophet's grandsons, championed by the Shii, were harassed by the Sunni Umayyads, and the younger grandson, Husayn, was ultimately martyred. As a result, from its earliest days Shii Islam was a voice of vigilance and protest against injustice and suffering for the cause of justice. As Mohammad Khatami, former president of Iran put it:

> In the Muslim world, especially in Iran, whenever oppressed people have risen against tyranny, their activism has been channeled through religion. People have always witnessed the fiery and bloodied face of religious revolutionaries who have risen to fight oppression and despotism.
>
> Our social conscience is replete with memories of the clash of true believers with hypocrites who have used religion to justify people's misery. Our part of the world has witnessed the historical antagonism between truth- and justice-seeking religion and the oppressive and misguided views of religion that have been the tool of oppressors.
>
> Is it not true that in the history of Islam, religion has opposed religious and secular tyranny?[9]

It was during the Safavid period that Twelver Shii Islam's ethos of suffering in the struggle against injustice was institutionalized. The martyrdom of Imam Husayn in 680 by Umayyad troops took place at Karbala on the tenth of Muharram (the first month of the Islamic calendar). Karbala, in Iraq, became—as it remains today—a major site pilgrimage for Shiis. The month of Muharram became a time of mourning (*ta 'ziyyah*), similar to the Christian period of Lent, in memory of the suffering of the martyrs. It is still marked by poetry recitations and reenactments of the martyrdom of Husayn, similar to Christian Passion plays.

Safavid Persia also became a place of high cultural achievement. As in Ottoman Turkey, the peace provided by political equilibrium allowed for prosperity and cultural productivity. By the time Islam came to the Persians, they already had a long history of urban society and efficient bureaucracies. In fact, it was a Persian family who organized the Abbasids' bureaucracy for them. The Safavids therefore readily developed an efficient state administration, which was headquartered in Isfahan. The great Safavid Shah Abbas (r. 1588–1629) made Isfahan his capital and set about beautifying it with parks and fountains and architectural monuments unrivaled to this day. The city is centrally organized around an enormous plaza surrounded by bazaars (*bazaar* is the Persian word for *market*), parks, palaces, schools, and other public buildings. It is dominated by mosques, including the magnificent mosques of Shah Abbas and Lotfallah. The Lotfallah mosque is considered one of the world's most beautiful religious buildings. Its facade is covered with tiles of various shades of blue; its graceful Persian-style dome is decorated with an elegant turquoise floral design on a white background. People who visit the mosque say its overall effect is so awesome as to inspire spirituality even in unbelievers. Shah Abbas also patronized other arts, including one of Persia's most unique contributions, the painting of miniatures. Among the oldest surviving examples of this exquisite art form are those from Isfahan. Works by the city's undisputed master, Reza Abbasi, are on display at New York's Metropolitan Museum of Art.

Eventually, Safavid leaders succumbed to attacks from powerful neighbors. Interestingly, the last Safavid king was overthrown by an Afghan tribal leader, Mahmud of Kandahar in 1722. Later, another Persian dynasty would rise, the Qajars (r. 1794–1925), and they would be replaced by the Pahlavis in the twentieth century. But the influence of Safavid culture remained dominant. Among the first tasks undertaken by Reza Shah Pahlavi (r. 1925–1941) was the restoration of Isfahan's architectural beauty. Persian culture was also undoubtedly influential in shaping the culture of the third great center of Islamic life in the middle period, Mughal India.

India and the Rise of the Mughals

On the eastern borders of Persia was the autonomous Ghaznavid Empire. It had arisen during the decline of Samanid control of western Afghanistan. The Samanids were a Persian family who had gained autonomy under Abbasid rule and taken control of much of Afghanistan as well as the great Silk Road cities of Khurasan, Samarkand, and Bukhara, their capital. They were powerful and their reign was prosperous and was known for great art and culture. By the eleventh century, the Samanids' border guards, the Seljuks, had taken control and begun expanding westward. On the eastern side of the empire, another of their former slave guards (Sebuktegin, d. 997) had broken away and established himself as the ruler of Ghazna (present-day Ghazni, Afghanistan). His son Mahmud (d. 1030) then expanded his control. As the Samanids' power decreased, Mahmud took temporary control of parts of Persia, but his major impact was in the other direction. After a series of brutal raids, he gained control across present-day Pakistan. To that Hindu and Buddhist region, he brought what would become the permanent presence of Islam. His raids, particularly those on Hindu temples, also brought him vast wealth. (Mahmud, like Timur after him, was decidedly intolerant of other religions. He perhaps even set an example for the modern-day Taliban in his destruction of other people's religious icons.) He used this wealth to finance cultural development in his realm, particularly Persian high culture. Although he was of Turkic background and anti-Shii religiously, he established Persian as the language of culture in his realm. He also brought famous scholars such as the scientist al-Biruni and the poet Firdawsi to his court; the final version of Firdawsi's famous epic *Shah Nameh* (*Book of Kings*) was dedicated to this ruthless ruler. Written in verse form, the *Shah Nameh* tells the story of Persian history from ancient times to the Arab conquests. It remains a classic of Persian literature.

Successors to Mahmud's power base moved the capital to Lahore, the great ancient city of the Punjab, having lost eastern ground to Persian powers. There they remained for some time, and much of the region became Muslim. Then around 1190, the Persian Ghurid rulers who had taken control of Ghazna, began raids into Indian territory. They ousted the last of Mahmud's successors at Lahore and within ten years began a military campaign right across northern India. It was the slave-warriors (mamluks) who worked for the Ghurids who ultimately established what would become Islam's lasting power base in India: the sultanate of Delhi.

As Mahmud had done in Ghazna, once they had established peace, the sultans of Delhi introduced Persian-influenced Islamic high culture. Poets and artists were welcomed there, and merchants found ready markets. Sufi missionaries brought their mystical teachings, becoming the major source of Islamic religious learning in India. Indigenous Hindu society in the region was divided along caste lines and well-established in their localized realms. Muslim rulers had more expansive territorial designs. Free of caste restrictions and offering religious freedom to their subjects, the Muslims became in effect a ruling class. The sultans of Delhi built on the prosperity offered by trade and local agriculture and were able to expand their sovereignty during the thirteenth and fourteenth centuries. By 1350 they had gained dominance throughout much of the Indian subcontinent.

The sultanate of Delhi was effectively ended by another of Timur Lang's infamous attacks. This one was particularly brutal. Timur considered the Delhi sultans' policy of religious freedom to be unconscionable. For Timur, unlike most Muslims, religious freedom was not an essential feature of Islam; in fact, he was mortally opposed to it. In 1398 his troops destroyed Delhi and massacred its inhabitants. Fortunately for all concerned, however, Timur was dead by 1405, allowing Islam in India to recover from his near-fatal blow. Autonomous Muslim rulers outside Delhi survived, and eventually Islamic power was reconstituted in Delhi under the Lodi sultans from the highlands of Afghanistan in the late fourteenth century.

What would become the great Mughal (i.e., Mongol) Empire in India was begun by Babur (d. 1530). Babur had inherited Timur's Mongol power in Kabul and, in true Mongol fashion, began to look beyond his borders. In 1526 he defeated the Lodi sultans (at the battle of Panipat) and took control of Delhi. But Babur's Mongol successors would overcome their heritage of intolerance. They would foster a culture of interreligious respect that would allow them to maintain dominance in India until the British took control in the eighteenth century.

The architect of the Mughals' ecumenical culture was Babur's grandson Akbar "the Great" (r. 1556–1605). As we have seen, the stability and prosperity of the Ottoman and Safavid empires were established despite the challenges posed by the ferocious Timur. Akbar was the only ruler of the middle period who was a direct descendant of Timur (as well as of Genghis Khan). But defying his intolerant heritage, he was among Islam's most enlightened rulers. Inheriting control of virtually all of northern India, including parts of present-day Pakistan, Bangladesh, and Afghanistan, Akbar found himself not only a cultural minority but also a religious one. Muslims were and would remain a minority in India, along with dozens of other minorities, including Christians, Jews, and Zoroastrians. But Akbar welcomed religious diversity. He established a uniform tax system that did not discriminate against non-Muslims and incorporated Hindus into his administration. To preclude divisive and destructive religious discrimination, he promoted respect for a nonsectarian monotheism (called *din-i ilahi* or "divine religion"). Allowing full expression of the rich cultural heritage of his many diverse subjects, Akbar thus gave rise to one of the most unique and culturally productive regimes in Islamic history.

Although Islamic rule in India ended more than two centuries ago, and hostility between the Hindus and Muslims remains, Mughal architecture still offers enduring and cherished evidence of its legacies. The planned city of Fatehpur Sikri, for example, built by Akbar, is a wonder of sixteenth-century engineering. Its monumental gateway clearly reveals the combined Hindu and Islamic styles. It is ornately carved with multiple arches over a post and lintel structure and opens directly into the Great Mosque of Fatehpur Sikri. Unfortunately, Akbar and his technicians overlooked one essential aspect of life in their planning: water. The city had to be abandoned for lack of this vital resource, but it remains a popular tourist attraction. A massive gate, the Delhi Gate, was a feature of another of Akbar's achievements, the Agra Fort.

Akbar's son and grandson provided even greater architectural monuments to India. Jahangir (r. 1605–1627), who was born on the site of Fatehpur Sikri, added to the beauty of the Mughal landscape, creating the Shalimar Gardens in Kashmir, for example. But his greatest devotion was to art. He was a painter himself and devoted enormous resources to patronizing the art. Earlier Mughal painting is known for its riotous colors and movement, but Jahangir's artists, known primarily for their portraiture, developed a more delicate, sedate, almost spiritual style. Jahangir's son Shah Jahan (r. 1628–1658) continued to support art (in the United Kingdom, examples can be found in Windsor Castle library) but not to the extent that his father did. He will always be remembered for his architectural monuments. Among them are the Great Mosque and Red Fort at Delhi—again, a massive structure of red sandstone, with rows and rows of columns and arches under a flat roof. He also built the Shalimar Gardens of Lahore, eighty acres of lush gardens beautifully landscaped and accented by reflecting pools and fountains of white marble. But none is more famous than the Taj Mahal, the splendid mausoleum he commissioned at Agra for his wife Mumtaz Mahal. Its white marble dome and towers, complemented by its trademark reflecting pool, remain a symbol of love and spirituality for people of all faiths and none.

The respect for religious diversity institutionalized by early Mughal rulers certainly contributed to the peace and prosperity of the realm, reflected in its refined cultural achievements. The period is also noteworthy for its intellectual sophistication. In Mughal India science and scholarship continued to flourish. A unique reflection of this openness and sophistication is seen in the genre of humorous social satire, for example in the stories of Raja Birbal, Emperor Akbar's court poet. Birbal was a peasant from outside Agra who had helped the emperor find his way to Agra one day. In gratitude, the emperor told the boy to visit him someday in his capital. When he was a bit older, Birbal decided the time had come. He approached the guard at the royal court and found him skeptical, to say the least. He managed to convince him to let him in, but only by promising to share half of any gift the emperor might bestow on the young man. He entered Akbar's chamber and the king remembered him at once and was delighted he had come. "Ask for anything your heart desires and it shall be yours," he said. Birbal said, "If [Your Majesty] pleases, my dearest wish is to be given fifty lashes of the whip!" Naturally, people thought he was crazy but when the king asked him why he wanted such a strange gift, Birbal explained that the guards would only let him in if he split any gift with them. "Are our people to be kept away by a greedy, wicked guard?" he thundered. "Send for the rascal!" The guard was sentenced to the entire "gift" of fifty lashes and never again tried to bully poor people who sought an audience with the emperor. And [the young man] was given a place at the court, with all the comforts that went with it. "We confer on you the title of Raja Birbal from this day on," the emperor declared. "And you shall stay near us and amuse and guide us henceforth!"[10] From then on, Birbal both entertained and gently criticized the mighty and meek alike.

Even more interesting as a reflection of the times are the stories of Nasroddin. Nasroddin was a legendary figure who symbolized both wisdom and foolishness, or perhaps wisdom and social commentary disguised as foolishness. Satire of any aspect of society could be clothed in a story about Nasroddin. If the story were cleverly enough presented, it might circulate far and wide as a vehicle of people's concerns.

One of the stories told about Nasroddin reveals a growing concern about the excessive mysticism in Indian popular religion. According to this story, Nasroddin was sent by the king to find out about the spiritual leaders who had become so famous in India at the time. Nasroddin traveled the countryside, interviewing members of the mystical communities and listening as they outdid one another with stories of their leaders' wondrous and miraculous works. He then returned home and wrote his report for the king. It contained only one word: "Carrots." The king asked him what that was supposed to mean. What did carrots have to do with mysticism? Nasroddin explained that, like a carrot, most of the reality of mysticism is hidden from view; few people recognize it when they see it growing; it must be cultivated and if it isn't, it will deteriorate; and "there are a great many donkeys associated with it."[11]

In fact, Indian Islam had traditionally been dominated by Sufi teachers, particularly those from the Chishti and Suhrawardi orders. Islamic political sovereignty in the Indian subcontinent was established by military force. But spreading the religion was left primarily to the Sufi preachers. As noted in Chapter 2, the Chishtis were deeply spiritual. Their preachers taught people to avoid materialism in all its forms. Poverty was considered a virtue and social involvement a distraction. The goal of spiritual life in Chishti thought was to achieve union with the divine One by transcending the self through chanting (*dhikr*). Chishti communal centers (*khanaqahs*) became major sources of Islamic teaching from the thirteenth and four-teenth centuries in northern India; for many people, they were the only source of Islamic teaching. The Suhrawardi order cultivated piety through dhikr based on the names of God. A number of other nontraditional forms of religious expression also developed on the popular level, such as those of the Qalandars. Less organized than Sufi *tariqas*, these "irregulars" often displayed unorthodox behavior and little respect for Shariah.

The Sufi approach to spiritual development allowed for a wide range of religious expression and was, as such, naturally tolerant. But it also gave rise to concern among scholars that the essential roots of Islamic teaching were being lost. They were afraid that Islam's core teachings were being replaced with a kind of amalgam of religious and spiritual teachings, and that many of them were distinctly un-Islamic, which was a development that was bound to displease the religious authorities. Beyond that, the mystical belief that all reality is in fact One seemed to be heretical. It was contrary to Islamic monotheism. Traditional religious scholars believed that it contra-dicted the Islamic view that God is the Creator of all individuals and that there is eternally an essential distinction between God and creatures. To claim that human beings share in any way in divinity seemed to be not only heretical but also blasphemous. In fact, this monism (belief that all existence is essentially unified) appeared to some scholars to be influenced by Hinduism. After all, Hindus, despite their multiplicity of gods, believe that ultimately there is only One, one reality in which all individual existents—inanimate, animate, and divine—participate. Traditional religious scholars therefore began to feel the need to root out what they considered un-Islamic influences.

The concern for orthodoxy in Indian Islam showed itself as early as the sixteenth century in response to the growing popularity of a new religion that seemed to combine Islam and Hinduism: Sikhism. There had been significant interaction between Hindu and Islamic spirituality. Many spiritual exercises of Hindu yoga practice—controlled breathing patterns, for example, and the use of meditation to achieve heightened religious awareness—found their way into Sufi practice, and Islamic monotheism found increasing expression in otherwise polytheistic Hindu thought. But Sikhism was a new religious movement that actively blended characteristically Islamic monotheism with Hindu monism. The Sikh religion was begun by Guru Nanak (d. 1539), a Hindu spiritual teacher from the Punjab (in northwest India). Nanak taught that there is only one God, but also that people undergo countless rebirths on the road to *moksha* (escape from the cycle of rebirth) and reabsorption into the divine One. He taught that people can escape this cycle through virtuous living and meditation on God's name. Both Muslim and Hindu scholars found fault with Nanak's teachings, but their popularity continued to spread under Nanak's successors, especially in the tolerant atmosphere created by Akbar. But during the reign of Jahangir, concern for religious orthodoxy began to gain political attention. At this time, leadership of the Sikh community had passed to Nanak's fifth successor, Arjun. In response to scholars' complaints, Jahangir demanded that Arjun remove from Sikh scriptures references that were offensive to either Muslims or Hindus. When Arjun refused, he was tortured to death.

There were also Sufis who believed that some mystics went too far. Sheikh Ahmad Sirhindi (d. 1625) was one of them. He was a leader in another Sufi order, the Naqshbandis, a more reserved order from Central Asia. Sirhindi was appalled by Emperor Akbar's religious initiatives, particularly his eclectic new "divine religion." He believed Akbar's and Jahangir's religious openness was dangerous to Islam and did not even think that Shii Muslims should be tolerated. But his most vehement criticisms were directed toward Chishtis and anyone else who believed that all existence is really One. He taught that this belief in the unity of existence (*wahdat al-wujud* or oneness of existence) was really just an illusion. He thought that such people achieved an altered state of consciousness through "artificial means"— various exercises such as chanting and rhythmic swaying. Sirhindi criticized the Sufis, saying that it only *seems* that all existence is One (*wahdat al-shuhud*); despite the appearance of unity in mystical consciousness, in reality creatures remain distinct from one another, as well as from the Creator. To claim that this perception is actually the way things are is heresy because it equates God with His creatures. What is more, people who claim that all existence is One, and that everything that exists is really a manifestation of God, also do away with evil, because God is necessarily all good. For this kind of Sufi, then, evil is just a perception, too. In this context,

Sirhindi says, the law of God becomes irrelevant. Straying from the Shariah, he concludes, people naturally fall into moral decline.

Jahangir thought Sirhindi's intolerance of Shiis was misguided. He had him imprisoned for a short time. But Sirhindi had obviously struck a sympathetic chord among many Muslims, and he became widely popular. He was declared Mujaddid al-Alf al-Thani, "the renewer of the second millennium" of Islam. Sirhindi also influenced some Mughals, in particular Akbar's great-grandson Aurangzeb (r. 1659–1707). When Aurangzeb was young, Sufism was still highly influential among the Mughals. His own brother, Dara Shikoh (d. 1659), next in line for their father Shah Jahan's throne, was among them. Drawn to mysticism, Dara Shikoh promoted the esoteric teachings of many religions. He surrounded himself with people of many faiths and personally sponsored the translation of Hindu scriptures. Aurangzeb took it upon himself to champion the cause of orthodoxy, first within his own family. He and two other brothers—all provincial governors—fought with Dara Shikoh for the right to take control of the empire. Dara's troops defeated one brother's army, but after a series of battles Aurangzeb's imperial forces emerged victorious. Aurangzeb then had Dara Shikoh executed as a heretic; two other brothers were exiled and killed. Aurangzeb had himself declared emperor. His sickly father was imprisoned, where he died seven years later.

This violent beginning of Aurangzeb's reign was only a taste of what was to come. Like his predecessors, Aurangzeb insisted on expanding Mughal control militarily, leading to numerous and ongoing rebellions that drained the Mughal resources during Aurangzeb's long reign. Internally, Aurangzeb began a campaign to impose Islam, in its traditional form, throughout the realm. That meant reversing many of Akbar's policies that had led to peaceful relations with non-Muslim religious communities, especially Hindus. He reimposed the tax on non-Muslims, had many Hindu temples and schools destroyed, and prohibited the building of new ones or even the repair of old ones. He imposed economic policies that disadvantaged Hindus and offered bribes to those who would convert to Islam. Naturally, these policies marginalized and alienated Hindus, severely weakening the social fabric of Mughal India.

Aurangzeb's relations with the Sikhs were no better than those with the Hindus. After Arjun's execution under Jahangir, the Sikhs had retreated from their pacifist stance and established themselves in a defensive position in the Punjab. In its largest city, Lahore, Aurangzeb built the colossal Badshahi mosque to symbolize the triumph of Islam. Aurangzeb also tried

Figure 4 Worshipers at Badshahi mosque in Lahore.
Source: © Christine Osborne/CORBIS

to force the Sikh guru Tegh Bahadur to convert to Islam. When he refused, Aurangzeb had him executed. This resulted in further militarization of the Sikh community and further hostility toward the Muslim rulers. This hostility often flared into open rebellion against their Muslim overlords in the Punjab, resulting in a cycle of vicious reprisals.

Succeeding Mughal leaders thus inherited a mortally wounded realm. Continued efforts to impose Islamic dominance on a mixed population, with a Hindu majority, resulted in ongoing uprisings and intercommunal warfare in India. Indeed, it was these rebellions that allowed Britain to impose direct rule over much of the subcontinent in 1757. They held it until 1947, when it was partitioned into the Hindu-majority state of India and the Muslim-majority state of Pakistan.

Understanding Developments in Islamic History

Following the classical period of Islam, when its texts and ideals were formulated and its basic institutions established, Muslims were subjected to a number of attacks—by plague and disease, but more importantly, by foreign invaders. The once-unified Muslim community became fragmented. After the decline of the Abbasid caliphate, Muslims would never again live as a single political unit. A period of division and almost continuous warfare was followed by reorganization. The Muslim world reconstituted itself into the three empires discussed, the Ottoman, the Safavid, and the Mughal, as well as several other autonomous Islamic communities in sub-Saharan Africa and South Asia. Muslim intellectuals felt the need to put these developments into perspective. Thirteenth-century historian Ibn al-Athir registered the concern of many that infighting among regional rulers was weakening the Islamic community. He believed that it was this infighting that allowed foreigners to be successful: "It was the discord between the Muslim princes ... that enabled the Franks [Crusaders] to overrun the country."[12] There is no question that Ibn al-Athir was right. We have seen that the majority of the battles fought by the Ottomans, Safavids, and Mughals were against Muslims as they jockeyed for position in the vacuum created by the decline of Abbasid power.

Yet we have also seen that when stability was restored, Islamic society continued to be prosperous and enormously creative. Many of the great scientific and artistic advances described in Chapter 2 were achieved not under the unified Umayyad or Abbasid caliphates but under the various regional units that developed after the demise of central authority. Many of the great thinkers and artists of the time ended up working under a number of different patrons depending on the political situation. There is the famous case of Nasr al-Din al-Tusi (d. 1274). Al-Tusi was the renowned Persian astrologer and mathematician who developed the most accurate table of planetary motion known to science at the time. He did it while working at the great observatory at Maragheh in Azerbaijan, which he himself commissioned to be built while he was a government minister under the Mongol leader Hulegu Khan. That was after he had worked with a branch of the Shiis known as the Ismailis. When they were attacked by the Mongols— some say with al-Tusi's assistance—al-Tusi, who was actually a Twelver Shii, joined the Mongols and encouraged them to destroy Sunni Baghdad in 1258.

The great historian Ibn Khaldun (d. 1406) also had experience working under a number of regimes, from Spain to North Africa and Egypt. But he used this experience as a laboratory for understanding political and histor-ical processes in general. As we saw in Chapter 2, Ibn Khaldun's *Muqaddimah* is often cited as the first work of historiography and the precursor of the modern disciplines of anthropology, sociology, economics, and political science. But he is perhaps best known for his theory of the cycles or patterns of power. In Ibn Khaldun's view, the rise and fall of regimes is quite predictable. His analysis is based on the world in which he lived, which was divided between nomads of the deserts and settled peoples of the towns. In his view, nomadic communities have a natural solidarity (*'asabiyyah*) resulting from the strenuousness of their lifestyle. They have to cooperate and assist one another or they will not survive. When a group of nomads decides to give up their wandering ways and settle in towns, their natural solidarity and expectation of cooperation in the face of challenges serves them well. It translates into a commitment to fairness and mutual assistance, both necessary for the continued survival of the group. But that solidarity only lasts for a few generations in a settled environment. The settled life is easier than the nomadic life, and people get soft. The first generations remember how difficult life was in the desert and work hard to maintain balance and order within their new domestic environment. But as prosperity develops, the natural solidarity fades. People forget how important fairness and cooperation are and begin to work for personal gain. This results in competition and rivalries that divide the community against itself and inevitably leave it weakened and open to conquest.

The world in which Ibn Khaldun lived was a perfect example of this cycle. He was surrounded by competing regimes—and survived a number of them. But he believed Muslims could transcend the cycle. Ibn Khaldun did not equate the strength of the Muslim community with political or military power. Instead, he identified it as the commitment to justice. As long as the members of the community remained committed to justice, which consisted in an ethic of fairness and cooperation among community members, the community would remain strong. When community members turn against each other, putting their own interests above those of the group, the social fabric is weakened and eventually splits. "Injustice," he said, "brings about the ruin of civilization."

Whoever takes someone's property, or uses him for forced labour, or presses an unjustified claim against him, or imposes upon him a duty not required by the religious law, does an injustice to that particular person. People who collect unjustified taxes commit an injustice. Those who infringe upon property commit an injustice. Those who take away property commit an injustice. Those who deny people their rights commit an injustice. Those who, in general, take property by force, commit an injustice. It is the dynasty that suffers from all these acts, inasmuch as civilization, which is the substance of the dynasty, is ruined when people have lost all incentive. This is what Muhammad actually had in mind when he forbade injustice.

Ibn Khaldun then concludes by reiterating the classic formulation of the objectives (*maqasid*) of Sharia, arguably the earliest articulation of human rights in history: "This is what the religious law quite generally and wisely aims at in emphasizing five things as necessary: the preservation of (1) religion, (2) the soul (life), (3) the intellect, (4) progeny, and (5) property."[13]

For Ibn Khaldun, the ultimate purpose of the Islamic community was to establish justice. God established the Muslim community and commissioned its members as his stewards to spread justice throughout the world, by protecting people's rights to religion, life, education, family, and property. Commitment to this purpose was to be the basis of their solidarity. When that commitment weakened among various rulers, inevitably their regimes fell into decline.

But Islamic civilization as a whole need not decline, provided people maintain their commitment to justice. Ibn Khaldun actually chastises people in his era who take a passive attitude toward establishing justice. These are the people who sit back and wait for the Mahdi to appear. Ibn Khaldun says that all Muslims believe that at the end of time a man from the family of Prophet Muhammad will appear and lead Muslims back to a just society. Because the society will be just, it will also be powerful. The Mahdi or Jesus will then overpower the Antichrist, ushering in years of justice before the final judgment. (The Mahdi is not mentioned in the Quran. Belief in the Mahdi comes from oral traditions, which are not consistent. That is why some people believe that Jesus will come after the Antichrist appears so that he can do away with him, whereas others believe that Jesus will come with the Mahdi and help him get rid of the Antichrist.) Ibn Khaldun notes that some scholars criticize belief in the Mahdi, although he himself does not. But he does criticize people in his own time who simply assume that injustice will be corrected soon, when the Mahdi appears.[14] He believes that all people must work for justice by maintaining their commitment to fairness and cooperation in all their social dealings. In the same way, he criticizes people who rely on fortune-tellers and astrologers to predict the future. (He uses as evidence of their unreliability the fact that, at the time of Prophet Muhammad, there were reports that the world would end 500 years after the coming of the Prophet. Ibn Khaldun was born 723 years after the Hijra.)

Instead of waiting for the Mahdi or allowing fortune-tellers to control their destiny, Ibn Khaldun says that people should use reason to understand their religion and the world and figure out how to establish Islamic values in the world's ever-changing circumstances. Furthermore, he criticizes those mystics who believe that all existence is One, that only God exists, and that we are all a part of God. He says that this is just a passing perception, and it is foolish to trust such passing perceptions, like blind people who are not aware that there is an entire dimension of perception beyond their abilities.

Rather than trying to understand things beyond their perceptive abilities, people should concentrate on things they can understand. Ibn Khaldun then gives an elegant description of empirical science, the kind of understanding of their environment that human beings can develop through observation and reasoning in an orderly way. Pursuit of science has obvious practical uses that promote human well-being. Practical sciences can help us build better homes, for example, and grow better crops. But of all the kinds of science, law is the most important because it details the ways to promote justice and prevent injustice. And this is the reason for which human beings were created.

Conclusion

Ibn Khaldun's analysis of the rise and fall of nations is brilliant. It became a classic of historiography. And his articulation of the source of strength of Islam is an eloquent tribute to Islamic values. But it still leaves unanswered the question of Islamic trauma in the modern era. How did the Muslim world—the world of Suleiman the Magnificent, Shah Abbas, and Akbar the Great, the world of universities and public libraries, great architects and artists, literature and learning—become subject to European colonialism and emerge in the modern world weak, underdeveloped, and associated with extremists and terrorists? How did these magnificent states of the middle period of Islamic history become subjected to European powers? These are the questions addressed in the following chapters.

Notes

1. See his "Dialogues between a Christian and a Saracen," in *Migne Patrologiae Graecae*, vol. XCIV (Paris, 1860), col. 1585; vol. XCVI (Paris, 1864), cols. 1335–1348.
2. Cited in Philip K. Hitti, *Islam and the West* (Princeton, NJ: D. Van Nostrand, 1962), 51.

3. See Guibert of Nogent, *RHC Historiens Occidentaux 1844–95*, IV: 137–110, cited in Terry Jones and Alan Ereira, *Crusades* (London: Penguin/BBC Worldwide, 1996), 13.
4. See Jones and Ereira, *Crusades*, 52.
5. Francesco Gabrieli, *Arab Historians of the Crusades* (Berkeley: University of California Press, 1984), 11.
6. Gabrieli, *Arab Historians of the Crusades*, 12.
7. Gabrieli, *Arab Historians of the Crusades*, 93–145.
8. Ross E. Dunn. *The Adventures of Ibn Battuta: A Muslim Traveler of the 14th Century* (Berkeley: University of California Press, 1989), 174–176.
9. Mohammad Khatami, *Islam, Liberty and Development* (Binghamton, NY: Institute of Global Cultural Studies, 1998), 73.
10. See Monisha Mukundan, *Akbar and Birbal: Tales of Humour* (New Delhi: Rupa & Co., 1994), 7–11.
11. Quoted in Marilyn Waldman and R. Waldman, "Islamic World," *The New Encyclopaedia Britannica* (Chicago, 1991), 22:127. Nasroddin had counterparts in other parts of the Muslim world as well. He is known as Juha in the Arabic-speaking world, Nasreddin Hoca in Turkey, and Musfiqi in Tajikistan, for example.
12. Gabrieli, *Arab Historians of the Crusades*, 11.
13. Ibn Khaldun, *The Muqaddimah*, 238–240.
14. He calls them "stupid" and "weak-minded." See Ibn Khaldun, *The Muqaddimah*, 258.

4

Colonialism and Reform

The twentieth century was disastrous for the Muslim world. It opened with European powers in control of large portions of former Ottoman and Mughal lands, as well as other parts of the Muslim world, and dominating in Iran. World War I ended the caliphate and consolidated European control over most Muslim lands. Muslims in all these regions therefore had to struggle with multiple challenges and against overwhelming odds. As the vitality of Muslim societies declined, reformers had begun to work in many Muslim majority countries. But their work was complicated by the threat of further foreign domination. A number of trends thus emerged: agitation for reform in declining Islamic empires; the struggle for independence from growing European influence; efforts to modernize Islamic societies and reform religious thought in order to deal with contemporary challenges. This chapter will survey the takeover of the Muslim world by European powers and examine reformers' efforts to deal with it.

Colonialism

By the early the twentieth century, almost the entire Muslim world was under the control of European countries. The French controlled North Africa and Syria; the British controlled Egypt, Palestine, Iraq, and India; the

Islam: History, Religion, and Politics, Third Edition. Tamara Sonn.
© 2016 John Wiley & Sons, Ltd. Published 2016 by John Wiley & Sons, Ltd.

Dutch controlled Indonesia; and the Dutch and then the British controlled Malaysia. From this vantage point, it began to look like the Crusades were on again. But it took some time before the overall patterns of colonization became clear because the processes by which Europe gained control of these regions were diverse, gradual and, in some cases, subtle. Colonialism also developed sporadically, one city or region at a time, over a wide geographic range. Spain established a beachhead here; France set up control there; Britain took over areas in North Africa, the Middle East, and India; Italy and Holland operated at opposite ends of the Islamic world; and so on. European countries gained control through a combination of strategies, including gradual assumption of economic power, playing off rivals against one another, and military campaigns when necessary. As a result, Europe's overall domination of the Muslim world did not become apparent to most people until it was almost complete.

After the Crusades, the first European inroads were by way of the sea, when the Portuguese took control of the Indian Ocean spice trade from the Arabs. As we saw in Chapter 3, this was a wound to the Mamluk economy from which it never recovered. Eventually, the Ottomans were able to overpower the Mamluks and take control of almost the entire Arab world. For centuries, the Ottomans had been a formidable force. They were strong enough to be able to play a role in Europe's premodern power struggles, when regional powers tried to assert themselves against the old imperial families who wanted to control the entire continent. We saw that Suleiman the Magnificent was able to manipulate those struggles to Ottoman advantage in the Balkans. However, in the bargain Suleiman gave French subjects the right to travel and trade in Ottoman lands. French traders were also given the protection of French laws and courts even while they were in Ottoman lands; they were exempted from Ottoman laws, including taxes. Suleiman also granted the French king Francis I the right to control access to trade in the Middle East for other European subjects in the Capitulations of 1536.

These special privileges (*imtiyazat*) were later demanded by the British as well, and expanded throughout the Ottoman Empire. They assured the Europeans safety of life and property and freedom of religion, but the exemption from Ottoman law and taxes also gave the Europeans distinct trade advantages. These advantages, later obtained by the Europeans in the Persian world as well, were often passed on to local Christian and Jewish communities. This proved to be the critical factor in the Capitulations. They allowed Europeans and their allies in the Muslim world to amass greater wealth than was possible for local Muslims to obtain.

Obviously, the brilliant Suleiman would not have given the Europeans such rights if they had posed any threat at the time. But as it turned out, French cultural and economic influence in Syria (which included Lebanon until after World War II) grew exponentially. Religious missions were founded by Roman Catholics, and later by other denominations, catering to the area's Christians interested in the advantages provided by European learning. European merchants had established lucrative trade in Syrian cotton, silks, and handicrafts by the seventeenth and eighteenth centuries. But soon the balance of trade began to shift. European manufactured goods were being imported, replacing indigenous crafts and enriching those merchants with close relations to Europe. By the late nineteenth century, it began to appear to Syria's Muslim majority that the Christians (including the Orthodox, who had benefited from Russian missions) were developing economic advantages based on foreign support. This inevitably undermined trust and resulted in communal hostilities. Those conflicts brought increased attention from Ottoman officials and Europeans, and foreign influence continued to expand. France built railways connecting Syria's three major cities—Damascus, Beirut, and Aleppo. The American University of Beirut (originally called the Syrian Protestant College) was established in 1866, and the French Jesuit Université Saint-Joseph opened in Beirut in 1881.

By the outbreak of World War I in 1914, Christians were among Syria's most highly educated and Western-influenced population, and France treated the region as part of its eminent domain. In the Treaty of Sèvres in 1920 after that war, France was granted a "mandate" for control over Syria that would not end until France itself was occupied by Nazi Germany in World War II and could no longer afford to manage its Syrian territories.

By the early twentieth century, France, locked in competition with other European colonial powers, had already taken control of North African territories in Morocco, Algeria, and Tunisia. In 1830 France had attacked Algiers, technically part of the Ottoman Empire but virtually autonomous. The French proclaimed that they had nothing against the people of Algeria, only their Turkish rulers. Their original complaint was against piracy, a venerable tradition in the Mediterranean and elsewhere; it had been practiced by the Greeks, Romans, Carthaginians, and Europeans. The famous Barbary pirates (named after the non-Arab inhabitants of North Africa, the Amazighen, known in the West as the Berbers) followed the same practice, demanding tribute from ships passing through their waters and seizing them along with their crews and cargo if they refused. The wealth acquired from this enterprise helped in their efforts to maintain their independence from Istanbul. But the threat of piracy was a constant worry among the European states whose economies were increasingly dependent on sea trade. Piracy became such a menace that Europe and the newly formed United States demanded a halt to it and fought several battles when the pirate states refused to give in. President Thomas Jefferson even sent in the U.S. navy, which struggled with the pirates for four years (the Tripolitan War, 1801–1805). The British had bombed Algeria in 1816 in an effort to stop piracy and had largely been successful. Nevertheless, the French claimed that their goal in attacking Algiers in 1830 was to put a stop to piracy. Their attack was successful, and the Ottoman officials were sent packing. But the French did not leave. The region quickly attracted French settlers, and France appointed a "governor general of the French possessions in Africa," headquartered in Algiers. Resistance by Algerians began immediately, but it only intensified French resolve to take full control of the area. After years of Algerian attacks on settlers' farms and French reprisals against Algerian villages, France declared itself the ruler of Algeria. In 1845 Paris appointed a "governor general of Algeria." By 1871 Algerian resistance had been crushed. Algeria was considered a part of France. It only regained independence after a brutal war (1954–1962), in which an estimated one-tenth of the population lost their lives and another one-fifth to one-third were displaced (relocated by the French).

From its North African headquarters in Algeria, France was able to expand its control westward to include Morocco. Morocco had never been a part of the Ottoman Empire, enjoying an independence that allowed it to be a refuge for Algerians fleeing the wrath of France. But Moroccan assistance to the struggling Algerian resistance brought on French attacks. The French military easily defeated the Moroccans in the 1840s. But European countries were always in competition for colonial holdings, which were the source of enormous wealth for these industrializing powers. So, in the 1850s, Britain negotiated for special trading privileges in Morocco, promising to protect Moroccans from the French. Meanwhile, Spain claimed territories in the western portion of Morocco and declared war to secure them. Morocco was quickly losing its independence under a succession of weak rulers in the late nineteenth century. This led to rebellions that further weakened their leaders and allowed the Europeans to press their own claims. In a classic example of European colonial gamesmanship, in 1904, Britain, Spain, and Italy agreed to let France take over in Morocco if France allowed England to keep Egypt, Spain to dominate northwestern Morocco, and Italy to take Libya. A futile rebellion by the Moroccan sultan's brother ended in the Treaty of Fez in 1912, which declared Morocco a French protectorate.

On the other side of Algeria, Tunisia had also asserted autonomy from its nominal Ottoman overlords. But at the same time Tunisia felt threatened by its much larger neighbor Algeria. So when the French came into Algeria in 1830 and promised to look after Tunisia's interests, Tunisia did not protest. But when it became clear that France actually intended to take direct control in Algeria, Tunisian rulers recognized the threat to their own independence and desperately tried to strengthen themselves against the modern European power. Unfortunately, they could only attempt this by raising taxes and taking out loans—from Europe. Popular discontent erupted in rebellions that further strained government resources. The Europeans finally decided to take control of Tunisia's government to recoup their debts. The only real suspense was over which of Tunisia's major lenders, Britain or France, would take ultimate control. The European colonial powers each worried that the other was taking unfair advantage in staking their increasingly high-stakes claims in the disintegrating Ottoman Empire. They came together at the Congress of Berlin in 1878 to deal with a number of related issues. One of the outcomes was that Britain gave France permission to take control in Tunisia. On the pretext of securing Algeria's borders, France set up a resident governor in Tunisia and assumed direct control in 1881. France kept control of Morocco and Tunisia until 1956, officially, but in reality kept control of certain strategic areas until the 1960s.

France attempted to expand its North African dominance into Egypt, but Britain was keenly competitive. Napoleon had sailed into the port of Alexandria in Egypt in 1798 and announced to the Egyptian people that he was going to overthrow the Mamluks, who were ruling Egypt with virtually no interference from Ottoman officials. Napoleon claimed that the Mamluks were unworthy to rule Egypt because they were not good Muslims. He then told them that the French were better Muslims than the Mamluks, and his proof was that the French had destroyed the power of the pope, who had called the Crusades, and then evicted the notoriously anti-Muslim Crusader knights from Malta. The French would also protect the Egyptians from the Turks, they claimed, whose greed had destroyed Egypt. Although Napoleon may have been personally sincere, it seemed to the Egyptians that his real goals were more mundane. They included protection of French trade, already well established in Egypt, just as it had been in Syria because of the favorable trade conditions provided to Europeans by the Capitulations. As well, the reliability of Egypt's annual grain production was an attractive prize, given France's periodic domestic shortages.

Indeed, Egyptian suspicions were well founded. French administrators settled in and set about modernizing Egypt in their own image. They established a new bureaucracy, with new tax policies, and began confiscating Mamluk lands and redistributing them to those who would support their administration. They also built hospitals and made other contributions to the country, but they were still intruders, and their continued occupation met with stiff local and international resistance.

By 1801, the French had to vacate Egypt after the Ottoman military defeated them in a series of battles, supported by a naval blockade set up by France's chief European competitor, England. (As they departed, the French took with them the Rosetta Stone, which their archaeologists had discovered; it was confiscated by the British and taken to London where it formed the basis of the British Museum's famous Egyptian Collection. They took other ancient Egyptian artifacts as well, which would become the inspiration for a new style in French design motifs: art deco.) One of the leaders of the Ottoman campaign, Mehmed (Muhammad) Ali (d. 1848) was then put in charge of Egypt. He tried to reorganize the country in ways that would allow Egypt to regain its pride of place among the world's nations and secure it against foreign invaders. He centralized control of the economy and government, executing the Mamluk chiefs who competed for power and confiscating their properties as well as those endowed through religious foundations (*waqf* properties). He revived and modernized the country's irrigation system and introduced improved crops for export. He modernized the education system, using French instructors and advisors and encouraging Egyptians to study abroad. And he modernized the military, initiating a draft so that Egyptians could defend themselves rather than rely on Ottoman troops.

Mehmed Ali also gained enhanced stature in Istanbul by using his military to help out in their campaigns against a rebellious group in the Arabian peninsula, the Wahhabis. The Wahhabis were a narrowly traditionalist reform movement, determined to revive the strength that characterized the early Muslim community by wiping out "innovations," practices that had developed after the days of the Prophet and his Companions, such as Sufism. They were also militant. In their view, contrary to that of other Muslims since the first century of Islam, Muslims who violate their strict rules must be encouraged to reform, and if they refuse, should be declared infidels and brought into submission by force. This applied to people involved in folk practices such visiting the tombs of holy people and praying for their intercession. The movement, which still

exists, was based on the teachings of Muhammad ibn Abd al-Wahhab
(d. 1791) and was spread by the tribe of Ibn Saud with whom they allied
in the mid-eighteenth century. The combined Wahhabi–Saudi forces
gained dominance in much of the Arabian peninsula without undue
concern to Ottoman officials. When they began to spread northward into
Iraq and Syria, however, the Ottomans took notice. They asked for and
received Mehmed Ali's assistance in confining the movement to the
Arabian peninsula. Autonomy in Egypt and Sudan, the eastern portion of
which he had already conquered, was Mehmed Ali's reward.

Mehmed Ali's successors, though more conservative, continued efforts to
develop Egyptian economic power. They wanted to keep their independence
from Istanbul and knew they needed outside help to continue developing.
But they were suspicious of Europe's growing influence in the region, so they
tried to balance the influence of their major investors, the French and the
British. For example, the British built a railway from Alexandria to Suez
(1858), which allowed them a faster route to India; the French then built the
Suez Canal (1869), making the trip even easier. But all this development was
expensive, and much of the capital was borrowed—again, from European
sources. Many of the reforms did improve Egypt's financial status. In
addition, its long staple cotton became extremely valuable when the U.S.
Civil War eliminated U.S. cotton from the world market, significantly
increasing Egypt's export revenues. But when the war was over, Egypt was
again faced with mounting debt, which would ultimately end the country's
independence. In 1875, the Egyptian ruler was forced to sell his shares in the
Suez Canal to Britain. The following year an international commission was
set up to deal with Egypt's debt. The commission put all Egyptian finances
under the control of a British and a French agent. When the Egyptians protested, France and Britain pressured the Ottoman sultan to oust the Egyptian
ruler (1879). The Europeans took over again, which infuriated the Egyptians.
Opposition groups organized within the National Assembly, which had been
established in 1866, and the military, resulting in the establishment of Egypt's
first political party, the National Party (*al-hizb al-watani*). The French and
British sent naval forces to Alexandria in 1882 to protect their investments.
Riots erupted, and British ships responded by bombing Alexandria and
occupying Cairo. Britain kept control of Egypt, declaring it a British "protectorate" at the beginning of World War I and installing a compliant monarch
at the end of the war. Officially, Egypt was independent, but the monarchy
implemented British policy. Actual independence was not achieved until a
military coup overthrew the monarch in 1952.

Meanwhile, Britain had been extremely busy expanding its empire in South Asia. India became the jewel in England's imperial crown by processes similar to France's occupation of Syria. By the end of the fifteenth century, as we saw, Portugal had achieved dominance in trade in the Indian Ocean, by virtue of the superiority of its sea routes over the Arab land routes. By the seventeenth century, the British, French, and Dutch were competing for trade advantages in the region. The British East India Company, established by royal charter in 1600 specifically to gain control of trade in India and points east, acted as more than a commercial enterprise. As with many of today's mega-transnational corporations, it is difficult to say whether the company acted as an agent of the home government or vice versa. Either way, the effect on India was the same. To achieve its monopolistic goals, the company required military force, as well as administrators to control foreign populations, and the government was happy to oblige. In 1612 British forces defeated Portugal in battle and won concessions from the Mughals to engage in trade in cotton, silk, indigo, and spices. This was during the period in which Mughal power was declining; the intolerant policies of the successors of Akbar were increasingly unpopular, and regional powers struggled to assert their autonomy. The resulting weaknesses in various parts of India provided opportunities for the East India Company. It gained control of Bengal in 1757, defeating the local Muslim ruler and competing French forces in the decisive Battle of Plassey. This was a major victory; Bengal province, larger than France, was one of India's richest. It was a major exporter of rice, sugar, spices, fruits, meats, silks, cottons, to name just a few of its valuable products. From Bengal, the Company began to expand its control, defeating the forces of the central Mughal authorities, regional principalities, and other colonial competitors. Soon the British extracted from the Mughal emperor the right to collect taxes in Bengal. This further weakened the central government in Delhi and exponentially increased Britain's profits, but with devastating effects on Bengalis. Traditional Mughal administrative policy had included maintaining tax-exempt fields for the poor and surplus supplies of grain to sustain the population during the region's periodic droughts. The British did not follow these practices. The infamous Bengal Famine of 1770 resulted in the deaths of an estimated 10 million people, one third of Bengal's population.

The British government gradually assumed authority over what was effectively its Indian foreign policy (the Regulating Act of 1773 and Pitt's India Act in 1784), but that policy continued to focus on expanding British power in the subcontinent. Decisive defeats of local forces in 1818 brought capitulations from other leaders. India was in the process of transition; what had been the Mughal Empire became a British trade monopoly and ultimately a British colony—indeed, Britain's most valuable. In 1846, the British defeated the Sikhs, who had established a state in the Punjab (northwest India) in the late eighteenth century. They annexed Sikh territory in 1849.

The final stage came in 1857. By that time, Britain controlled, either directly or through compliant local leaders, virtually all of India. A revolt erupted among Bengali troops employed by the British. The cause of the rebellion was the widespread suffering caused by British exploitation; expropriation of land; exorbitant taxes on Indians while British traders, who were exempt from tax duties, grew rich; disruption of traditional life; and imposition of foreign institutions and cultural norms. But the British explained the rebellion in terms of concerns over dietary restrictions. They claimed that the sepoys—Indians serving in the British-run military—had been ordered to use a new kind of rifle; to load this rifle the ends of the cartridges had to be bitten off. Supposedly, the soldiers believed the grease on the cartridges was a mixture of both cow and pig fat, offending both Hindus and Muslims. In fact, the British were so unpopular overall that the revolt quickly spread to Delhi and turned into a general rebellion against British rule. It took more than a year for the British to put down the rebellion, and they did so with extreme brutality. It was then that Britain instituted direct rule of the subcontinent. By this time it was possible to say that "the sun never sets on the British empire." (Their colonial subjects explained that that was because God couldn't trust the British in the dark.) The British did not exit the subcontinent until 1947, when they "partitioned" it into the majority Hindu state of India and the Islamic state of Pakistan, consisting of two sections (East Pakistan and West Pakistan) separated by language and culture and more than 1,000 miles of India. The status of Kashmir, a Muslim majority state ruled by a Hindu, has yet to be settled.

To the southeast, the Dutch East India Company secured hold over what would become Indonesia and, for a time, Malaysia. Islam had been introduced to the Malay peninsula and the islands that would become Malaysia and Indonesia by Indian traders in the thirteenth and fourteenth centuries. By the early sixteenth century, Portuguese merchants were well established in the region's Moluccan Islands, the "Spice Islands." But within a century the Dutch East India Company outmaneuvered both the Portuguese and local traders and gained control of the region. Apart from brief interludes of French control (1811–1816, when France had conquered Holland and incorporated Indonesia into its empire) and Japanese control (1942–1945, during World War II), the Dutch remained in power in Indonesia until 1949. They were ousted from what would become Malaysia (as well as Singapore) by Britain in the mid-nineteenth century. Except for the Japanese occupation during World War II, Britain kept control of Malaysia until 1957.

Italy, following on its great Roman heritage, also engaged in colonization in regions that would become Somalia and Libya. Somalia, with its ports on the Horn of Africa, was traditionally prosperous, based on Indian Ocean trade, and never part of the Ottoman Empire. Britain, France, and Italy competed for dominance there but by the late 1880s, Italy successfully established itself as the "protector" of the sultanates that controlled the Horn. (Ultimately, Britain would take control of "Italian Somaliland," and the country would declare independence in 1960.) Nearer to home, Italy pursued interests in Ottoman North Africa. The coastal regions of what would become Libya had gained semi-autonomy during the eighteenth century. The Ottomans reasserted direct control in 1835, but it was loosely held. The Ottoman province of Tripolitania comprised the Western city of Tripoli and the eastern city of Benghazi, and south of them a vast desert region known as Fezzan. All three regions were dominated by tribal groupings intent on maintaining their independence. With France dominating Tunisia and Algeria to the west, and Britain in charge of Egypt to the east, Italy emerged as a less threatening trade partner. But after successfully establishing a number of financial interests along the fertile coastal strip, Italy set about asserting direct control of the country. With the assistance of troops from their Somiland territories, Italy defeated Ottoman forces in 1912. Fierce tribal resistance continued for two decades and was brutally crushed. Italy consolidated its power in 1934, but following its defeat in World War II, lost control of Libya to British and French administrators. The country declared its independence in 1951.

The Outcome of World War I

This pattern of commercial and political domination played out across the Muslim world as Europe expanded its control. But as we saw, Europe did not operate as a single unit following a preplanned scheme to take control of the whole Muslim world. Individual European countries used the rest of the world, including the Muslim world, as a kind of Monopoly board to play out their colonial competition. As one European power moved into one region, another moved into a neighboring region in an effort to block its opponent's expansion. European countries bargained with one another and traded countries in an effort to gain strategic advantage, with utter disregard for the rights and welfare of the countries being traded.

The best examples are to be found in the Middle East, particularly Iraq and Syria. The land between the two great rivers, the Euphrates and the Tigris, has a long and illustrious history as Mesopotamia, part of the famous Fertile Crescent. But the modern state of Iraq was created by the Europeans from parts of three Ottoman provinces: most of Basra province in the south with its primarily Shiite Arab population, Baghdad province in the center with its mixed Sunni and Shiite Arab population, and parts of Mosul province in the north, with its large Kurdish population, primarily Sunni but including Assyrian Christians and others. (Kurds are an unique, if diverse ethnic group whose language is related to the Iranian language group.) The region had come under Ottoman rule in the sixteenth century but, as we have seen, Ottoman power was in steep decline by the beginning of the twentieth century. The Persian Gulf had been familiar territory to European traders since the early seventeenth century. But the discovery of oil in Iraq sharpened competition for this corner of Ottoman territory.

By the early twentieth century, the Ottoman sultan had been dubbed "the sick man of Europe." He was pictured in cartoons as a carcass, over which European-named vultures circled. Among those predators were Britain, Holland, and Germany, or more precisely, British Petroleum, Royal Dutch Shell, and the Deutsche Bank. In 1914 these three companies formed the Turkish Petroleum Company and began negotiations for the rights to develop Iraqi oil reserves. Local rulers were relatively autonomous by this time but still weak. They were therefore willing to trade the rights to this subterranean mineral for hard cash. But the outcome of World War I forced a slight modification in Europe's commercial and colonizing agreements. Germany's defeat in the war resulted in its exclusion from the company, and Britain took control of its shares. Britain also landed a military force from India. The British took over control of Basra and Baghdad provinces by 1917, claiming they were not planning to stay; they only wanted to help the Iraqis get rid of their unpopular Turkish rulers.

European colonial competition had proceeded unabated during the war. Britain had sought Arab cooperation in the war, knowing they were increasingly unhappy under Ottoman Turkish rule. Arab leaders had been agitating for independence, both from the Turks and the Europeans who had gained dominance in Arab lands despite Turkish rule. Debate often centered on strategy: should the Arabs work for reform of the Ottoman system and greater autonomy or for full independence? If they chose independence, should they struggle against the foreigners first and then the Turks, or vice versa? The British offer to support a rebellion against the Turks seemed risky but worthwhile. It had come in the run-up to the war from British administrators in Egypt to the leading family of Mecca, the Hashemites, who were descendants of Prophet Muhammad ("sharifs") and traditionally responsible for maintaining Islam's two holiest cities, Mecca and Medina. The British knew that the Turks had been modernizing, largely with German help. They assumed that in the impending war, the Turks would ally with Germany against the British, French, and Russians. The British therefore looked for a way to weaken Turkish forces. Exploiting Arab discontent with Turkish rule, the British offered to recognize Arab independence in all liberated territories in return for the Arabs' assistance in the war. The Arabs were to rebel against the Turks, effectively opening a second front in the war and preventing the Turks from providing significant assistance to Britain. This was a lot to ask, given that the Ottomans were not only the political rulers of the Middle East but also technically the spiritual leaders of the Muslim world. It was a momentous decision; among the earliest rules established in Islamic law was the prohibition on collaborating with non-Muslims against Muslim rulers. Nevertheless, after consultation with regional leaders, the Hashemite leaders decided to trust the Europeans. That, as it turned out, was a colossal mistake.

Along with the famous Lawrence of Arabia, the British officer assigned to work with the Arabs, the Arabs fought the Turks in the Middle East. They thus undoubtedly assisted in the defeat of the Germans and their allies. But after the war, instead of granting the Arabs independence as promised, the Europeans distributed Arab territories among themselves. This was what they had secretly agreed to do, at the same time as they were publicly promising the Arabs independence.[1] In the secret Sykes–Picot Agreement in 1916, France was designated "protector" of Arab Syria and the Kurdish Mosul province. Britain would "protect" Arab Baghdad and Basra provinces, and the Palestinian portion of traditional Syria, as well as what would be called Transjordan (the land on the eastern side of the Jordan River, all the way to Iraq). (Russia's claims, for example, that the west bank of the Jordan River from Gaza to Tyre should be international were ignored as a result of the 1917 Bolshevik Revolution.) The treaties ending World War I established the independent state of Turkey but ignored the promises made to the Arabs. Instead, they imposed the provisions of the Sykes–Picot

Agreement, changing the term *protectorate* to *mandate*. But France now wanted a share of the company that was exploiting Iraqi petroleum resources. So France traded Mosul to Britain in exchange for defeated Germany's share in the Turkish Petroleum Company. (Later, the United States insisted that its companies be included in the deal. In 1928, a consortium of U.S. petroleum companies was incorporated into the company, and it was renamed the Iraq Petroleum Company.)

Now Britain could put together Iraq: Mosul was added to Baghdad and Basra provinces to form the country. But what about a leader? The idea of the mandates was that the Europeans were supposed to watch out for the interests of the countries they were assigned, helping them along until they were ready to assume independence. They were not supposed to be colonial overlords. So Britain and France had to find Arab leaders they considered suitable for their new countries. Fortunately for them, there was a family of leaders available for work: the Hashemites. Their betrayal at the hands of the Europeans had left them with only their domains in western Arabia. Around this time the Saudi family began to expand from its realms in central Arabia, to which it had been limited since Egypt's Mehmed Ali had driven it back from Iraq. The Saudis eventually defeated and exiled the Hashemites and named nearly all of Arabia after themselves. The sons of the elderly Sharif Hussein had vigorously protested the violation of the Arab trust by the British. Faisal had gone north to Syria and set up a government in Damascus. But when he refused to accept the French mandate he was forced out of Syria. Meanwhile, Iraqi tribes, Sunni and Shii together, were rebelling against their British overlords. The British responded with punishing force, including aerial bombardments and the burning of villages. Perhaps most notoriously, Kurdish rebels in the early 1920s were suppressed with aerial bombardment and the threat of poison gas. But these efforts were expensive and exhausting. Winston Churchill, newly appointed Colonial Secretary, agreed with advisors that indirect rule of Iraq would be more effective. So the British offered the deposed Faisal the title of king of Iraq in 1922. He accepted, but only if the British changed their "mandate over" to "alliance with" Iraq, and with the concurrence of the Iraqi people. Faisal finally had a throne, and Britain had a compliant Sunni Arab ruler for its diverse but oil-rich Iraq.

According to the treaty of alliance, Iraq was technically independent, but Britain would oversee the army and appoint advisors to run the economy and foreign policy. And the pernicious Capitulations were reasserted, exempting the British from local laws and taxes. The fact that Iraq had not, in fact, been independent was made clear when the League of Nations recognized its independence in 1932. But even then Britain maintained control of the economy and the military, and petroleum resources continued to be exploited by the foreign-controlled Iraqi Petroleum Company. Throughout this time, political opponents of the British-dominated monarchy were jailed, exiled, or executed, and insurrections were mercilessly suppressed. Foreign domination of Iraq was not actually ended until a violent revolution in 1958.

The betrayal of the Arabs by the British and French resulted in the creation of other new states as well. Sharif Hussein and his son Faisal, when they were still in charge of western Arabia and Syria respectively, decided to split Transjordan, that southern portion of traditional Syria situated between the Jordan River and Iraq, in 1918. But after Faisal's defeat in Syria and transfer to Iraq, the British decided to offer the rule of Transjordan to Faisal's brother Abdullah, provided he accept their ultimate dominance, as in the case of Iraq. Jordan received nominal independence in 1946 but, characteristically, Britain maintained control of the economy, the military, and foreign policy. In 1955 the sovereign kingdom of Jordan was admitted to the United Nations, but complete independence came only with the departure of British military leaders in 1956.

As noted previously, traditional Syria included Lebanon as well. Lebanon's mountains had separated it geographically from the rest of Syria and its long coast had opened it to cultural influences that had given the region a unique identity since the days of the ancient Phoenicians. Its strong local leaders had near-autonomy under Ottoman rule, but Lebanon was included in the French mandate over Syria. Under French control, the region was reorganized into a separate government, with a slight Christian majority. The government got its own constitution but, like Syria, was still controlled by France. Christian-dominated Lebanon was particularly pro-French; the language of administration and education was French, and the French dominated the economy. When France fell to Nazi forces during World War II, Lebanon and Syria were occupied by Vichy (pro-Nazi French) administrators. British and Free French troops defeated them and declared Lebanon and Syria independent, promising the locals the right to choose between separate countries or a united Syria. But in fact, French administrators remained. In 1943 contending Lebanese factions agreed on a National Pact: the Muslims would accept a Lebanon independent of Syria, provided the Christians would commit to a Lebanon independent of France. The agreement was not put in writing, but it was accepted that the president of

Lebanon would always be a Maronite Christian (a unique sect of Eastern Christianity, dating from the seventh century, that entered communion with Roman Catholicism in the twelfth century), the prime minister would be a Sunni Muslim, and the speaker of the National Assembly would be a Shiite Muslim. Emigration of wealthy Christians to better economic fields abroad, and immigration of Sunni Muslims escaping war in Palestine/Israel would shift the demographic balance, severely straining communal relations in Lebanon.

The last portion of traditional Syria was given to Britain to rule, and it remains among the most problematic places in the region: Palestine. The League of Nations granted Britain control of the area in 1922, and included the Balfour Declaration within the mandate. The Balfour Declaration had been issued in 1917 by the British foreign secretary Arthur James Balfour in response to requests by Zionist leaders for British support for their movement. In view of centuries of European Christian persecution of Jews, leaders of the World Zionist Organization had given up hope that European Christians would ever allow Jews to live in peace and security, with equal civil and political rights. They therefore wanted to establish a homeland for Jews in Palestine, as the ancient Jewish homeland had been called by the Romans (after the name of its "Philistine" inhabitants). Lord Balfour wrote that the British government viewed

> with favour the establishment in Palestine of a national home for the Jewish people and will use their best endeavours to facilitate the achievement of this object, it being clearly understood that nothing shall be done which may prejudice the civil and religious rights of existing non-Jewish communities in Palestine, or the rights and political status enjoyed by Jews in any other country.[2]

Under British control of Palestine, the Jewish population increased exponentially, as Jews sought escape from intensifying anti-Semitism in Europe. According to Ottoman statistics, there were around 24,000 Jews in Palestine in 1882. By 1914, there were some 60,000. The British census in 1922 recorded 83,790 Jews, about 11 percent of the population. Within nine years, that number had increased to 174,610.[3] Arab leaders supported limited Jewish immigration on humanitarian grounds, but having been betrayed by the British and lost their autonomy in their own homelands, they were not surprisingly bewildered that Britain had now decided to distribute these lands to Europeans.

Figure 5   The Dome of the Rock (687–691) in Jerusalem.
Source: © Dominique Landau/Shutterstock

As Nazism grew in Europe, threatening the very survival of the Jewish people, more and more European Jews emigrated to Palestine. Native Palestinians began to rebel against this mass immigration into their land. Zionist activists in Palestine became anxious to evict the British and form a sovereign state. The British Mandate authorities in Palestine thus faced Arab uprisings against increased foreign immigration, and Zionist terrorism against both Arab opponents and the British presence. The pressure on Britain became too much, especially with its economy at home devastated by World War II. By the late 1940s, the British had to give up their troublesome colonial holdings. They made plans to leave not only India but also Palestine. They handed the problem of Palestine to the United Nations. And, as Britain had done in India, the United Nations decided to partition Palestine. There were to be two states, one for Jews (regardless of national origin) and one for Arabs (regardless of religious identity), with the Jewish state receiving 55 percent of the land. The partition plan was rejected by the people whose land was being partitioned, of course, but it was passed anyway. Immediately, Zionist leaders declared Israel a state, on 15 May 1948, and Arab leaders declared war. The Arabs were no match for the zealous European refugees. As a result of their defeat, some 800,000 Palestinians became refugees. Today, after two major wars in 1967 and

1973, several more limited engagements (including Israel-Gaza wars in 2008 and 2014), and countless United Nations resolutions later, Palestinians remain stateless.

The Effects of Colonialism and Themes of Islamic Reform

The cumulative effects of colonialism have been monumental. Most obviously, colonized peoples experienced overwhelming frustration of their aspirations for true independence, empowerment, and development. As a result, colonization produced resentment and a profound sense of betrayal and humiliation by Western powers that had claimed to be concerned for the best interests of the peoples under their control. This frustration only increased as colonized and formerly colonized peoples struggled to develop in a fiercely competitive world market, at the cost of self-sufficient traditional economies. Deepening rural poverty typically led to rapid urbanization: the mass migration of rural people into cities in search of work. But work was often unavailable, leading to growing unemployment and underemployment. The migration to cities also put intense pressure on traditional family structures as men left home in search of work and women were forced into single parenthood. Men unable to fulfill their traditional roles as providers and protectors often experienced shame and despair, while women—burdened with running the family alone—began to question their traditionally subservient roles.

In addition to these economic and social impacts, the Muslim world experienced a leadership crisis. In some cases there was a backlash against traditional leaders who had failed to foresee the threat posed by European powers. And colonized communities lost many qualified people through the emigration of the wealthier and better-educated classes to regions where they could live in greater freedom and prosperity. When independence did come, military governments often took the place of civilian leadership, a result of the fact that force was required to evict colonial powers. But ultimately the military governments were no more popular than the colonial ones. Compounding their frustrations, formerly colonized countries often experienced intensified militarism and authoritarianism as they protested against their own dictators.

These economic, social, and political effects of colonialism have influenced developments in the Muslim world since the end of the nineteenth century. Since that time, the challenge facing Muslims has been to understand how their societies plunged from the pinnacles of affluence and influence, high culture, and advanced learning in the Middle Ages to the depths of subjugation and despair in the modern world, and then figure out what to do about it. Virtually all modern Islamic discourse is characterized by efforts to overcome the effects of colonialism and revitalize Islamic societies.

"Renewal" (*tajdid*) and "reform" (*islah*) remain the hallmarks of modern Islam. But it would be a mistake to think that reform in the Muslim world began solely as a reaction to colonialism. In fact, voices of reform began to be heard as early as the thirteenth century. A century before Ibn Khaldun discussed the cycles of political life, scholars living in the turbulent days of ongoing Crusader and Mongol invasions and the fall of the Abbasid caliphate discussed the challenges facing Muslim communities. A major voice among them was the famous—and still widely quoted—legal scholar Ibn Taymiyya (d. 1328).

Ibn Taymiyya believed that many of the problems of the Muslim world in his time resulted from competition among regional leaders as they vied for control of a politically united Muslim community. Ideally, he said, the Muslim community would be politically united, but in reality it was divided into regional units. But lack of political unity need not compromise the strength of Islamic society because that strength was based on solidarity in commitment to a common moral vision, rather than on political leadership. The entire Muslim community could be morally united, cooperating throughout history to carry out God's revealed will, regardless of time or place. Differences of language, ethnicity, and culture paled in light of a shared commitment to Islamic principles. Although Arabs had the advantage over non-Arabs in that their native language was Arabic, which is the language of the Quran, all believers are equal in the eyes of God. Ethnic and cultural diversity are part of God's plan, as the Quran confirms (11:118). Because of Christian and Mongol invasions, Ibn Taymiyya was distrustful of non-Muslims. Still, he insisted on religious freedom and security for Jews and Christians in accordance with the Quran. To do otherwise would violate the purpose of the Islamic state: to establish justice. Like Ibn Khaldun, Ibn Taymiyya believed that the goal of all revelation is to guide human beings in the struggle to establish justice and prohibit oppression. And that, rather than political unity, is a task in which all Muslims must cooperate.

In discussing this goal, Ibn Taymiyya brought up two issues that would become themes of modern Islamic reform. The first is rejection of fatalism, passivity in the face of injustice, and relying on the intercession of saints rather than taking responsibility in one's society. Ibn Taymiyya argued forcefully against determinism, the idea that human beings have no free will. Despite the Quran's insistence on personal responsibility, determinism had become a dominant position among Muslim theologians by the time of Ibn Taymiyya, as a result of a series of scholastic debates which remain relevant today. As we have seen, in Islam as in Judaism there is greater emphasis in daily life on correct action than on correct belief. Nevertheless, a core tenet of Islam was, as it remains, commitment to absolute monotheism. God is one and undivided in the Islamic perspective, absolute, all-knowing, and all-powerful, the merciful creator and judge, from whom all come and to whom all return. Acceptance of this ultimate reality is considered to be the basis of submission (*islam*), which will manifest itself in righteous behavior and, in turn, result in a just and peaceful society, one whose success is measured by the well-being of even its weakest members. In other words, Muslims' primary concern is with actualizing God's will, rather than defining or categorizing beliefs. Nevertheless, challenges to belief did arise from time to time, and scholars had to formulate responses. In the process, they developed a set of beliefs that became part of official Islamic teaching.

One such challenge came from the Kharijites. The Kharijites ("Seceders") were religious zealots who had supported Ali, Prophet Muhammad's cousin and son-in-law and thus closest surviving male relative, in his dispute with the dynastic Umayyads over who was the legitimate leader of the Muslim community. But the Kharijites had turned against Ali when he agreed to arbitration in his dispute with his opponents. They saw this decision on Ali's part as compromise with evil. They believed the Umayyads sought leadership of the community out of sheer greed. To the Kharijites, this was a betrayal of Islam, meaning that Ali himself and all his supporters, in their compromise with people whose behavior violated Islamic norms, had also ceased to be true Muslims. They were convinced that true Islam/*islam* can only be manifested in correct behavior. Someone who acts unjustly cannot be considered Muslim because a *muslim* is someone who does the will of God. They took literally the Quran's directive that "[t]ruth comes from your Lord, so let anyone who wishes to, believe; and let anyone who wishes to, disbelieve" (18:29). To the Kharijites this indicated ultimate individual responsibility, not only for belief but also for actions. If people behave badly, then it is their own choice and therefore their own responsibility. At the same time, the Kharijites believed, it is the responsibility of the righteous to make sure that those who are causing problems are stopped. They believed that the community had to be vigilant against those who did not live up to the Islamic model and who undermined the goal of establishing a just society. They believed it was especially important that Muslims rise up against an unjust leader. They therefore continued to fight Ali, forcing him into a battle in 658 in which most of them were killed. The rest escaped to remote areas and carried out sporadic attacks against rulers who, they believed, acted in ways unbecoming of a true Muslim.

Unfortunately, it is difficult to maintain social order based on such a model of human perfection, and that is how the Kharijite model looked to the majority of Muslims. The issue was particularly significant because excommunication had become a serious matter in Islam. The Quran insists, "There is no compulsion in religion" (2:256). It stresses that a plurality of religious communities is part of the divine plan. "If your Lord had so willed, He would have made mankind one community, but they continue to be divided" (11:118). "For each of you [religious communities: Jews, Christians, Muslims] We have appointed a law and a ritual. If God had willed it, He could have made you all one religious community. But [He has not] so that He may test you in what He has given you. So compete with one another in good works" (5:48). This acceptance of religious diversity and freedom was reinforced when Prophet Muhammad established the constitution for the various tribes of Medina, some Muslim and some Jewish. "The Jews ... are a community along with the believers. To the Jews their religion and to the Muslims theirs."[4] Accordingly, as we have seen, religious pluralism was a basic feature of Islamic societies and, in fact, a source of much of their strength and dynamism.

However, the matter of apostasy—rejecting Islam after having accepted it—was something different. As the Islamic community developed in history, belonging or not belonging to the community became a political matter. A Muslim was someone who accepted not only the word and will of God, but also the chosen leader of the community. As in medieval Europe, people believed that everyone who accepted a particular religion had to be part of the same political community. Like pre-modern Europeans, the early Muslim leaders believed that anyone who rejected their religion also rejected their leadership and was thus declaring himself an enemy. As a result, as we saw in Chapter 1, they made the decision to force the rebellious tribes to submit to their leadership or face death.

This decision became a precedent in Islamic law. From that time on, the charge of apostasy was a grave matter. So when the Kharijites began labeling professed Muslims apostates, it had to be taken seriously. After significant debates, the majority of Muslims asserted their commitment to the Quran's emphasis on divine mercy and forgiveness. They stressed the struggle for social justice and the need to do good works but chose to leave judgment of individuals to God. In a characteristic verse, the Quran claims, "God lets anyone He wishes go astray and guides whomever He wishes" (35:8). To most Muslims this meant, as it still does, that only God can judge people's souls. If someone claims to be Muslim, the community must accept that. No one has the right to declare a professed Muslim an apostate based on the person's actions. Only God can judge the sincerity of a believer's heart. This majority position was developed by religious scholars (*'ulama'*) as a theory of divine judgment based on mercy and forgiveness. They were known as Murjites ("Postponers"), claiming that if people identify themselves as Muslims, others must accept them as Muslims. In legal codes, the position was expressed by Abu Hanifa, who claimed that no one can judge a professed Muslim to be a non-Muslim based on his or her behavior.

The practical implications of this view were obvious. Kharijite-style radicalism was marginalized, their rebellions were put down, and people could once again live in peace and security. But acceptance of this position had other implications. After accepting the position that only God can judge people, some scholars concluded that the Umayyads' victory in the battles against Ali and the Kharijites was itself an expression of God's will. Because God is all-powerful, nothing can happen without God's will. Therefore, if the Umayyads are in power, that must be the will of God, and people should not resist it.

This position may have resulted in political stability, but it also led to an attitude of fatalism about what happens in daily and political life. Scholars continued to raise the question of people's moral responsibility. A central feature of the Quran's teaching is that people will be judged by God based on their actions. They will be rewarded for good choices and punished for bad ones. But if God has predetermined everything, including people's individual choices, then what about moral responsibility? What can we make of God's mercy and compassion if He is going to reward or punish people for doing things over which they really have no control? In other words, what about free will? Muslims found themselves face to face with the age-old question of how to reconcile the notion of God's omnipotence (all-powerfulness) with human responsibility. This discussion gave rise to another school of thought among Islamic religious scholars, the Mutazilites. Known as Islam's rationalists, the Mutazilites chose to stress God's justice, rather than God's omnipotence. God revealed that He is just, and that He will judge people based on their choices. Therefore, we must assume that human beings have moral responsibility. But other scholars found this position offensive. They believed that the Mutazilite position placed requirements on God, as if to say that God would be forced to judge in specific ways based on what human beings did.

There were many other issues involved in the scholars' discussions about the question of God's omnipotence and justice. But eventually the rationalist position was overruled, and the position of an anti-rationalist scholar, al-Ashari (d. 935) became official teaching. The Asharite rejection of excessive rationalism in religion became associated with fatalism and determinism. It was this that Ibn Taymiyya argued against. He found it particularly evident in Sufi mysticism, with its emphasis on personal enlightenment, rather than social issues. He considered determinism worse than heresy because it makes a mockery of God's promises of reward for good behavior and punishment for evil. Ibn Taymiyya was not opposed to Sufism as such; he believed that Sufi spirituality was an effective means to internalizing a moral outlook. But he rejected some practices associated with Sufism, such as praying to saints rather than relying on God, personal initiative, and group cooperation in the struggle to create and maintain a just society. He was, in fact, an inspiration in this regard to the Wahhabis, although the Wahhabis would take the position further, rejecting Sufism altogether.

As we saw in Chapter 3, this theme would arise again in seventeenth-century India, where Sufism was most dominant, with the reform movement of Sheikh Ahmad Sirhindi. Sirhindi was particularly concerned with the kind of Sufi teaching that undermined the significance of everyday reality. According to some Sufi thinkers, all reality is One, and external appearances are just illusions. Through meditation and other spiritual practices, people should rise above appearances and focus on the oneness of all reality. Sirhindi believed this attitude distracted people from commitment to following the law. Later, another Indian reformer, Shah Wali Allah of Delhi (d. 1762), taught that Sufis must purify their practice and conform to mainstream Islamic teaching in order to achieve the goal of a strong, just, and united Islamic society.

Another major theme of Islamic reform stressed by Ibn Taymiyya is the need to keep Islamic law flexible through ijtihad. As noted in Chapter 2, Islamic law is the core of Islamic society. Because of Islam's emphasis on good works and the creation of a just society, concern with actions, rather than doctrine, tends to dominate public discourse. True belief is assumed to be an essential prerequisite to righteous behavior, but intellectual analysis of belief was not a priority. The focus of religious thought in the first several centuries of Islam was law. By the tenth century, four major schools of Sunni jurisprudence had been established, and a fifth developed in Shii Islam. During the early years of Islam, Islamic law was open and flexible. Its goal was to provide ongoing guidance for the ever-expanding Islamic community regarding what was permissible in view of the Quran and the example set by Prophet Muhammad. Flexibility was especially important, given that the Muslim world quickly came to include multiple, diverse cultures. In addition, circumstances rarely remained static: new conditions arose as societies developed economically, culturally, and politically. Yet, by the tenth century, Islamic law began to lose its flexibility. As described in Chapter 2, the interpretive element of Islamic law is called ijtihad. Sometimes called "intellectual jihad" because the two terms share a single root (meaning "to struggle"), ijtihad was the means by which scholars derived legislation concerning new or changed circumstances from the sources: the Quran and the Sunna. But as we saw, eventually the scholars added another source of Islamic law: consensus (*ijma'*) among the scholars concerning the legal implications of the Quran and the Sunna. And using that source, some scholars allegedly determined that no new ijtihad would be needed.

No specific date is given for this decision; no one individual is given credit for it; nor is it alleged that the opinion was ever unanimous. The idea that "the gate of ijtihad is closed" seems to have developed gradually and probably refers generally to a conservative tendency among legal scholars, rather than a clear mandate. That tendency was evident by the beginning of the tenth century, says historian of Islamic law Joseph Schacht:

> [T]he point had been reached when the scholars of all schools felt that all essential questions had been thoroughly discussed and finally settled, and a consensus gradually established itself to the effect that from that time onwards no one might be deemed to have the necessary qualifications for independent reasoning [ijtihad] in law, and that all future activity would have to be confined to the explanation, application, and, at the most, interpretation of the doctrine as it had been laid down once and for all.[5]

In place of independent reasoning as a means for developing Islamic law in changing circumstances, following and expanding on precedent (*taqlid*) was recommended.

Presumably, the goal of the scholars in discouraging ijtihad and encouraging taqlid was to maintain continuity in Islamic law, particularly during the perilous years when the central power of the caliph was giving way to autonomous regional powers (see Chapter 3). But in the view of many reformers, the cessation of ijtihad made Islamic law inflexible and unable to deal effectively with change, with detrimental effects on society. First, Islamic law was marginalized. Political authorities began to legislate independent of the legal scholars to suit their own needs. As we saw, Suleiman the Magnificent was known as Suleiman the Lawgiver at home because of his penchant for legislation. But his law was not based on the Islamic sources; it was not called Shariah. Suleiman's law was called *qanun*, civil law as opposed to religious law. This pattern was followed by many other regional rulers and especially by the European colonial powers. As non-Muslims, European citizens were exempt from Islamic personal law, and the Capitulations made them exempt from Islamic civil law. When European powers took control of Islamic governments, they continued the process of marginalizing Islamic law, setting up their own systems of economic, commercial, and civil law.

A related consequence of ending ijtihad was that people were left without religious guidance on new developments as they arose. In classical times, Islamic legal scholars (*fuqaha'*) were the bulwark of civil society. They were the people's protection against the autocratic tendencies of the caliph or sultan (ruler). Religious authority was the only protection against the sultan's awesome power. But the less flexible Shariah scholars were, the more people turned to secular law for guidance. By the modern era, religious law was restricted to ritual and personal matters: prayer, fasting, pilgrimage, charity, marriage, divorce, and inheritance. Shariah was considered a closed set. If Muslims wanted guidance on other matters, they would have to seek elsewhere.

Ibn Taymiyya had recognized the danger of this trend even in the fourteenth century. He argued that ijtihad must remain active, lest Islamic law become irrelevant. Even during his day, the tendency was to consider Islamic law as a fixed code rather than a dynamic process of deriving guidance for human life from divinely revealed sources. For this reason, Ibn Taymiyya stressed the difference between Shariah and *fiqh*. Shariah is God's will for humanity, revealed in nature, in history, in the Torah and the Gospels, but it was revealed most perfectly in the Quran and the example set by Prophet Muhammad (the Sunna). It is eternal and changeless, and many specific regulations have been made explicit in it. These include regulations concerning ritual, some dietary restrictions, and major moral issues such as murder, theft, and usury. But human beings must use reason to derive legislation from the revealed sources for circumstances not specifically dealt with in revelation. The regulations derived in this way by human beings are the realm of fiqh, and they are not changeless or infallible. Ibn Taymiyya cautioned that fiqh must not be confused with Shariah and criticized those who failed to distinguish between the two. "Indeed, some of them think that Sharia is the name given to the judge's decisions; many of them even do not make a distinction between a learned judge, an ignorant judge and an unjust judge. Worse still, people tend to regard any decrees of a ruler as Sharia, while sometimes undoubtedly the truth (*haqiqa*) is actually contrary to the decree of the ruler."[6] In other words, Muslims in every generation must continue to seek guidance from the revealed sources, rather than relying on decisions made by people in the past. Not only are people fallible, so that their interpretations must be reexamined in light of new evidence or circumstances, but the fact that a decision was suitable for a given time and place does not necessarily mean it will remain suitable for all times and places. Ibn Taymiyya therefore insisted that ijtihad was a religious duty, essential to the vitality of the Muslim community.

Modern Iterations of Islamic Reform and New Challenges

Colonialism gave renewed urgency to the classical themes of Islamic reform. As noted previously, in the early modern period the critique of Sufism was reiterated and intensified by Muhammad ibn Abd al-Wahhab, founder of the Wahhabis, in the eighteenth century. He also echoed Ibn Taymiyya's call to revive ijtihad, treating both Sufi saint worship and the stress on legal precedent as the result of following precedents set by human beings (taqlid), rather than the guidance of revelation.

Several other scholars during the eighteenth and nineteenth centuries echoed the same theme. One of the best known was Egyptian scholar Muhammad Abduh (d. 1905). In his view, taqlid was equivalent to intellectual servitude. He says that the Quran:

> forbids us to be slavishly credulous and for our stimulus points [to] the moral of peoples who simply followed their fathers with complacent satisfaction and were finally involved in an utter collapse of their beliefs and their own disappearance as a community. Well it is said that traditionalism can have evil consequences as well as good and may occasion loss as well as conduce gain. It is a deceptive thing, and though it may be pardoned in an animal, is scarcely seemly in man.[7]

It was the creativity of ijtihad that had allowed the Islamic community to thrive, responding dynamically to changing historic circumstances and, within a few centuries after the death of Prophet Muhammad, become one of the world's major political and cultural forces. But when people began to simply imitate their ancestors, elevating tradition to the status of virtue, they lost their initiative and fell into obscurity. They became easy prey for more energetic forces.

Abduh associated the need for reform of Islamic law through ijtihad with Islam's inherent rationality. He described the rationality of the universe as a reflection of divine unity. Rejecting the tendency to split the world into the spiritual (religious) realm and the physical (nonreligious) realm, Abduh insisted that the divine is revealed through all creation. That is why the Quran frequently reminds people to examine the world and see the signs of God in it. Considering the Quranic command to "read the signs" and "seek knowledge," Abduh actually considered the exercise of reason to be essential to the practice of Islam, even a form of worship. Failure to exercise one's reason was a religious failing: "So the Quran directs us, enjoining rational procedure and intellectual enquiry into the manifestations of the universe, and, as far as may be, into its particulars, so as to come by certainty in respect of the things to which it guides."[8]

Abduh's emphasis on rationality reflects a related theme of Islamic reform developed in the twentieth century: the call for renewed commitment to the Islamic tradition of scientific excellence. It is based on the perception that Muslim societies had lost their commitment to learning. Among the first to voice this theme was Abduh's mentor, the famous Persian anti-imperialist Jamal al-Din al-Afghani (d. 1897). Europe's exploitation of colonized people's resources was the major problem, of course. But many reformers found it particularly galling that it was often rationalized on the basis of claims that Islamic culture was backward and unscientific. This view was perhaps best articulated by the French Orientalist Ernst Renan (d. 1892) in his famous lecture at the Sorbonne in 1883. Responding to Renan, Afghani reminded his readers that it was Islam's commitment to learning that had produced the highest scientific culture in the Middle Ages. Scholars in the Muslim world had pulled together the ancient traditions of Greece, Rome, Egypt, Mesopotamia, Persia, India, and China, revising and developing them, and then transmitted them to Europe. Where would modern Europe be without Arabic numerals and algebra, for example? This is the way science works, he noted. It is "continually changing capitals. Sometimes it has moved from East to West, and other times form West to

East." Science does not belong to any single culture; it is a world heritage to which various communities have contributed at various times. Muslims have made major contributions to science, as history demonstrates, and so the Europeans are mistaken when they claim that Islam is inherently unscientific or backward. In fact, he says, of all the major religions Islam is the most supportive of science. When Islam came to the Arabs, they had no science. But Islam encouraged study and the acquisition of knowledge, and that's why Muslims quickly developed the highest degree of learning known to the Western world.

But Afghani also believed that Muslim societies had lost the scientific spirit. They had passed it on to the Europeans and, he believed, that is why the Muslim world had been overcome by the Europeans. Afghani was particularly critical of people who called themselves religious scholars and yet discouraged modern science. He said that their minds were actually "full of every superstition and vanity." They were unable to even take care of their communities, but they were nevertheless "proud of their own foolishness." These scholars were "like a very narrow wick on top of which is a very small flame that neither lights its surroundings nor gives light to others." And then Afghani pointed out the defensiveness of their position. He said they have mistakenly "divided science into two parts. One they call Muslim science, and one European science." Having lost their commitment to learning, Muslim scholars did not even recognize their own scientific heritage when confronted with it in modern form. They thought it was all foreign. He concludes, "Those who forbid science and knowledge in the belief that they are safeguarding the Islamic religion are really the enemies of that religion. The Islamic religion is the closest of religions to science and knowledge, and there is no incompatibility between science and knowledge and the foundation of the Islamic faith."[9]

Indeed, modern Islamic reformers agreed that there is no distinction between religious and secular science. As Ibn Khaldun had pointed out five hundred years previously, human beings were created with reason; that is the difference between them and animals. They were then commissioned by God to use their reasoning capabilities to carry out the "trust," which was their responsibility to create and maintain a just society. Whether attempting to understand the lessons of revelation, history, or nature, reason is required on an ongoing basis.

Among the most eloquent expressions of this theme is found in the work of Indian reformer Muhammad Iqbal (d. 1938). Iqbal said that Islamic societies had fallen into stagnation when they substituted inertia for Islam's essential dynamism and adaptability. Like Ibn Khaldun, Iqbal saw ijtihad as the key to Islam's ability to adapt to ever-changing circumstances, and traced its roots to human rationality. He criticized traditional scholars for their conservatism and fear of change. Although deeply spiritual himself, he also criticized Sufis for excessive concern with the inner meanings of things. Muslims must be concerned with the practical world. Also like Ibn Khaldun, Iqbal criticized those who take a passive attitude toward life, waiting for God to send a great man to lead the community properly. In Ibn Khaldun's case, it was the Mahdi that people were waiting for; in Iqbal's critique, it was the popular belief that God would send a *mujaddid* ("renewer") at the beginning of every century to guide people. Iqbal traces this belief to the sixteenth century. Addressing some traditionalists' claim that all necessary ijtihad had been done, he said the "closing of the door of *ijtihad* is pure fiction" resulting from "intellectual laziness. ... If some of the later doctors have upheld this fiction, modern Islam is not bound by this voluntary surrender of intellectual independence."[10]

For these early modern reformers, the renewal of Muslims' activism and commitment to learning and science was not just the source of high culture; it was the basis of power. Afghani proclaimed, "If someone looks deeply into the question, he will see that science rules the world." Recounting the stories of the Chaldeans, the Egyptians, the Phoenicians, and the Greeks, he concluded:

> The Europeans have now put their hands on every part of the world. ... In reality this usurpation, aggression, and conquest has not come from the French or the English. Rather it is science that everywhere manifests its greatness and power. Ignorance had no alternative to prostrating itself humbly before science and acknowledging its submission.[11]

When Muslim scholars lost their commitment to careful reasoning, relying instead on the past and making a virtue of imitating it, and when Muslim societies lost their commitment to the sciences, the Muslim world began to lose its cutting edge. It fell into stagnation and became easy prey for foreign adventurers.

So early modern reformers such as Afghani, Abduh, and Iqbal were recalling classical themes of Islamic reform. Their critiques of scholars' comfortable traditionalism, Sufi practices that resulted in passivity and superstition, and the habitual practice of taqlid (following precedent) among legal scholars rather than ijtihad (independent reasoning) had a distinguished history. But in the context of the massive socioeconomic and political disruptions caused by colonialism, it sometimes was difficult to distinguish between Western attacks on Islam and Islamic reformers' critiques. Colonial domination brought profound suffering for all but the elites. It also brought foreign lifestyles into the streets—fashion, music, drinking, and public mixing of the sexes. The greater the disruption of traditional lifestyles by colonialism, the more important symbols of tradition became to many people living under the European yoke. As a result, some reformers were denounced as "Westernizers," trying to conform Islam to European standards.

The case of nineteenth-century Egyptian reformer Qasim Amin is a good example. Amin joined in an ongoing debate about the need for reform in the status of women. Abduh, like other reformers, had insisted on the need for educational reform in the Muslim world. Also like other reformers, he insisted that women as well as men must be educated. The education of both sexes was both an Islamic value and essential to social development. At the same time, several reformers added, Muslims must reexamine their overall treatment of women. They must recognize that in many ways the standards of dignity and equality established by the Quran had not been implemented for women. This was the theme developed by Qasim Amin. In a book called *Tahrir al-Mar'a* (The Liberation of Woman, 1899), he argued that women's education and improved status in marriage, including ending the seclusion of women, were necessary for the overall health of Islamic society. But Amin's criticisms took the form of an attack on traditional religious scholars. He said that they had absolutely no interest in science. They could discuss the grammar of a single phrase from the Quran "in no fewer than a thousand ways," he said, but if you asked them anything about history, geography, or science, "they shrug their shoulders, contemptuous of the question." Amin concluded that the religious scholars were greedy and lazy.[12] This, combined with sarcastic descriptions of how unattractive traditional Egyptian women were, naturally turned popular opinion against his reforms. His criticisms of Islamic society sounded just like the criticisms leveled by the Europeans.

Islamist Approaches to Reform

For new generations of Muslims, coming of age in the wake of World War I, the dominant issue facing the Muslim world was the need for solidarity in the face of external threats. Yes, reform was necessary, but to call too enthusiastically for change, especially in the areas where European criticisms were most direct, appeared to be collaboration with the imperial enemies. And this was exactly how Amin's work was received. Dozens of extremely hostile articles appeared in the newly developing Egyptian press, some even accusing Amin of carrying out his "attacks against Egypt" under orders from the British colonial government. Even today Amin is described as an unrepentant Westernizer—in effect, a "self-hating Muslim." Actually, the reforms he urged were not revolutionary; many others before him had called for improvement in the status of women, in accordance with Quranic standards. But under the negative impact of colonialism, and because of the association of such critiques with the foreigners who had taken over, defending society from colonialism increasingly took the form of defending Islam. Whereas many earlier reformers had stressed the consistency of Islamic values with those exemplified by modern Western society, reformers who stressed the perfection and sufficiency of Islam, properly practiced, became more and more popular. Rather than having to justify Islam on the basis of external standards, people were anxious to embrace their Islamic identities.

This shift was perceptible on the issue of women's status, where some reformers began to valorize traditional roles. Indeed, many women chose to reject Western styles in favor of traditional dress. Interestingly, whereas some older generation women saw veil as a sign of marginalization of women and cast it off in the name of reform, for many younger women the headscarf (generically called by the Arabic *hijab* in modern usage) would become a symbol not only of Islamic identity but of personal empowerment and political assertion.

The shift in emphasis also became evident in the area of education. There is no question that education was in need of renewal. Islam's traditional commitment to learning had been undermined when the great medieval empires began to fade, chiefly because of the way traditional Islamic education developed. Although the sciences continued to flourish in the Muslim world well into the sixteenth century, they did so generally under the patronage of royal sponsors. Scientific study was not institutionalized as part of Islamic education. It was left to private scholars supported by wealthy sultans and princes. As well, the natural sciences sometimes produced unorthodox speculation, such as the possibility of the eternity of the world and the impossibility of the resurrection of a dead body. As a result, traditional religious scholars spurned such studies and, as we saw in Ibn Taymiyya's fourteenth-century critiques, often limited their own studies to those of their respected forebears. This often meant focusing on complex discussions of the Quran's grammar, style, and meaning, and on discussions of the ancestors' commentaries on its grammar, style, and meaning.

In the nineteenth and twentieth centuries, many reformers addressed this particular phenomenon. They expressed deep concern that reverence for tradition, combined with distaste for controversy, effectively precluded innovation in Islamic education. During Europe's "Dark Ages," Muslim religious scholars' lack of engagement with the natural sciences did not appear to be a problem, and early reformers' critiques fell on deaf ears. But when European scholars began to develop the sciences they had inherited from the Muslim world, and European powers gained control of the Muslim world, it became clear that the tables had turned. Muslim reformers recognized the need for reform. But again, in the face of colonialism and the Orientalist critique of Islam, calls for reform were compromised. Traditional scholars may have fallen into a comfortable traditionalism, but they still enjoyed the status of respected elders in society and undoubtedly felt a responsibility to their communities. Thus, the more Islamic reformers criticized the traditional scholars as an impediment to development and independence in the Muslim world, the more they sounded like the Europeans who justified their imperialism by claiming the Muslims were incapable of running their own affairs. As a result, many educational reformers, in fact, alienated people in their own societies. In the eyes of people already under the pressure of colonization, these internal criticisms, despite their good intentions, seemed to be betrayals. Not all religious scholars rejected reform, of course. But tradition was well entrenched. Muhammad Abduh could not even get his own university—the famous center of Sunni Islamic learning, al-Azhar University—to teach Ibn Khaldun's *Muqaddimah*. "It would be against the tradition of teaching at al-Azhar," he was told.[13] So again, we see a shift from the need to reform, to the need to revive.

The desire to reclaim tradition while at the same time reviving the strength of Islamic societies evolved into a new theme of Islamic reform in the wake of World War I: the need for self-reliance. Younger generation reformers insisted that Islam alone was sufficient for all human needs. This new discourse served the dual purpose of appealing to the broadest possible audience in largely undereducated populations and motivating them to become politically involved. Thus, rather than criticizing people's passivity and superstitions as the earlier reformers had done, the more populist post-World War I reformers focused on what could be called consciousness-raising. As in the U.S. Civil Rights movement and certain quarters of feminism, listeners were regaled with accounts of the suffering they had undergone at the hands of an essentialized enemy and encouraged to rise up and assert their rights. (Interestingly, in all three cases, the stereotyped enemy was usually the same: white men.)

A natural corollary of the emphasis on the absolute sufficiency of Islam was its overt politicization. Islam was more than mere belief and rituals, as Western Christianity appeared to be. After World War I, reformers stressed that Islam is a comprehensive worldview, a set of values and principles designed to guide all aspects of life: personal, social, economic, and political. From the perspective of this politicized Islam (called political Islam or Islamism by scholars or, less accurately, fundamentalism), secular political organization, which relegates all things religious to the private sphere, was inappropriate for Muslim societies. The order they envisioned would be wholly Islamic. Unlike the established political parties, generally populated by educated elites from the cities who had often gone to European schools and were comfortable with modern life, postwar reformers represented the majority of people—still largely rural or newly urbanized and generally traditional in outlook. Motivating them to become politically active to achieve independence and good governance became a major task of the Islamists. Competing with secular governments with far greater resources, often supplied through close relations with foreign powers, the Islamists demanded that foreign models of government be replaced with authentic Islamic governments and that Islamic law be restored to its rightful place.

The first and still the most widespread Islamist organization was the Muslim Brotherhood. It began in Egypt in the late 1920s and gradually spread throughout much of the Arabic-speaking world. Its founder, Hasan al-Banna (d. 1949), described his reasons for founding the Brotherhood in a story with characteristic emotional appeal. He told of a group of laborers working for the British on the Suez Canal who came to him and begged him to lead them to freedom. According to al-Banna's account, they said:

> We are weary of this life of humiliation and restriction. ... [W]e see that Arabs and Muslims have no status and no dignity. They are no more than mere hirelings belonging to the foreigners. ... We are unable to perceive the road to action as you perceive it, or to know the path to the service of the fatherland [*watan*], the religion and the *ummah* [Muslim community] as you know it. ... All that we desire now is to present you with all that we possess, to be acquitted by God of the responsibility, and for you to be responsible

before him for us and for what we must do. If a group contracts with God sincerely that it live for his religion and die in his service, seeking only his satisfaction, then its worthiness will assure its success however small its numbers or weak its means.[14]

The perception of Europe's contempt for the colonized peoples is palpable. It became a common theme as early Islamist activists built their movements. Empathizing with the suffering of the weak and marginalized was both recognizably Islamic and closer to the hearts of the majority than complex issues of jurisprudence and theology. The impact of this emotional appeal was then compounded by identifying the villain responsible for the tragic plight of these workers and, by extension, of the Muslim people as a whole. It is "the West." Like the Crusaders of yore, "The West surely seeks to humiliate us, to occupy our lands and begin destroying Islam by annulling its laws and abolishing its traditions."[15] Whether it is capitalist Europe or Communist Russia, al-Banna tells his listeners, the West is lacking in moral guidance. The West's intellectual freedom and democracy are good, and there is nothing wrong with capitalism as such, al-Banna explains, but the West is hopelessly materialistic and always willing to oppress the poor for the sake of the wealthy. Similarly, Communism's emphasis on social justice and solidarity is admirable, al-Banna says, especially by contrast to Europe's selfish individualism. But Communism's atheism and tyranny (its "Red barbarism") are no better than tsarist Russia's degenerate culture. Altogether, he concludes, Western ideologies have resulted in "a deadening of human sentiments and sympathies, and … the extinction of godly endeavors and spiritual values."[16] The solution to society's woes, then, is perfectly clear:

> We believe the provisions of Islam and its teachings are all inclusive, encompassing the affairs of the people in this world and the hereafter. And those who think that these teachings are concerned only with the spiritual or ritualistic aspects are mistaken in this belief because Islam is a faith and a ritual, a nation and a nationalism, a religion and a state, spirit and deed, holy text and sword.[17]

Popular ideologue of the Muslim Brotherhood, Sayyid Qutb (d. 1966), further developed the themes of al-Banna. Writing in the context of the Cold War, Sayyid Qutb explained that the world is divided between two hostile blocs, the Communists and the capitalists. Each of them is determined to control the world for its own benefit, with no thought for the well-being of anyone else. "[N]either the Eastern Bloc nor the Western Bloc gives any credence to the values they advocate, or consider us ourselves as of any consequence. … We will receive no mercy from either bloc. We are oppressed strangers in the ranks of both. We are therefore the tail end of the caravan regardless of the road we take."[18] In what would become a motivating perception among contemporary radicalized Muslims, Qutb claimed that the West actually seeks to destroy Islam. What was the reason for this hostility toward Islam? The West knew Islam was the source of Muslim societies' strength; by destroying Islam, or at least marginalizing it and keeping it out of the public sphere, they could control Muslim societies and exploit their resources. Qutb claimed that the secular West is "angered only because of the [Muslim] believers' faith, enraged only because of their belief."[19] As well, the West appeared to have abandoned moral values and was therefore against a society that was committed to them. The source of people's problems, then, is nothing less than the perennial struggle between good and evil, and the answer to all their problems is clear. Islam "is capable of solving our basic problems, of granting us a comprehensive social justice, of restoring for us justice in government, in economics, in opportunities and in punishment." There is no need to turn to any other system.[20]

Anyone tempted to follow Western models only has to look at the misery in which Western people live, according to Sayyid Qutb. They walk around in

> grief, sorrow and uneasiness. [Western man] is miserable, distressed and prey to confusion. He seeks to escape from life. Sometimes he takes refuge in opium, hasheesh and wine and sometimes wishes to forget his inner anxieties through the craze of rapidity and idiotic ventures. … It seems as if it were a hoard of demons who were chasing man and he were trying to flee and evade it, but it were always taking hold of his neck.[21]

Obviously, then, people must avoid Western innovations. Islam is the only proper course. It is the "only path that grants man excellence, bestows on him true freedom, and saves him from the curse of slavery." Islam, by granting sovereignty over human beings to no one but God, is the only religion that truly liberates humanity from earthly bonds.[22]

Qutb was influenced by Abu'l Ala Mawdudi (d. 1979), the founder of South Asia's largest Islamist movement, the Jamaat-i Islami (established in the 1940s). In Mawdudi's works Islam is again the ideal cure for all of society's ills. Unlike other systems, says Mawdudi, Islam does not allow one group to dominate another.

> In fact, it is an all-embracing order that wants to eliminate and to eradicate the other orders which are false and unjust, so as to replace them by a good order and a moderate program that is considered to be better for humanity than the others and to contain rescue from the illnesses of evil and tyranny, happiness and prosperity for the human race, both in this world and in the Hereafter.[23]

Unlike Western secularism, Islam "is a complete scheme of life and an all-embracing social order where nothing is superfluous and nothing lacking."[24] Without Islam at the center of governance, society descends into a new *jahiliyya*—a state of "ignorance" like that before the coming of Islam.

Conclusion: Mainstream Islamists and Radicals

Unlike previous generations of reformers, Islamist reformers after World War I developed broad social appeal based on empathy with people's daily experiences and appealing to their cherished values and aspirations. This appeal, in fact, resulted in the growth of grassroots movements, as more and more people found solace in Islamist leaders' vision of human dignity and hope in their promise of Islamic renewal. Islamist movements also commonly provided social services, including education, health care, and vocational training that were not provided by the state. As grassroots movements, however, their growth was gradual. From humble beginnings in small Egyptian towns in the 1920s, for example, the Muslim Brotherhood grew into massive organization with branches throughout Egypt and other parts of the Arab world by the 1940s.

The Muslim Brotherhood also became politically involved. Its members supported the Arab uprising when Palestine was partitioned in 1947. Accused by the British-backed Egyptian government of plotting a coup, the Brotherhood was banned in 1948. Al-Banna was assassinated in 1949. Yet the Brotherhood survived and continued to grow. They assisted the Egyptian military officers' coup that overthrew the government of King Farouk in 1952. Brotherhood leaders then reminded the new Egyptian leaders of the Islamic values of social justice and participatory governance and the need to take measures to achieve them. Included among those measures were the need for economic reform, health care, improved education, and civilian rule.

It was this last demand that proved most problematic to Egypt's new military government. A failed attempt on the life of Lt. Col. Gamel Abdel Nasser, who had taken control of the government following the coup, was attributed to the Brotherhood, and the organization was again banned. Thousands of its members were arrested and subjected to torture. Among them was Qutb. Qutb had begun his life as a secular education reformer. After a sojourn in the United States in which he was shocked by racial discrimination and licentious lifestyles, he had joined the Brotherhood, intent on gradual social reform. In prison, Qutb wrote a commentary of the Quran that met with wide acclaim. But Nasser's government found it offensive and accused Qutb and other Brotherhood members of plotting to overthrow his government. The accused denied the charges, but Qutb and two colleagues were nevertheless convicted. They were hanged in 1966.

Sayyid Qutb thus became a hero of the Islamist movement; he was declared a martyr (*shahid*). His works focused on mainstream themes of Islamic thought: human dignity and equality, personal responsibility, and freedom of conscience. But he also developed political theories that differed from those of the Muslim Brotherhood founder Hasan al-Banna. Whereas al-Banna called for constitutional, representative government, Qutb focused on the need for divinely guided government and, under the impact of his imprisonment and torture, did not hesitate to condemn the governments led by rulers such as Nasser as ignorant and oppressive. As well, although al-Banna stressed the gradual nature of social reform, Qutb began to stress the need for the devout to separate themselves from mainstream society, steeped as it was in ignorance (*jahiliyya*) of true Islam. Under the impact of prison and torture, Qutb also introduced a new element into his writings—the need for active struggle (*jihad*) against tyranny. Whereas the mainstream Brotherhood focuses on nonviolent struggle and allows fighting only in self-defense, Qutb argued that all fighting against tyranny is defensive, whether the tyrants attack first or not.

Qutb's writings stopped short of violating the prohibition on *takfir*— declaring self-professed Muslims to be infidels—a prohibition that has been in place since the atrocities carried out by the Kharijites in the seventh-century. But some of his followers took that next step. As well, some took his call to separate (perform *hijra*) from societies ignorant of Islam to heart. Takfir and hijra, in combination with the call to fight tyranny, became the motivating ideology of radicalized Islamic groups. Because of their permission to declare people infidels and to launch preemptive strikes on them, they are often called *takfiris, jihadis,* or simply terrorists.

That term applies to a group that emerged following the execution of Qutb. Some younger members gave up on mainstream Brotherhood strategies for gradual reform. Many mainstream Muslim Brotherhood members participated (as independent candidates; the Brotherhood was not a political party) in Egyptian elections. But a handful radicalized, broke away from the Brotherhood and formed new organizations dedicated to the goal of forcefully ridding Egypt of "jahili" rule and replacing it with their version of Islamic governance. They named themselves in accordance with their innovative teachings: *Al-Jihad,* and *Takfir wa [and] Hijra* (also known simply as *Jamaat al-Muslimin,* Association of Muslims), for example. Members of both groups were involved in the assassination of Nasser's successor, President Anwar al-Sadat in 1981, and a devastating attack on tourists in Luxor in 1997. Most famously, the current leader of al-Qaeda, Ayman al-Zawahiri, quit the Muslim Brotherhood following Qutb's assassination, and joined the new *Al-Jihad* organization.

The upsurge of terrorist activities in the last quarter of the twentieth century overshadowed mainstream Islamist activism. And despite the Brotherhood's consistent condemnation of terrorism, because of the overlap in mainstream Islamist and jihadi opposition to authoritarian governments, many governments characterized all Islamists as terrorists. This designation justified, in the government's view, further suppression of Islamists, which led to further radicalization. But as we will see in Chapter 5, the Muslim Brotherhood and other Islamist organizations remain active participants in their countries' struggles for good governance and democracy, although setbacks in that process have resulted in continued radicalization at the fringes of society.

Notes

1. For a discussion of the various agreements between the Arabs and the Europeans see Don Peretz, *The Middle East Today* (New York: Praeger, 1983), 101–159.
2. See George Antonius, *The Arab Awakening* (New York: Capricorn Books, 1965), 266–267.
3. See Janet Abu-Lughod, "The Demographic War for Palestine," *The Link,* 19/5 (Dec. 1986), 1–14.
4. For the entire text of the Constitution of Medina, reportedly dictated by Muhammad, see W. Montgomery Watt, *Islamic Political Thought: The Basic Concepts* (Edinburgh: Edinburgh University Press, 1968), 130–134.

5. Joseph Schacht, *An Introduction to Islamic Law* (Oxford: Clarendon Press, 1982), 70–71.

6. Translated by Fazlur Rahman in *Islam* (Chicago: University of Chicago Press, 1979), 112, from Ibn Taymiyya, *Al-Ihtijaj bi'l-Qadar*, in his *Rasa'il* (Cairo, 1323 AH), II:96–97.

7. Muhammad Abduh, *The Theology of Unity*, trans. Ishaq Musa'ad and Kenneth Cragg (London: Allen & Unwin, 1966), 39–40.

8. Abduh, *The Theology of Unity*, 39–40.

9. Nikki R. Keddie, *An Islamic Response to Imperialism: Political and Religious Writings of Sayyid Jamal ad-Din "al-Afghani"* (Berkeley: University of California Press, 1983), 103–107.

10. Muhammad Iqbal, *The Reconstruction of Religious Thought in Islam* (Lahore: Institute of Islamic Culture, 1986), 118–121, 141.

11. Quoted in Keddie, *An Islamic Response to Imperialism*, 102.

12. See the discussion in Leila Ahmed, *Women and Gender in Islam: Historical Roots of a Modern Debate* (New Haven, CT: Yale University Press, 1992), 156–157.

13. See Fazlur Rahman, *Islam and Modernity: Transformation of an Intellectual Tradition* (Chicago: University of Chicago Press, 1982), 64.

14. Quoted in Richard P. Mitchell, "The Society of Muslim Brothers" (Ph.D. diss., Princeton, 1960), 524.

15. Mitchell, "The Society of Muslim Brothers," 379.

16. Mitchell, "The Society of Muslim Brothers," 373.

17. Mitchell, "The Society of Muslim Brothers," 374.

18. Quoted in Yvonne Y. Haddad, "Sayyid Qutb: Ideologue of Islamic Revival," in John L. Esposito, ed., *Voices of Resurgent Islam* (New York: Oxford University Press, 1983), 73.

19. Sayyid Qutb, *Milestones* (Indianapolis, IN: American Trust Publications, 1990), 137–138.

20. Haddad, "Sayyid Qutb," 70.

21. Syed Qutb Shaheed, *Islam, the True Religion*, trans. Rafi Ahmad Fidai (Karachi: International Islamic Publishers, 1981), 3.

22. Haddad, "Sayyid Qutb," 79.

23. See Rudoph Peters, *Jihad in Classical and Modern Islam* (Princeton, NJ: Markus Wiener, 1996), 107–108.

24. Abul A'la Mawdudi, *Islamic Law and Constitution*, ed. and trans. Khurshid Ahmad (Lahore: Islamic Publications, 1967), 53.

5

Contemporary Islam: The Challenges of Democratization and Complications of Global Politics

There is a story, popular among medieval scholars, about a king who wanted to know why the weight of a pail of water with fish in it was less than the combined weight of the pail of water and the fish, weighed separately. He gathered his wise men together and charged them with figuring out the explanation. After a few days the scholars returned to the king's chambers and each provided a detailed explanation for the phenomenon the king had described. The king listened dutifully and then laughed out loud and called for a pail of water, some fish, and a set of scales to be brought forth. He then told the sages to carry out the measurements in question. They found that, in fact, the combined weight of the pail of water and the fish was exactly the same as when the fish were in the bucket. So all the wise men's learned explanations were wrong. The point of the story is that it is difficult to find the right answer to an improperly formed question.

This bit of wisdom could be applied to the many observers who look around the Muslim world today, and finding intractable wars, autocratic governments, and atrocious levels of violence, wonder what it is about Islam that accounts for all these phenomena. U.S. talk-show host and comedian

Islam: History, Religion, and Politics, Third Edition. Tamara Sonn.
© 2016 John Wiley & Sons, Ltd. Published 2016 by John Wiley & Sons, Ltd.

Bill Maher famously claimed in October 2014, for example, that Islam is "the only religion that acts like the mafia," indicating that it was Islam that accounts for the atrocities committed by the so-called Islamic State (also known as ISIS or ISIL).[1] U.S. Evangelist Rev. Franklin Graham explained simply that the root of terrorism, whether al-Qaeda, the Taliban, Boko Haram, or the Islamic State, is Islam. "Islam has not changed in 1,500 years. It is the same. It is a religion of war."[2] British biologist and outspoken atheist Richard Dawkins, puts it even more starkly: "I think Islam is the greatest force for evil in the world today."[3]

There is no doubt that since the last quarter of the twentieth century, there has been an extraordinary escalation in violence committed by people claiming to be motivated by their religion. But it is important to ask whether or not it is the religion that motivates the violence. In fact, there was a great deal of violence before the rise of so-called Islamic extremism that was not committed by people claiming religious motivation. Throughout the nineteenth and early twentieth centuries, colonial powers' exploitation of their subjects' resources caused untold suffering, and subject peoples struggled mightily to regain independence. Few of those uprisings were launched in the name of religion, even if religious leaders participated. The 1857 rebellion in India, for example, was fought by Hindu and Muslim soldiers working together, and the 1920 uprising in Iraq—both against British rule—was joined by Muslim, Jewish, and Christian Iraqis. It was not unusual, then, as now, for colonial authorities to characterize the rebels' motivation as religious. Winston Churchill, describing his experiences as a young lieutenant in the British cavalry trying to impose British rule on the Afghans in 1898, claimed that it was Islam's "incentives to slaughter" and "merciless fanaticism" that drove the Afghan resistance.[4] The following year, attributing Sudanis' fierce resistance to British forces to their religion, Churchill claimed, "No stronger retrograde force exists in the world."[5] Yet the long sweep of history makes it clear that neither resistance to colonial policies nor postcolonial violence is adequately explained by religious ideology. Although one can cite both Biblical and Quranic references to rationalize violence, there exist far more immediate explanations for the phenomena. Like the sages in the medieval story, those who look to Islam to explain tyranny and the rise of terrorism will look in vain. In fact, the explanations are not to be found in Islam.

Quite the contrary. The most popular Muslim voices have been those advocating peaceful, democratic reform, and Islamic sources universally condemn unprovoked violence. As we saw in the previous chapter, World

War I was a turning point for Muslim majority countries from North Africa to Southeast Asia. Before the war, European countries had imposed colonial control throughout most of the Muslim world. The war brought hopes—and in the case of Arabs, promises from the Europeans—of independence. But those hopes were dashed; foreign domination continued and, in some cases, intensified after the war. As a result, longstanding campaigns for renewal and reform of Islamic societies assumed greater urgency. Under new generations of religiously oriented leaders, these campaigns emerged as fully fledged organizations. There were secularist groups as well, including socialists and Communists, primarily among the urban elites. But Islamist organizations, representing the voices of ordinary people, became the most popular. Islamist movements were indeed, as they continue to be, populist.

Eventually, various regions within the Muslim world did gain political independence from their colonial overlords over the course of the twentieth century. But independence was achieved through enormous struggle, leaving liberated populations exhausted, in social and economic upheaval, and without stable governmental structures. Often those who led the liberation struggles took political control after independence by default. Throughout the formerly colonized ("developing") world, it would take decades for communities to develop stable, representative governments. In the meanwhile, many post-independence rulers remained as unpopular as the colonial occupiers had been, and in many cases, it was Islamic leaders who continued the struggles for democracy.

This chapter will examine the complicated interplay between religion and politics in several representative countries in which Muslims struggle to establish good governance following decades of foreign domination. That struggle will be complicated by global and regional geopolitics, as well as by radicalization of some factions and the development of terrorist organizations. A survey of challenges facing Muslim countries in the past century, however, indicates that it is not radicalism that represents the majority of Muslims, but rather ongoing efforts, against overwhelming odds, to establish effective, stable democratic governments.

Turkey

Among the classic examples is Turkey. What is now the Turkey had been the headquarters of the Ottoman Empire. During the nineteenth century, most its Arab provinces had been colonized by Europeans. Allied with

Germany during World War I, the Ottoman Empire was defeated and emerged as the Republic of Turkey. The Allies maintained colonial control over the Arab provinces and briefly occupied portions of Turkey. They were evicted by the "father of Turkey," Mustafa Kemal "Ataturk," and the country declared its independence. But efforts to democratize Ottoman governance had begun long before the fall of the empire. In 1876, a group of reformers known as the "Young Ottomans" had pressured Sultan Abdul Hamid II into establishing a parliament with legislative authority in accordance with a constitution. The Sultan paid scant attention to the constitution, but in the early twentieth century, around the same time that Russians were agitating for constitutional controls on monarchical power, another group known as the "Young Turks" mustered sufficient popular pressure that the Sultan was forced to abide by it. Multiparty elections were held in 1908. The constitution remained in effect until the defeat of the Ottomans. When the Western Allies occupied Istanbul following World War I, they abolished the constitution.

Neither the Young Ottomans nor the Young Turks were Islamic in orientation; modernization, including democratization, was their goal. The vestiges of Ottomanism, with its basis in the caliphate and religious orientation, seemed archaic to them. Traditional religion seemed to stand in the way of progress. The post-Ottoman government of Ataturk was therefore militantly secularist, banning religious broadcasts, closing religious associations and schools, and prohibiting public expressions of religious identity such as turbans and veils. But despite energetic development programs, Ataturk's government failed to improve the lives of the rural majority. They continued their traditional lifestyles, both economic and social, and religion remained central to their lives.

Thus, in suppressing popular religion, Ataturk's government became decidedly undemocratic. It was failed economic policies and the suppression of popular religion that gave rise to a new and overtly Islamic democratization movement. The popularity of Islamic themes in political discourse was also enhanced by fears of Communist expansion from neighboring Russia, particularly after World War II. Turkey became a member of the North Atlantic Treaty Organization ([NATO], an alliance of Western countries for mutual defense against Communist aggression). But Turkey's economy continued to languish and its government continued to be dominated by secularists and the military. In this context, Islam began to appear as a source not only of democratic institutions but also of values that would protect Turkey from both Western decadence and Communist atheism.

In 1970 Necmettin Erbakan (d. 2011) organized the National Order Party (NOP) to promote the moral renewal of society as well as modernization and democracy. However, Turkey's powerful military remained highly skeptical of both religion and populism, and imposed a ban on the NOP. The NOP re-formed as the National Salvation Party (NSP) in 1972. The NSP demonstrated its growing popularity through electoral successes throughout the 1970s. At the same time, leftist movements were growing and clashing with militant right-wing secularists. The military had launched coups in 1960 and 1971 to maintain control over a restive society. They did so again in 1980, suspending Turkey's democracy and banning political parties.

Democracy was not restored until 1983 when the NSP reemerged as the Welfare Party ([WP], in Turkish, *Refah Partisi*). By far the most popular Islamist party, the WP was, however, not the sole representative of an Islamic-oriented democracy. The Motherland Party, led by former Islamist Turgat Ozal (d. 1993), also campaigned on a platform that included the importance of religious values in Turkey's social and democratic progress. But the WP dominated 1994 municipal elections and emerged with a plurality of votes in 1995 general elections. Again, populist issues were the determining factors. Polls indicated that voters were primarily concerned with the economy, social services, and good governance; they were disappointed in secular parties and looked to the Islamist parties for hope.

Erbakan was named prime minister in 1996, but like the French remembering the era of religiously legitimated authoritarianism, secularists remained skeptical of the public role of religion. Pressure from the military resulted in WP's coalition government collapsing in 1997. The party was banned in 1998, its assets seized, and its leaders tried for sedition. The WP's successor, the Virtue (Fazilet) Party, suffered under similar pressure from the secularists. It was banned in 2001.

But religiously oriented populism would not be forever suppressed. The same year the Virtue Party was banned, a new Islamist party, the Justice and Development Party (AJP), was founded by people formerly associated with the WP. The 2002 parliamentary elections resulted in a major victory for AKP, running on a platform of "conservative democracy," with an emphasis on pluralism, prosperity, and pragmatism, and AKP has dominated Turkey's government since then. The AKP's Recep Tayyip Erdogan led Turkey to significant economic and political progress in the early twenty-first century. The gross domestic product (GDP) improved, as did social services and minority rights. By 2010, Turkey's economy was among the top twenty in the world.

Turkey's remarkable economic progress, in turn, empowered the government to limit the role of the military and its potential for interfering in politics. A series of allegations of military plots against the democratically elected government between 2007 and 2013 resulted in hundreds of arrests and convictions of military personnel. These events predictably raised concerns, both among secularists and Islamist critics, about increasing government authoritarianism. Erdogan's efforts to strengthen the presidency relative to the legislative and judiciary branches further heightened concerns. Widespread popular protests against the government erupted in the summer of 2013. Nevertheless, AKP supporters continue to see the party as the protector of Turkey's democracy and accuse the military and its supporters of plans to sacrifice democratic rule on the altar of secularism. The continued popularity of the party was demonstrated in the AKP's electoral successes, including the presidential elections in July 2014. June 2015 general elections resulted in the loss of AKP's parliamentary majority but the party remained Turkey's most popular.

Iran

Iran is another example of a country whose populist, democratic movements have been led by religious figures. Iran's democratization path, however, has been more problematic than that of Turkey. Like Turkey, Iran was never directly colonized. But its warm water ports and natural resources, including massive petroleum reserves, made it an irresistible target for Russia, Britain, and the United States. As a result, and despite the long and glorious history of monarchy in Persia (the ancient name for Iran), the country's struggle to establish democratic governance in the modern era has been complicated by concurrent struggles to maintain national autonomy.

Iran's first oil concession was granted in 1901, giving the right to exploit all of Iran's petroleum and natural gas for sixty years to the forerunner of British Petroleum, the Anglo-Persian Oil Company (APOC), in return for a cash payment of £20,000, 20,000 shares, and 16 percent of the annual profits. At that time the Qajar family dominated Iran. They had already sold the rights to develop Iran's infrastructure—roads, communications, and industry—as well as mining, in the famous 1872 Reuter Concession, which granted British Baron Julius de Reuter the right to 60 percent of profits from these enterprises for the next twenty years. The Qajar rulers had also granted sole control over Iran's tobacco industry for fifty years to British Major G. F. Talbot, for a mere £15,000 and 25 percent of profits. Both concessions had met with popular displeasure. The tobacco concession led to major protests against foreign intervention, which were led by members of the clergy. (In Shii Islam, religious authorities are often referred to a clergy; Sunni religious authorities are usually referred to as scholars ['ulama'].)

But the Qajars were undeterred. They were intent on modernizing the economy, the bureaucracy, and the military. Oil revenues had not yet begun to flow, so the Qajars were forced to rely on foreign loans, chiefly from Russia and Britian, to finance their projects. Popular protests among the Iranians against growing foreign influence increased, again led by members of the clergy. Despite their efforts to weaken the clerical leaders by confiscating religious properties, the Qajars could stop neither the protests against their policies nor the country's growing subjugation to foreign interests.

Protests turned into revolution in 1906. The Qajar *shah* (king) was forced to establish a constitutional government with an elected parliament. But that shah died and his successor was subjected to the Anglo-Russian Entente of 1907, whereby Britain and Russia split the country into respective zones of influence, complete with their own militias, the Russian-trained Cossack Brigades in the north and British-trained South Persia Rifles in the British zone. The new shah attempted to use the foreign-backed militias to his advantage; he had the Cossack Brigades bomb parliament in 1908. But the constitutionalists struck back, launching an attack on the capital, Tehran, and overthrowing the new shah in favor of his son.

World War I and the Bolshevik revolution brought more instability. When Soviet-backed factions in northern Iran attempted to assert independence, the leader of the Cossack Brigades, Reza Khan marched on Tehran. Balancing British and Russian powers, he subjected rebellious regions to strong central control, increasing his popularity among nationalist reformers. He appointed himself minister of war and then prime minister, and by 1925 his assertion of central control earned him sufficient support to overthrow the reigning Qajar dynasty. He had himself crowned shah, taking the name Shah Reza Pahlavi.

The new king was determined to maintain independence from foreign powers. In 1932 he decided to take control of Iran's oil production, but a British fleet of warships and the League of Nations convinced him to simply accept a higher percentage of profits in the company (and an extension of the agreement for another three decades). With the increased profits, the shah was able to increase the rate of modernization. He improved infrastructure, expanded industry, and modernized and enlarged the military, purchasing new hardware, weapons, ships, tanks, and airplanes.

Like his hero Mustafa Kemal Ataturk, also a military man, Reza Shah's policies were devised and implemented from the top down. In addition to economic and military reforms, he engaged in social engineering, imposing new lifestyles on traditional peoples. Nomadic herders were forced to adapt to settled life, and people who had always been farmers found themselves living in towns or moved to different agricultural areas to make way for new industrial developments. Traditional Persian dress was banned. Men had to wear European-style hats, and women had to remove their veils, ostensibly to make for a more efficient and modern workforce. Traditional "Persia" now was dubbed modern "Iran," and APOC became the Anglo-Iranian Oil Company (AIOC). But there was more to it than that. Again like Ataturk, Reza Shah saw traditional religion as a hindrance. He attempted to exert control on the religious establishment by regulating their education and introducing state-controlled licensing for religious teachers. And most egregiously, he issued legal directives, without consulting Islamic legal authorities. For a people accustomed to traditional authorities and religious terms of reference in public discourse, these transitions seemed jarringly abrupt. When people began to speak out, he silenced their media; when they organized politically, he banned political parties.

Reza Shah also attempted to bypass limits on his authority imposed by Britain and the Soviet Union, with somewhat less success. By the late 1930s Germany was Iran's major supplier of industrial equipment, technical support, and trainers. Nazi Germany even established an official news agency in Iran. Inevitably, this deepened Britain's and Soviet Union's hostilities toward the country, particularly when the Nazis invaded the Soviet Union during World War II. Britain and the Soviet Union again occupied Iran to maintain its neutrality in the war and keep its petroleum resources from falling under Nazi control. And again Britain and the Soviet Union divided the country into spheres of influence. In 1942 they pressured Reza Shah into abdicating, replacing him with his son, Muhammad Reza Pahlavi. The new shah agreed to be compliant with Western interests, and the Westerners agreed to withdraw their troops from the country.

Following World War II, Muhammad Reza Shah continued the industrialization and Westernization of Iran, with results similar to those of his father's policies. British Petroleum maintained sole control of petroleum production in the country; its revenues were so high that the portion paid to the shah of Iran made him enormously wealthy and allowed him free rein in his country. But the rapid pace of change and introduction of foreign practices continued to result in social dislocation and unrest. Opposition to the shah increased and was increasingly politically organized. A pro-democracy Communist party, Tudeh, was established in the 1940s, as was a conservative Muslim organization, the Fedayan-e Islam, calling for an end to all foreign influence, both political and cultural. A coalition of parties calling for Iran to take control of its own resources (to "nationalize" Iran's oil)—the National Front—was established in the late 1940s, under the leadership of veteran politician and leading voice of economic autonomy and democracy, Mohammad Mosaddegh.

As the Westernized elites became increasingly prosperous, the gap between them and the majority of Iranians drew more and more support for the National Front. Appointment of the country's prime minister was a prerogative of the shah, and in 1950 he had appointed an opponent to nationalization of oil to the post. But in March 1951, that prime minister was assassinated, and parliament immediately voted in favor of nationalization and renamed the AIOC the National Iranian Oil Company (NIOC). In the face of such popular pressure, the shah appointed Mosaddegh as prime minister who was then responsible for dealing with the British.

Prime Minister Mossadegh led unsuccessful negotiations with AIOC for equal shares of profit from Iran's oil. Britain's efforts to press its claims with the United Nations and the International Court of Justice likewise led nowhere, as did arbitration efforts by the United States. Britain therefore took measures to cripple Iran's oil industry, pulling out its technicians, freezing Iranian funds in British banks, leading an international boycott on the country, and blockading the country's export hub, Abadan.

The shah, though a supporter of nationalization in principle, believed that Mosaddegh was a Communist and that he and parliament were leading the country to a Soviet takeover. This suspicion was shared by Western powers and heightened when parliament granted the prime minister emergency powers that effectively suspended the constitution for a period of six months. It was then, in 1953, that British and U.S. intelligence agencies collaborated with Iranian anti-Mosaddegh forces in a clandestine operation—code-named "Ajax" (or "Operation Boot," on the British side)—to oust the prime minister and reverse nationalization. When the coup succeeded, the shah returned from Rome, where he had taken refuge. Britain regained control of its petroleum company, now renamed British Petroleum, and agreed to split its profits with Iran.

With increased support from the United States, and increased wealth from the new profit-sharing arrangement, the shah was able to reassert the monarchy's dominance of Iran's government. As he states in his autobiography, he assumed the right to veto parliament's legislation and dismiss it, if need be. "As King I appoint the Prime Minister. I also appoint the other ministers, usually with his advice; likewise I sign the decrees appointing governors-general, higher judges, ambassadors, military officers, and certain other officials. I serve as Commander-in-Chief of the armed forces, both declaring war and concluding peace."[6] Or, as political scientist Mehran Kamrava puts it, "The crown, and more specifically the person of the shah, became the state."[7]

From this time on, the United States gradually increased its influence in Iran, replacing Soviet and British influence. As a result, the shah's continued Westernization, financed by ever-increasing wealth, became associated with U.S. influence, particularly as the shah's popularity in the West increased. In 1971 he staged an enormous celebration of Persia's pre-Islamic history, inviting dignitaries from all over the world. He built luxury accommodations for the international guests, hiring French decorators and couturiers to design the costumes for servants to wait on them. Cuisine for the four-day celebration was provided by Maxim's of Paris, and guests were toasted with the finest French wines. The Shah was interviewed favorably on U.S. television and was regularly named one of the world's "best-dressed men," along with various Hollywood celebrities.

But in Iran, opposition was growing. The gap between the rich and poor continued to widen. Modernization and development were directed primarily toward urban centers, rather than the country's traditional agrarian base. That gap became more conspicuous, as well, as the urban rich became increasingly Westernized. No longer were upper classes enjoying their wealth behind splendid garden walls; younger generations appeared in co-ed schools and public work and entertainment spots clad Euro-American style—and in the 1970s that meant mini-skirts, skin-tight jeans, and long, uncovered hair. Not only were these transformations unequally distributed and culturally jarring for the traditional masses, but they resulted from unilateral policies. Traditional leaders were not consulted, and most importantly, religious authorities' opinions were distinctly unwelcome. But as opposition grew, so did the shah's intolerance. Extrajudicial arrests, imprisonment, and torture at the hands of U.S.-trained security forces and the dreaded secret police SAVAK were common. Rumors of tens of thousands of deaths by torture were no doubt exaggerated, but there were enough known cases to give the rumors credibility and the rumors, in turn, were effective in spreading fear and loathing of the regime.

The final straw was perhaps a symbolic one. One New Year's Eve (a western holiday), the Shah was toasted with champagne (a forbidden drink) by U.S. President, Jimmy Carter, as a great humanitarian. The next year, 1979, the shah was overthrown in the Islamic Revolution.

Ayatollah Ruhollah Khomeini (d. 1989) had long since become the nominal leader of opposition to the shah. Khomeini's religious authority allowed him to speak with sympathy and authority to a broad spectrum of Iranians, effectively galvanizing disparate centers of opposition and transforming them into a mass movement. In impassioned speeches, he focused attention on Islamic themes of social justice in stark contrast to the suffering of the poor and marginalized. A famous example occurred in 1963, following the bloody suppression of a protest by seminarians in Iran's holy city of Qum. They had protesting the Shah's Westernization of the country, including the opening of a liquor store in their neighborhood. The event shocked Iranians and left a lasting impression on the Shah's growing opposition. In an address in June of that year, Ayatollah described the attack as nothing short of an attack on Islam itself:

> What did [the Shah's regime] have against the students of theology? … What had our eighteen year-old sayyid [a student who had been killed in the attack] done to the Shah? What had he done against the government? What had he done against the brutal regime of Iran? Therefore we must conclude that it wanted to do away with the foundation. It is against the foundation of Islam and the clergy. It does not want this foundation to exist. It does not want our youth and elders to exist.[8]

Reflecting the sense of alienation shared by many Iranians and solidarity with Palestinians whose destiny was also controlled by Western elites, the Ayatollah described the shah as merely a tool of foreigners. A typical example: "All of our troubles today are caused by America and Israel. Israel itself derives from America; these deputies and ministers that have been imposed upon us derive from America—they are all agents of America, for it they were not, they would rise up in protest."[9] True Muslims would rise up against the "agents of the enemies of Islam," the Ayatollah claimed, and expose the sinister and destructive designs of imperialism.[10]

Khomeini's skillful articulation of populist anti-autocracy and pro-justice themes resulted in a mass following. He was able to fill the streets of Iran's cities with hundreds of thousands of people protesting against the shah's regime. He was exiled by the shah, but his voice could not be silenced. His speeches continued to circulate on cassettes. Ultimately, his followers brought so much pressure on the regime that it collapsed. Protests turned violent and martial law was declared, but it was too late. A mutiny in the air force prompted the shah to leave Iran. Ayatollah Khomeini returned to Iran on January 17, 1979, to wildly exultant crowds.

Ayatollah Khomeini was now not just the symbol of popular protest but of the end of tyranny. It seemed that Iranians had finally gotten a chance to regain control of their government, overcoming the setbacks symbolized by the 1953 overthrow of Prime Minister Mosaddegh. But a number of factors, both internal and external, have made the development of suitable government challenging for Iran. For one thing, popular anger against the United States exploded when the shah went there for medical treatment after his overthrow. Crowds of students burst into the U.S. embassy. Students had already taken over the embassy right after the revolution, but the government evicted them and restored the embassy to U.S. control. But this time, perhaps preoccupied with the occupation of neighboring Afghanistan by Iran's erstwhile enemy, the Soviet Union, the government did nothing. The United States responded by freezing Iranian assets, which compounded the difficulties the new government was having as it attempted to recover from revolution. Within less than a year, Iran's other neighbor—Iraq—invaded Iran.

The hostage crisis was resolved after 444 days, following more clandestine U.S. activity involving the sale of weapons to Iran. But the Iran–Iraq War lasted for eight years and resulted in hundreds of thousands of deaths on both sides. The fact that the United States supported Iraq in the war intensified anti-American hostility, but the end of hostilities allowed Iran finally to focus on the more immediate concern of establishing good governance.

In the confusing days of postrevolutionary triumph, Ayatollah Khomeini had imposed a unique and rather vague form of governance which was a parliamentary system overseen by clerical authorities. The clergy of Ayatollah Khomeini's generation were empowered to determine who stands for election and to strike down laws it considered un-Islamic. But in keeping with their intensely traditional orientation and the association of social innovation with foreign intervention, the clergy's notions of what constituted Islamic norms often failed to reflect the expectations of many of the revolution's supporters. Soon after the end of the war, parliament amended the constitution in an effort to streamline governance and allow for arbitration when the elected legislature disagreed with the decisions of clerical authorities.

The new constitution was passed by a popular referendum, just after the death of Ayatollah Khomeini. Elections brought Akbar Hashemi Rafsanjani to the newly important office of president. A former student of Ayatollah Khomeini but also a member of a wealthy landed family, Rafsanjani focused on rebuilding Iran's war-ravaged economy and infrastructure during his two terms as president. But the 1990s also brought significant change in Iran's demographics. Iran's youth generation was expanding, and this generation had different expectations from those of their elders. With little experience of the tyranny of the shah's regime, and increasingly connected electronically to their global peers, younger generations chafed under the strict social restrictions imposed by the elder clergy. Their aspirations for a more open and globally integrated Iran were addressed by respected reformist cleric Mohammad Khatami.

Khatami was elected president of Iran in 1997 by an overwhelming majority with wide voter turnout. His focus on the need to establish what he called a "new Iran" and to reintegrate Iran into the family of nations clearly struck a popular chord.[11] Khatami acknowledged that colonialism had impeded Iran's progress but argued that recovery remained the responsibility of Iranians. He believed that what was needed were freedom of thought and expression. People should develop their own intellects and knowledge to help guide society collectively, and they must be able to do so without fear of censorship or persecution. And in a radical departure from previous Islamist anti-Westernism, Khatami said that there are positive strengths and achievements in Western society that Muslims should try to incorporate into their own societies, such as rejection of "autocratic and whimsical rulers." Returning to themes articulated by Afghani and Abduh (see Chapter 4), Khatami concluded that lack of freedom has resulted in fatalism and excessive mysticism, distracting people from their communal responsibilities. Once Islamic societies regained their freedom and intellectual momentum, they could work on becoming contributing members of the world community. But they could not achieve their goals in a vacuum. The West must be constructively engaged, through "rationality and enlightenment," not fanaticism. That merely harms Islam. Islamic societies do not need martyrs; they need what he called "religious intellectuals," able to explore new options and develop new ways to deal with a world traditional authorities could never have imagined. Overall, Khatami argued that Iran should be a society "where the government belongs to the people and is the servant of the people, not their master, and is consequently responsible to the people."[12]

President Khatami's reformist platform was extremely popular, but progress toward implementing it remained agonizingly slow. Many members of the bureaucracy retained older generations' suspicions of the West; their suppression of reformers led many into exile. And then, again, external events impacted Iran's internal development. The residual suspicions of the West harbored by many conservatives appeared validated by events following the al-Qaeda attacks in New York and Washington, DC. The United States launched its "Global War on Terror" (GWOT), occupying Iran's eastern neighbor, Afghanistan. And in January 2002, President George W. Bush announced to existence of an "Axis of Evil," which would be the focus of the GWOT: North Korea, Iraq, and Iran. The U.S. invasion of Iraq in early 2003, a former U.S. ally that had nothing to with 9/11, lent credibility to old fears of Western aggression. The next elections, with low voter turnout, brought the outspoken anti-American isolationist Mahmoud Ahmadinejad to the presidency.

Ahmadinejad, an early supporter of Ayatollah Khomeini, appealed not only to conservative elements of the clerical establishment but also to the rural poor. Western sanctions imposed on Iran following the 1979 Revolution and expanded in 1995 crippled Iran's efforts to recover from the Iran–Iraq War. Campaigning on a platform recalling Khomeini's concern for the marginalized poor, Ahmadinejad advocated fairer distribution of the country's wealth. But his economic policies ultimately did little to help the poor, and his efforts to distract public attention with denunciations of Israel and the United States did little to enhance his popularity.

Iranians' frustration with continually delayed progress toward reform dominated the 2009 presidential elections. Running against Ahmadinejad were Mir-Hossein Mousavi and Mehdi Karroubi. Both were popular among reform-minded people, especially the youth. Neither was revolutionary but both supported democratization of Iran's Islamic government. Mousavi called for loosening of restrictions on the media and expanded women's rights. Karroubi also called for expanded rights for ethnic and religious minorities. But when election results were announced and Ahmadinejad won, supporters of reformist candidates were convinced they were fraudulent and demanded a recount. In the face of public outcry, demonstrations were banned, and hundreds of reformers were arrested.

Defying official bans, Mousavi led a massive silent protest in Tehran, in which a reported three million supporters participated. Dubbed the

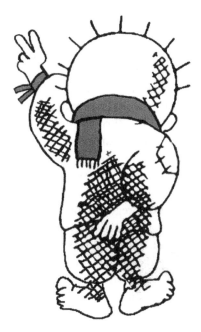

Figure 6   Handala cartoon, original version by Naji Al-Ali.
Source: published with the permission of Naji Al Ali family

"Green Movement," reformers adopted the slogan "Where is my vote?" and continued to hold regular silent protests throughout 2009. (The Green Movement adapted as its symbol Handala, Palestinian resistance cartoon character developed by slain cartoonist Naji al-Ali [d. 1987]. See illustration above.)

Green Movement activists threw their support to progressive candidate Hassan Rouhani in the 2013 presidential elections. With a strong mandate to return Iran to the path of reform and integration into the global community, Rouhani's first task was to settle the nuclear standoff with the West. Iran's nuclear power program began in the 1950s, with U.S. President Dwight Eisenhower's "Atoms for Peace" program. The country ratified the Non-Proliferation of Nuclear Weapons Treaty (NPT) in 1970, confirming its program's peaceful intentions, and has worked with the International Atomic Energy Association (IAEA) on monitoring nuclear facilities. Official U.S. National Intelligence Estimates claim that Iran "is not on the verge of a nuclear weapon."[13] Nevertheless, the United States and other Western powers suspect Iran of secretly developing nuclear weapons and demanded, in 2006, that the country cease its nuclear program. Citing its peaceful intentions and legal right to develop nuclear power, in accordance with the NPT, Iran refused the demand. The United Nations Security Council therefore passed resolution UNSC 1929, imposing punishing economic sanctions on Iran. Since then the country has been involved in ongoing negotiations for a comprehensive agreement to guarantee both its sovereign rights and peaceful intentions in return for the lifting of sanctions.

High-level negotiations over Iran's nuclear program resulted in an agreement in July 2015 that would allow Iran to maintain its nuclear energy program under strict international oversight, but it faces stiff opposition among some of Iran's neighbors and their supporters in the U.S. Congress as of this writing. As well, Iran's regional foreign policy remains embroiled in the Syrian civil war, But Iranians themselves express primary concerns consistent with those demonstrated over the past century. Human Rights Watch notes that Iranians still contend with discrimination against women and minorities; severe press restrictions; restrictions on freedom of information, expression, and assembly; and very high rates of capital punishment, which can apply even to juveniles.[14] Not surprisingly, in a 2013 Zogby poll, Iranians indicated employment opportunities, democracy, civil rights, and women's rights as their top priorities.[15] Thus, although modern Iran is often characterized on the basis of the image of its most conservative clerical establishment, the longer view of history sees the Iranian people returning time and again, after numerous setbacks, to the struggle for democracy. As political scientists Ali Gheissari and Vali Nasr put it: "A century after the Constitutional Revolution of 1906, Iran is still grappling with how to achieve a democratic state."[16]

Pakistan, Afghanistan, and al-Qaeda

Pakistan, with a population of 180 million, is the world's second-largest Muslim country. Like Iran, it has had to contend with the impact of regional and global geopolitics in its struggle for political and economic development. But unlike Iran, with its ancient tradition of grand monarchies, Pakistan— one of the world's youngest countries and the only one established specifically for Muslims—was created as a democracy. Yet Pakistan's rocky path toward effective governance provides another example of how ideals can be compromised in the context of colonial and postcolonial politics.

Pakistan was created in 1947 when Britain partitioned India. It was to be an Islamic state, ruled in accordance with Islamic values. The idea of Pakistan was developed by the progressive reformer Muhammad Iqbal (see Chapter 4) in the 1930s. On the level of practical politics, however, the cause of Pakistan had been taken up Muhammad Ali Jinnah (d. 1948), still known today as the "Great Leader" (*Quaid-i Azam*). Jinnah, a Shiite Muslim from Karachi, was a highly sophisticated man, trained in law in England. When he returned to India he became a successful attorney and active in the independence movement, working with people like Jawaharlal Nehru in the Indian National Congress Party and Iqbal in the Muslim League to free India of British control. His original goal was for a united, democratic India. He was known as the "ambassador of Hindu–Muslim unity." His orientation shifted, however, when elections in British India in 1937 resulted in Hindu governments that excluded Muslims from provincial cabinets. This convinced Jinnah that Muslims, even in a democratic India, would be totally marginalized. He therefore adopted the call for a separate Muslim state, becoming leader of the Muslim League. But his vision for Muslim Pakistan was a progressive one, where there would be no religious test for citizenship. It was to be a democracy where peoples of all faiths could live in freedom and equality. Within this ideal Islamic state, all people would be free to develop and contribute constructively to the global community.

The vision for Pakistan was, in fact, a template for a modern Islamic state. Jinnah was elected the first president of the Constituent Assembly of Pakistan, which met on August 10, 1947, to begin the process of forming a government and drawing up a constitution. He died before that process was completed, however, without expressing a preference for parliamentary over presidential democracy, for example. But there is no doubt that Jinnah insisted on constitutional democracy. In speeches to the Constituent Assembly, he stressed pluralism and popular sovereignty as the critical elements in the new state:

> If you … work together in a spirit that every one of you, no matter to what community he belongs, no matter what relations he had with you in the past, no matter what is his colour, caste or creed, is first, second, and last a citizen of this State with equal rights, privileges and obligations, there will be no end to the progress you will make. … My guiding principle will be justice and complete impartiality, and I am sure that with your support and cooperation, I can look forward to Pakistan becoming one of the greatest Nations of the world.[17]

Jinnah and his followers agreed that these principles reflected essential Islamic values, and that their democratic government would always be guided by Islamic principles. According to the Objectives Resolution passed in 1949, which has survived through the ups and down of successive Pakistani governments, Pakistan will be a democratic state whose power is exercised "through the chosen representatives of the people." This power is delegated by God to the people based on popular sovereignty and Islamic principles. Those principles are "democracy, freedom, equality, tolerance and social justice," as well as an independent judiciary.[18]

The mass popularity of Jinnah's plan combined with Jinnah's effective leadership ultimately convinced Britain to agree to an independent Pakistan. However, the state was inherently unstable: divided by more than 1,000 miles between East and West Pakistan and covering populations of widely divergent geographic regions, differing languages and cultures; deprived of the industrial infrastructure that had developed in India; and in some cases even left without control of its own water resources. These conditions created overwhelming challenges for the new state's leadership. The ideals of an enlightened Islamic society—nurturing human dignity, committed to learning, acting as a positive force for peace and social development—were quite overwhelmed by the struggle to maintain stability under increasingly difficult circumstances.

Pakistan's military, organized by the British, was the best organized institution in the country. As happened in many newly independent countries, the military took control of maintaining stability. This was not an easy task, given the challenges initially faced by the country. Not only was it divided East and West, but also even within Muslim West Pakistan, enormous ethnic diversity further stressed national unity. The name of the country is an acronym for the regions known as Punjab, Afghania (at the time known as North-West Frontier Province, and now known as Khyber Pakhtunkhwa), Kashmir, Sindh, and Baluchistan. The British had already split "Afghania" between India and Afghanistan in 1893, a 1500-mile boundary through some of the world's highest mountains, which is not recognized by ethnic Afghans (also known as Pashtuns, Pakhtuns, and Pathans). Kashmir is a Muslim-majority region. At the time of partition it was ruled by a Hindu, and not included in Pakistan. The diversity of these regions is reflected in their languages, of which there are dozens. The declaration of English and Urdu as the country's official languages did little to overcome that diversity.

"Pakistan" can also be interpreted as "the land of the pure," a name that reflects national ideals. But the challenges to those ideals began with partition itself. Many Muslims living in areas designated part of Hindu India felt compelled to move to Pakistan, and many Hindus in regions designated Muslim Pakistan likewise fled, fearing marginalization. This mass migration was marked by riots, untold loss of life and property, and general chaos. As well, the exclusion of Muslim-majority Kashmir from Pakistan led to immediate war as Pakistani tribal fighters invaded. In 1948 the United Nations Security Council imposed a cease-fire and call for plebiscite on the part of Kashmiris (UNSC 47). That plebiscite has yet to be held, and disputes over Kashmir have led to more wars with India and an uneasy military standoff that has continued to this day.

Obviously, these circumstances constituted enormous challenges for the fledgling government of Pakistan. Following Jinnah's death, the National Assembly appointed Muslim League leader Liaquat Ali Khan prime minister. He was assassinated in 1951, allegedly over the partition of Kashmir. By this time the world was deeply embroiled in the "Cold War" between the capitalist "West" (United States and Western Europe), and the communist "East" (the Soviet Union and its satellite states in Central and Eastern Europe). The new Indian government of Jawaharlal Nehru was socialist and, although technically non-aligned, received significant development assistance from the Soviet Union. The West was therefore keen to keep Pakistan in its bloc and inveigled Liaquat's immediate successors to include Pakistan in security treaties such as the 1954 Southeast Asian Treaty Organization (SEATO). The treaty involved a massive military build-up for Pakistan; this not only strengthened the military's stake in Pakistan's governance, but also alarmed neighboring India.

Pakistan gained independence from the British monarch in 1956, ratifying its first constitution, but within two years the constitution was suspended in a military coup. It would be fifteen years before democratic governance was reinstated in Pakistan—a period of intense militarization in the context of unresolved hostilities between India and Pakistan and East–West politics. In 1962, for example, India's border disputes with China erupted into war. The United States provided military assistance allowing India to strengthen its military. Predictably, India's military build-up resulted in reciprocal escalation of militarization in Pakistan. The civilian foreign minister under Pakistan's military government, Zulfikar Ali Bhutto, became convinced of the need for Pakistan to develop nuclear weapons. As he famously put it in a 1965 interview in the Manchester *Guardian*, if India produced a nuclear weapon, Pakistan would have to build or buy one, even if "we should have to eat grass."[19]

That was the year Pakistan began its second war with India. Determined to settle the Kashmir dispute before India's military build-up would make victory against the much larger neighbor impossible, Zulfikar Ali Bhutto encouraged border crossings that led to the war. Though a Western-educated socialist, Bhutto was more convinced than ever of the need for further militarization. Under U.S. President Eisenhower's "Atoms for Peace" program, the same one that set Iran on its nuclear path, Pakistan began construction of its first nuclear reactor in 1965.

At the same time, Pakistan felt betrayed by the U.S. support for socialist India believing it was holding the line against the Communist Soviet Union. Pakistan's concerns about the expansionist Soviets were not just theoretical. Pakistan's border with its western neighbor, Afghanistan, was just as unstable as that with India, and Afghanistan had also developed a strong relationship with the Soviet Union. When Kabul showed support for militant Pashtuns on the border with Pakistan's divided Pashtun province, Pakistan suspected a plan to foment rebellion in its own Pashtun regions.

Meanwhile, competition between East and West Pakistan burst into open hostilities. The divided Pakistan had always been dominated by its western section, headquarters of the military. In 1970 General Yahya Khan, who had succeeded Field Marshal Ayub Khan as president, allowed national elections to be held. East Pakistan's Awami League received a majority of seats, but the West-dominated government did not allow the League to form a government. Discontent in East Pakistan led to calls for independence in 1971. West Pakistan sent in the military, resulting in a brutal war that split the country; West Pakistan became Pakistan, and East Pakistan became Bangladesh. Estimates of war dead vary wildly, from 26,000 to 500,000. But the reality of mass carnage and displacement of millions of Bengalis is undeniable and has left lasting enmity between the now two states created specifically for Muslims.

The fact that India assisted West Pakistan in the war only intensified Pakistan's distrust of its Hindu-majority neighbor. This distrust found its way into a revised school curriculum. In national textbooks developed during the 1970s and 1980s, Indians came to be portrayed in ways that justified continuing hostilities—and continued militarization. As the Pakistani government attempted to forge a national identity, government-approved textbooks stressed the distinction between Hindus, alleged to be treacherous in the new histories, and Muslims, with their "pure" and upright religion. Whereas the country's founding documents stressed the openness of Pakistani society, with no religious test for citizenship and equal rights for all, the new curriculum stressed Islam's exclusively Islamic identity.

But if Pakistan was to become a "completely Islamized State," who would set the standards? As we saw, the views of Pakistan's founding fathers—Muhammad Iqbal and Muhammad Ali Jinnah—were progressive and inclusive. Their orientation was reflected in early developments in the country's legal system. The government of Field Marshal Muhammad Ayub Khan had established the Islamic Research Institute (IRI), tasked with developing Islamic legislation suitable for a modern state. Qualified scholars would examine traditional Islamic legal codes and recommend ijtihad in cases in which circumstances had changed and traditional legislation no longer was conducive to achieving established Islamic goals of social justice. By the mid-1960s Pakistan had implemented a number of the institute's recommendations for reform of some traditional statutes. For example, the medieval law limiting the legitimacy of women's testimony in court was revised in accordance with Quranic teaching on human equality and recognition of the change in women's social status through education. Polygyny (the right to marry more than one wife) was also limited, and the medieval equation of *riba*, which is forbidden by the Quran, with any level of interest whatsoever, was revised. According to the new interpretation, riba was identified as usurious interest rates, which continued to be forbidden, while reasonable interest rates were determined to be permissible to allow Pakistan to participate in the global economy.

With the increasing "Islamization" of Pakistan, however, the views of more conservative—and exclusivist—religious leaders assumed privileged status in Pakistan's government. Chief among them was Abu'l Ala Mawdudi, founder of South Asia's largest Islamist organization, the Jamaat-i Islami (see Chapter 4). Mawdudi opposed the partition of India in the first place, but once it had occurred, he settled in Pakistan and continued to advocate its Islamization. Like other Islamists, Mawdudi called for renewal of Islamic society through ijtihad. And he was a proponent of Islamic democracy. He rejected the term "democracy" in favor of "theo-democracy" because he taught that all legislation must conform with revelation, but he believed that legislation in an Islamic state must remain flexible and responsive to the needs of society through ijtihad.[20] But in his view it was all Muslims who had the right to participate in legislation. Non-Muslims would be able to vote only in special electorates reserved for them and would be ineligible for key governmental posts. He was profoundly critical even of heterodox Muslims, such as the Ahmadis. The Ahmadis are a Muslim sect that began in nineteenth-century India and are accused of calling into question the finality of Prophet Muhammad's teaching. The growing influence of the Jamaat-i Islami became evident when, in 1974, the government acceded to the demand to have the Ahmadis declared non-Muslims. As a result, Ahmadis have been systematically discriminated against and, in many cases, persecuted.

Yet even Islamization could not relieve Pakistan's economic woes, despite successive initiatives aimed at stimulating the economy, including nationalization of industry, land redistribution, and the establishment of labor protections. Nationalization of industry had led to decline in production and increased capital flight. And continued military development further strained the national budget. Democracy had returned to Pakistan in 1973, and Zulfikar Ali Bhutto had become prime minister. The country's mounting economic woes seriously eroded his popularity, however. When his party dominated the 1977 elections, protests erupted across the country. In an effort to gain the support of Islamists, Bhutto's government passed more Islamization measures, this time banning gambling and the sale of alcohol. It did not help. Escalating social unrest prompted the military to intervene again; army chief General Zia ul-Haq declared martial law. Bhutto was charged with conspiracy to commit murder, and following a highly questionable legal process, he was hanged in April 1979.

As we have seen, 1979 was an eventful year. It was the year of the Islamic Revolution in Iran. It was also the year of the Soviet invasion of Pakistan's neighbor Afghanistan. That invasion led to a protracted war against a brutal occupation and brought Pakistan into a critical position in the Cold War. Zia ul-Haq, military dictator or not, became an essential ally in the West's attempt to defeat the Soviet Union.

Like his predecessor, Zia cultivated the support of conservative Islamic groups. It was under his regime that, in the name of authentic Islam, most of the modernizing reforms of Islamic law made during the 1960s were reversed. It is also in the context of the West's proxy war against the Soviet Union in Afghanistan that problematic aspects of Pakistan's Islamization become most apparent.

Afghans mounted formidable resistance to the occupying Soviet troops. Regular military forces were joined by volunteer militias of all varieties and mercenaries from around the Muslim world. Some were secular nationalists, some pro-democracy, and some specifically religious. The United States and its Arab allies provided enormous support—money, weapons, and training—for the Afghans fighting against Soviet occupation.

They channeled their support through Pakistan, specifically the military-dominated Inter-Services Intelligence (ISI). Given Zia's distinctly nondemocratic military background and his Islamist orientation, the ISI favored Islamist militias in Afghanistan in doling out Western and Arab largesse. These fighters believed they were involved in a religiously sanctioned war (*jihad*) and therefore were called *Mujahideen* ("those who fight jihad"), although that term was generally used to refer to all Afghan resistance fighters.

Among those who received this support was Gulbuddin Hekmatyar, who had established an Islamic party, Hezb-e Islami, in 1977. Hekmatyar, a Pashtun from the Afghanistan side of the border, opposed the secular Afghan government. That opposition was shared by then Prime Minister Zulfikar Ali Bhutto, and Hekmatyar was granted protection in Pakistan. His Hezb-e Islami reportedly became a favored conduit for Western training and support following the Soviet invasion.

But once established, militant Islamic groups proved difficult to control. Following the defeat of the Soviets in 1989, Hekmatyar competed with other Afghan fighting groups for dominance of the country. The competition was stiff, plunging Afghanistan into a civil war that was at least as devastating as the Soviet occupation had been. That set the stage for the rise of the Taliban, a group of madrassa "students" (*taliban*) who gathered around a charismatic teacher, Mulla Omar, in Kandahar.

The Taliban set out to stabilize the country, one city at a time. Boosted by clandestine support from Pakistan, they were able drive the warring factions northward and in 1996 take control of the capital, Kabul. The relief felt by the population at the cessation of open warfare was at first palpable. After nearly two decades of war, the streets were once again safe to walk—provided one adhered to the Taliban's notoriously strict regulations. Women were removed from mixed company, men were forced to grow beards and pray regularly, alcohol and music and all graven images were banned and destroyed—from Western videos and pornography to the massive Buddha sculptures that had stood at Bamiyan for fifteen centuries. But still prosperity did not appear. Despite being "students," these undereducated former refugees were unprepared for the demanding technical tasks necessary to rebuild Afghanistan. Civilian infrastructure was in tatters, the economy a shambles, and cultivation of opiate-producing poppies in the drought-stricken country was the only reliable source of income.

Under these conditions, the so-called "Afghan Arabs" found refuge. Following the Soviet withdrawal, many of the foreign volunteers had returned to their native lands. Some, however, found they were not welcome at home and stayed on in (or returned to) Afghanistan. Chief among them was Osama bin Laden, a former recipient of Western and Arab aid in the fight against the Soviets. When Bin Laden's efforts to bring the Mujahideen home to Saudia Arabia to replace U.S. troops (stationed there after the first Gulf War) were rejected, he turned against the Saudi regime, and the Saudi government, in turn, revoked his citizenship. The opposition of Bin Laden's close associate, Ayman al-Zawahiri, to the Egyptian regime left him like-wise in need of political sanctuary. Bin Laden, al-Zawahiri, and other former Mujahideen determined to carry on their work. The struggle against Soviet occupation may have ended, but there were still many instances of oppression in the broader Muslim world. Bin Laden established a "base" from which to carry on these diverse struggles—in Arabic, *al-qaʻidah.* Al-Qaeda then focused its efforts on a single set of enemies identified as common to all global problems, identifying the United States and Jews as the co-culprits. This was the origin of the International Islamic Front for Jihad against Jews and Crusaders [Western Christians], established in 1998. Al-Qaeda carried out a number of attacks against targets worldwide, culmi-nating in the simultaneous attacks on the World Trade Center and the Pentagon on September 11, 2001. (See below.)

The United States immediately identified the source of the attacks and sought out bin Laden. The Taliban leaders refused to hand him over, offering instead to extradite him to a third country to be tried according to international law. Apparently mistrusting the Taliban, the United States rejected that offer and launched its war in Afghanistan on October 7, 2001. The Taliban government was quickly replaced, but the Taliban rejected the Western-backed government of Afghanistan and continued to fight it, joined by other former Mujahideen, including Hekmatyar and his Hezb-e Islami. By summer 2008 it was clear that the conflict in Afghanistan had spread beyond that country's borders and had reached deep into neigh-boring Pakistan.

By that time, Zia ul-Haq had died in a plane crash (1988) and democracy had again returned to Pakistan. Zulfikar Ali Bhutto's Harvard-educated daughter Benazir was elected in 1988 on a platform of social justice and help for the poor, just as her father had been. But like her father, she continued militarization, including Pakistan's nuclear program. The United States had passed sanctions against the country due to its nuclear program, but during the Soviet occupation when Pakistan was so important for U.S. foreign policy, the sanctions had been ignored. In 1990, they were imposed for the first time. The cessation of U.S. aid to Pakistan severely impacted the country's economy. As well, Bhutto and her husband were charged with corruption and dismissed from government. New elections brought Nawaz Sharif to the prime ministership for the first time. Nawaz continued Pakistan's militarization but reversed the Bhutto-era socialist policies and reprivatized industry. But Nawaz, too, was charged with corruption and financial mismanagement, leading to his resignation in 1993. Benazir was reelected. Continuing support of the Taliban to secure a friendly government on Pakistan's western border, Benazir also continued Pakistan's nuclear program to deter the threat perceived from nuclear equipped India. More U.S. sanctions led to further weakening of Pakistan's economy and more charges of corruption against her government. It was dismissed in 1996, and new elections brought Nawaz Sharif back into office.

During Nawaz's second term as prime minister, Pakistan's relations with India reached a critical point. Pakistan successfully tested its nuclear-capable Ghauri missile in 1998. India immediately carried out its second test of nuclear weapons, prompting Pakistan to carry out its first tests of nuclear devices. Although Nawaz had worked with India's government to improve relations, Pakistan's military apparently believed the time was right for military confrontation. Chairman of the Joint Chiefs of Staff General Pervez Musharraf launched a surprise attack on Indian troops in Indian-controlled Kashmir. Nawaz ordered the military to withdraw, causing great resentment in the army. In 1999 General Musharraf ousted Nawaz in yet another military coup.

Initially, there was popular support for the coup and hope for an end to corruption and a return to stability. There was already concern in many parts of Pakistan that continued bad governance was giving rise to the "Talibanization" of Pakistan and the growing "street power" of the Islamist parties who had endeared themselves to the ISI because of their support of the Taliban. That power was formidable. For example, in the spring of 2000 Chief Executive General Pervez Musharraf attempted to revise the "Blasphemy Law" (Provision 295-C of the Constitution), which allows anyone accused of insulting Islam to be jailed. According to this law, which was passed during General Zia al-Haq's Islamization program, anyone found guilty of any sort of insult to Islam or Prophet Muhammad is subject to the death penalty. For the most part, the law has been used against minorities, primarily the Ahmadis and Christians. Many Pakistanis oppose the law, believing it is simply a tool used to settle vendettas, and a violation of Islamic principles, including the necessity for rule of law. Nevertheless, the conservative religious parties brought pressure against General Musharraf, in the form of mass demonstrations, and the government was forced to back down.

As well, Pakistanis' hopes for a rapid return to democracy were once more dashed in the face of yet another international crisis: the U.S. invasion of Afghanistan following the 9/11 attacks. The United States needed General Musharraf in its efforts to defeat the Taliban government in Afghanistan, and General Musharraf benefited handsomely from Western support. But, again, the support of Islamist fighters turned out to be a double-edged sword. Opposition to the U.S. invasion was widespread, especially in view of the recent history of Soviet occupation and the fact that no Afghans were involved in the 9/11 attacks. Of more immediate concern, however, was the fact that the Taliban could not be confined to the Afghanistan side of the border. Fighters seeking refuge from U.S. forces easily found it in Pakistan. When Pakistan's government launched campaigns against them, and in 2004 allowed the United States to launch drone strikes against them within Pakistan, the Taliban turned against the Pakistan government, as well.

Following a government attack on a conservative, anti-American mosque in Islamabad 2007, one of Pakistan's Pashtun tribal leaders and long-time supporter of the Afghan Taliban, Baitullah Mehsud, brought together a diverse group of tribal fighters opposed to Pakistan government policies— particularly its alliance with the United States in strikes against them. This was the official origin of the Pakistan Taliban Movement (Tehrik-i Taliban Pakistan [TTP]). They were joined by the Taliban of Khyber-Pakhtunkhwa (KPK) Province, the Movement for the Enforcement of Islamic Law (Tehrik Nifaz-i-Shariat-i-Muhammadi [TNSM]). Formed in 1992, the TNSM had been cultivated by one of Pakistan's major religious figures and intermediary between the ISI and the Afghan Taliban, Mawlana Fazlur Rehman. General Musharraf jailed its founder for activities in Afghanistan, and the group was banned in 2002, but it continued to grow in strength as opposition to the U.S.-led war increased. With the formation of the TTP in opposition to the government of Pakistan, the TNSM began its campaign to take over KPK's Swat Valley, imposing a combination of brutal Pashtun tribal governance with an overlay of conservative Islam. Thus, as noted previously, by 2008 "Talibanization" had taken deep root in Pakistan, and Pakistanis themselves were its victims.

Yet, despite the complications of international geopolitics, Pakistan's struggle for democratization continued. By 2007, popular pressure against military rule had become so intense that General Musharraf had agreed to allow elections. Benazir Bhutto, by then living in exile, was allowed to return to compete in the elections. She was assassinated in late 2007, allegedly by a member of the TTP. Bhutto's husband, Asif Ali Zardari, was elected to the presidency.

Democracy had finally returned to Pakistan, and Zardari served a five-year term, followed by elections that brought Nawaz Sharif to his third term as prime minister. This was the first-ever democratic transfer of democratic governance in Pakistan's brief history. But Pakistanis still have to contend with the disastrous consequences of decades of excessive militarism at the expense of civilian development and the radicalization of portions of its own population resulting from manipulation of religious sentiments for political gain. The government of Pakistan and the United States have continued to attack Pakistan's Taliban, and the Taliban have continued their strikes against military and civilian installations, including hotels and, most notoriously, schools. The shooting of schoolgirls in Swat in 2012 became famous because Malala Yousafzai brought her story to life in the best-selling *I Am Malala* (2013). The rationale in that case was Pashtun tribal ethic that prohibits women from traveling unaccompanied in public, much less promoting education that encourages women to break from traditional tribal roles. In December 2014, the TTP attacked a military school in KPK, killing 132 children and thirteen staff. The rationale in that case was revenge for attacks against Pakistan's Taliban that had killed countless civilians, including children. What is more, according to the distinctive ideology of some of Pakistan's Taliban, Shiism is an aberration from true Islam and must be eradicated. Anti-Shia attacks have led to radicalization of some of Pakistan's Shia minority.

Pakistan has one of the world's strongest militaries, yet its civilian infrastructure remains fragile. The United Nations Human Development Report ranks the country 146th in the world. Nearly 50 percent of its people live in poverty, and 20 percent live on less than $1.25 per day. Adult literacy is less than 55 percent. Addressing these issues is the main concern of the majority of Pakistan's population. According to a 2014 Pew Global Attitudes Poll, more than 90 percent of Pakistanis place rising prices, electricity shortages, and lack of jobs as the country's top priorities. Crime was listed by 87 percent of respondents, health care by 62 percent, and corruption by 59 percent. Public debt, poor quality schools, food safety, traffic, and air and water pollution come next. The situation in Afghanistan was listed by only 28 percent.[21] Because Pakistanis have expressed concern about radicalization since the 1990s and consider their own terrorists a dire threat, U.S. and Pakistani attacks against the Taliban are increasingly seen as counterproductive, resulting in increased terrorism.

The 2013 elections that brought Nawaz Sharif to his third term as prime minister were unique in Pakistan's history. For the first time, a third party— in addition to the country's founding party, the Muslim League, and the party founded by Zulfikar Ali Bhutto in the 1970s, the Pakistan People's Party—received a significant share of the votes. That party is the Pakistan Tehreek-e-Insaf ([PTI] Pakistan Movement for Justice) founded by philanthropist and former cricket start Imran Khan in 1997. Running on a platform of Islamic social justice, including development of civilian infrastructure, environmental protection, and government transparency and accountability, PTI earned 34 seats in the National Assembly (to PPP's 45 and the Muslim League's 166). With widespread allegations of voter fraud, PTI supporters continue to protest the election results. But the strong showing for all three parties demonstrates Pakistanis' ongoing commitment to the country's founding principles of democracy as an expression of Islamic governance.

Indonesia

In contrast to the high drama of Turkey, Iran, and Pakistan, Indonesia—the world's largest Muslim majority country—has had a history of gradual democratization. Like Pakistan, Indonesia was created (in 1949) within boundaries established by colonial powers—in this case, Holland—and within those boundaries are hundreds of ethnolinguistic groups. Sharing little in common beyond colonial experience and Islam, Indonesians' efforts to forge a coherent nation state fell, as in so many former colonies, to the military. But throughout the country's brief history, its democratic evolution has been guided by the "five principles"—Pancasila—enunciated by the country's nationalist leader General Sukarno in 1945: Indonesian nationality, international standards of justice, consultative/democratic governance, social welfare, and monotheism. Its democratization in particular has also been "guided," as President Sukarno put it in 1959, by the military.

In 1955, the government of Sukarno and his Parti Nasional Indonesia ([PNI] the Indonesian National Association) allowed the first elections for representatives to a national legislature. The legislature had little power and was soon replaced with one comprising political appointees in equal number to elected members. This was meant to maintain stability as the central government struggled with ethnic and ideological opposition groups, including socialist and Islamic parties. But Sukarno stifled media voices and limited other civil liberties, broadening popular discontent with his government. In an effort to strengthen his position, and despite his active role in the formation of the Non-Aligned Movement, Sukarno made an alliance with domestic Communist groups. This proved to be his undoing. In 1965 he was ousted by a military coup, leading to the long reign of Major General Suharto and a massive slaughter of alleged Communists.

Suharto's government established a "New Order" in 1971, in which the formation of political parties and elections for the legislative assembly would be organized by the government. Political parties merged into three major groupings. In addition to Golkar, which represented the government and military, diverse Muslim parties merged into the *Partai Persatuan Pembangunan* ([PPP] United Development Party), and generically nationalist parties, including the founding PNI, combined to form the *Partai Demokrasi Indonesia* ([PDI] Indonesian Democratic Party). Regular elections for the national assembly began in 1971. Still, under careful government "guidance," Golkar continued to dominate.

Opposition to this limited form of democracy mounted for the next quarter-century. The 1997 Asian financial crisis devastated Indonesia's economy, precipitating massive capital flight and the collapse of Indonesia's currency. As often happens during financial crises, economic fears turned Indonesians against one another, leading to ethnic clashes. The reelection of Suharto in March 1998 triggered widespread demonstrations and rioting as the economy continued to disintegrate. In May, massive student-led demonstrations, supported by the military, ultimately forced Suharto to resign. At the same time, an anti-corruption and pro-democracy reform movement—*Reformasi*—developed. It was led by Anwar Ibrahim and supported by Indonesia's major Muslim organizations. Anwar Ibrahim had been Deputy Prime Minister under long-time Prime Minister Mahathir Mohamad. In September 1998, Mahathir accused the reform-minded Anwar of corruption and sodomy and dismissed him from the government, causing more public demonstrations.

Abdurrahman Wahid (d. 2009), leader of the conservative pro-democracy organization of Muslim leaders Nahdatul Ulama (NU), was elected to the presidency in 1999—the first democratically elected president of the country. Wahid's curtailing of the military's ability to interfere in politics and establishment of a human rights tribunal to examine military abuses in East Timor were widely respected. But his overall administrative skills left much to be desired. In 2001 the national assembly removed him from office and replaced him with his vice-president Megawati Sukarnoputri.

Daughter of former President Sukarno, Megawati had led her reorganized party—the *Partai Demokrasi Indonesia Perjuangan* ([PDI-P] Indonesian Democratic Party/Struggle)—to electoral victory in 1999. Her presidency was opposed by some conservative Muslims, but the majority expressed strong support, especially when she moved decisively against al-Qaeda-linked terrorists after the bombing of a nightclub in Bali that killed 202 people 2002.

Indonesia's democratic progress was again demonstrated in the 2004 elections, in which Susilo Bambang Yudhoyono was elected in the country's first direct presidential election. Reelected in 2009, Yudhoyono, a military veteran, represented the PDI. A skilled administrator, he focused on continued economic recovery, free trade, improvement of education and healthcare services, and regional cooperation on environmental issues, including global warming and preservation of Indonesia's extensive tropical forests.

In 2014, Joko Widodo ("Jokowi") was elected president. From Sukarnoputri's PDI-P, Jokowi represents a new brand of Indonesian politics. Widely populist and known for his affinity for the music of Metallica and Napalm Death, he represents none of the traditional elites. Rather, his election reflects the views of the more than 60 percent of Indonesia's population that is now urban and middle class. As in Turkey, this demographic shift is undermining the networks of power maintained by traditional elites, including the military. More urbanized, upwardly mobile generations are making political choices based more on common interests than ideology.

Tunisia and the Arab Spring

In Indonesia, as in the other countries we have surveyed, political choices have never been framed as between Islam and democracy. Islam has always been among the social substrata supporting the country's democratic evolution. Nowhere is that more obvious than in Tunisia. Tunisia, home of the ancient Phoenician city of Carthage and its famed warrior Hannibal, is the country most closely associated with the "Arab Spring." As we saw in Chapter 4, France, which had already colonized neighboring Algeria, declared Tunisia a "protectorate" in 1881. In the mid-twentieth century, while Algeria fought its long and devastating war with the French for independence, Tunisian nationalists kept up steady political pressure on France for their country's independence. It was granted in 1956. Tunisia's independence struggle had been led by journalist and political activist Habib Bourguiba (d. 2000). A former Ottoman official had declared himself king of Tunisia upon independence, but Bourguiba's nationalists dismantled the monarchy and declared Tunisia a republic, with Bourguiba as president. A new constitution in 1959 gave the president sweeping powers, which he wielded autocratically. Unlike in former British colonies, French administration had left no strong military organization. The newly independent state founded its own military, which remained beholden to the powerful civilian president.

President Bourguiba was therefore in a position to lead Tunisia in rapid recovery from seventy-five years of French control. Tunisia is a small country (11 million population in 2015), largely desert but with nearly 20 percent of its land devoted to a well-established agricultural sector and sufficient petroleum, phosphates, and other mineral resources to support industry and make it a net exporter. It also has an 800-mile Mediterranean coastline making it an attractive destination for European and other tourists seeking relief from their long winters. Bourguiba indeed followed an aggressive development program, focusing on the country's petroleum and mining sectors and industries such as textile production, as well as the tourism industry. In addition, Bourguiba's government invested heavily in social services, including health care and education. Tunisia today has one of the Muslim world's highest literacy rates outside of the wealthy Gulf States.

However, economic development was slow, and Bourguiba's government was distinctly undemocratic. Like Ataturk and the Reza Shah, Bourguiba was militantly secularist. Deeply influenced by Europe's historical confrontation with church-supported autocracies, he considered religion a retrograde force. As a result, he tried to undermine religious authorities' power by dismantling traditional religious schools and secularizing universities. As well, like other secularists before him, he bypassed traditional religious legal authorities. Not only did his government assume control of civil legislation, but it also imposed secular legislation in family law, which is something even the colonial government had not done. The legal equality granted females and males by Bourguiba's 1956 Code of Personal Status was less controversial than the fact that his government had taken the right to legislate on itself, independent of traditional legal authorities. Banning polygyny and women's veils, in defiance of accepted precedent, were more controversial, and Bourguiba's 1960 rejection of the annual Ramadan fast because it undermined workers' productivity, even more so.

Improved policies resulted in economic growth for Tunisia later in the 1970s, but the country's increasing wealth was concentrated among the elites close to the president. The plight of Tunisia's poor resulted in widespread labor strikes and public demonstrations in 1978. Bourguiba, who had declared himself President for Life in 1975, used his military to suppress the demonstrations, transforming them into deadly riots.

This is the backdrop for the rise of Islamic leadership in the struggle for both democratization and development. Rachid al-Ghannouchi led the way. With advanced education at both traditional Islamic institutions and the Sorbonne, Ghannouchi became convinced there were better options to moribund Islamic traditionalism than wholesale importation of foreign models. Inspired by progressive Muslim reformers of the past and the success of the 1979 Islamic Revolution in Iran, Ghannouchi established the Islamic Association, calling for workers' rights and economic and social justice. In 1981, the Islamic Association became a political party, the *Mouvement de la Tendance Islamique* ([MTI] the Islamic Tendency Movement). Other Tunisian Islamic movements that developed during the same period denounced political systems associated with European colonialism, including democracy. But MTI insisted on the right of all Tunisians to political participation in democratic governance.

MTI's progressive agenda clearly struck a chord among Tunisians. Its calls for democracy and social justice consistent with Islamic values, combined with its focus on Tunisia's Arab Islamic identity, made it the most popular alternative to Bourguiba's elitist, secularist, and Francophile autocracy. But that popularity also made it highly threatening to Bourguiba's government. MTI's leaders were imprisoned and its membership silenced.

The 1980s saw further economic challenges for Tunisians as economic progress slowed. Demonstrations demanding a living wage and decent standard of living broke out again in 1984. In what had become a pattern among autocratic rulers since the 1979 Iranian Revolution, Bourguiba targeted "radical Islam" as the source of the riots and declared MTI an enemy of the state, despite the fact that MTI remained committed to non-violence. New government regulations banned public prayer and symbols of Islamic identity. In 1987 Ghannouchi was again arrested, and sentenced to life in prison. That sentence was commuted; he was released in 1988.

In 1987 the ailing Bourguiba was declared incompetent and replaced by General Zine El Abidine Ben Ali. Ben Ali continued Bourguiba's radical secularism and initially attempted to neutralize the appeal of Islamist reformists. He made frequent public references to Islam, reversed Bourguiba's closure of theology schools and banning of the annual Ramadan fast, and renamed his Socialist Destourian Party the Constitutional Democratic Rally. He also scheduled the country's first multiparty—if highly controlled—elections for 1989. Targeting MTI specifically, Ben Ali insisted that no party could monopolize Islamic identity. In response, MTI removed "Islam" from its name and became al-Nahda ("Renaissance") Party. Ben Ali's government still rejected the party, but nonetheless its candidates, running as independents, received widespread support in the elections.

This electoral success further alarmed the Ben Ali government, which continued to fan fears of Islamic radicalism. Fearing further arrests, Ghannouchi and other al-Nahda leaders left Tunisia in 1989. (Ghannouchi was granted political asylum in England in 1993.) Ben Ali's government kept up the pressure on al-Nahda supporters at home. In the early 1990s, thousands of activists were arrested and hundreds sentenced to long prison terms; reports of torture, blackmail, and threats circulated widely. Although al-Nahda leadership maintained its commitment to non-violence, frustration among the rank and file led to radicalization among some members, who broke away and formed their own groups. Terrorist activities undertaken by these fringe organizations were blamed on al-Nahda and, despite the group's condemnation of terrorism, the government used them to justify further rounds of arrests and repression. Several al-Nahda members died in custody, and hundreds were tried and sentenced to stiff prison sentences.

Radicalization was also occurring in other Islamic organizations, including the traditionally apolitical ultraconservative Salafist community. Many found common cause with the newly emerged transnational terrorist organization, al-Qaeda, particularly after its spectacular attacks in New York and Washington DC on 9/11. Some volunteered to fight with al-Qaeda abroad, and some carried out al-Qaeda-style attacks at home. Again, the actions of radical Islamists were used by the government to charge that all Islamic activists—including the nonviolent, pro-democracy majority, al-Nahda—were terrorists. Like many autocratic governments, Ben Ali's claimed to be assisting in the West's Global War on Terror (GWOT) by suppressing its own pro-democracy Islamic activists.

The first decade of the twenty-first century saw continued economic growth in Tunisia, but little improvement in the high unemployment and income disparity between the ultra-rich elites and the working poor. Ben Ali and his extended family controlled the lion's share of the economy and enjoyed conspicuously luxurious lifestyles, whereas the average per capita income languished below $4000 per year and average unemployment ranged upward of 30 percent even for university graduates. And the country's enormous police force notoriously suppressed civil liberties. A popular joke told of dogs crossing the border to Algeria so they could bark.

Opposition to the Ben Ali regime finally exploded into open rebellion, triggered by a single, iconic event. Twenty-six year-old Mohamed Bouazizi had had to quit high school to support his mother and siblings. Among his jobs was selling fruit from a wagon on the streets of Sidi Bouzid, a city in central Algeria. On December 17, 2010, a policewoman reportedly spat at him and slapped him when he could not produce either a vendor's permit or a bribe, and then confiscated his cart. Bouazizi sought assistance from the governor's office but was ignored. In utter desperation, he stood in the middle of traffic, doused himself with gasoline, and set himself alight. News of Bouazizi's self-immolation spread quickly via social media and sparked massive demonstrations, first in Sidi Bouzid and quickly spread throughout the country. Security forces attempted to disperse the crowds with their typical brutality but to no avail. Despite hundreds of deaths, the demonstrations continued. They ultimately led to Ben Ali's resignation on January 14, 2011, marking the beginning of the so-called "Arab Spring."

Al-Nahda leaders quickly returned from exile to join Tunisia's transition to democratic governance. Elections for members of a constituent assembly to draft a new constitution were set for October. Al-Nahda, well-organized and widely represented throughout the country during its long struggle for survival despite repression, was well positioned to campaign effectively. Its platform focused on key Islamic issues of economic and social justice, not specifically on Islam. But secular parties, particularly those developed by remnants of the old regime, alleged that the Islamists were determined to overturn Tunisia's legal system and impose traditional Islamic law in the country. Despite Ghannouchi's repeated denials of those allegations, staunch secularists remained skeptical. Opponents also alleged that al-Nahda was a covert terrorist organization, the same allegations they had used during the Ben Ali era. Terrorist acts by the real radicals were blamed on al-Nahda, heightening secularists' suspicions. Nevertheless, with a voter turnout of more than 50 percent, al-Nahda received 40 percent of the votes. Polling data indicated that the vast majority of al-Nahda supporters voted on the basis of the party's economic and human rights position, not on its religious affiliation.

Working with other parties, al-Nahda supported the Assembly's choice of Moncef Marzouki, of the secular Congress for the Republic party, as president. It was a turbulent time because the revolution effectively brought the economy to a standstill, exacerbating social and political tensions. Radical Salafists insisted on conservative social norms, attacking students they deemed immodestly dressed and arts and film galleries they believed were un-Islamic. Tensions escalated and reached crisis point with the assassination of anti-Islamist activist Chokri Belaid in February 2013. In July, Leftist Popular Front leader Mohamed Brahmi was also assassinated, and a number of other violent attacks against secular targets followed. Al-Nahda immediately condemned the deeds, but secularist suspicions and protests against the party mounted. The al-Nahda-led Assembly struggled onward to create a coalition government in which key ministries were divided among the strongest parties and independent candidates. But the stalled economy and escalating terrorist attacks led to increased pressure for a new government.

Mass demonstrations during the summer of 2013 prompted al-Nahda to withdraw from the new government in order to preserve the peace. The Assembly continued its deliberations on the new constitution. Secularists, Islamists, and technocrats alike finally agreed to a document presented to the country in January 2014. Parliamentary elections were then scheduled for October. The secular coalition party Nidaa Tounes received more votes than did the Islamist al-Nahda Party, and its leader Beji Caid Essebsi was elected president in December 2014. The government he presented to the country in January 2015 included no Islamist or leftist parties, yet al-Nahda representatives continue to participate in Tunisia's parliament, and the party accepted the government as an expression of the will of the people.

What about Terrorism? ISIS, Boko Haram, Islamic Jihad, Hamas, and Hezbollah

As we have seen in other examples, popular discontent in Tunisia centered on demands for socioeconomic justice and civil and human rights. These populist demands were championed by the mainstream Islamist party, al-Nahda. That is why the party was popular, and that is why the autocratic government suppressed it. Its Islamic identity was a secondary matter. And the party's willingness to compromise with secularists, including withdrawing from the coalition it had created, demonstrated its commitment to democratic governance and the well-being of the country. Tunisia's "Dignity Revolution" therefore confirms in microcosm what macro-scale polling data have shown. In 2008 Gallup World Poll published the results of the most extensive survey of Muslim opinion ever conducted, *Who Speaks for Islam?* The poll sampled views of more than fifty thousand Muslims in more than thirty-five countries, over a period of six years. It demonstrates that Muslims overwhelmingly support democracy and human rights, including the right to freedom of religion for all people. Subsequent Pew Research Center polls have confirmed the Gallup data. Although secularists fear the involvement of religion in public life, polling data indicate that the majority of Muslims believe the influence of their religion in public life would enhance, not limit, human rights and democracy.[22]

This strong connection between Islam, human rights, and democracy in the minds of majorities of Muslims, supported by the long history of democratization described previously, may surprise those familiar with the "clash of civilizations" theory, which claims that Islam rejects human rights and democracy.[23] It will undoubtedly seem counterintuitive to those whose only impression of Islam comes from headlines featuring terrorism committed by people identified as Muslim. Headlines, by nature, feature the extraordinary, the spectacular, the terrifying. And there is little more extraordinary, spectacular, and terrifying than terrorism. What we have focused on so far are mainstream Islamic values, history, and contemporary developments. They are not particularly spectacular or extraordinary and therefore rarely make headlines. But what about the non-mainstream? What about the headline makers, the terrorists? Although they are aberrations from mainstream developments, they are real. How do they fit into the overall history of Islam?

Surprise is among the defining characteristics of irregular warfare, also known as terrorism. Regular warfare involves public announcement of the onset of hostilities, by duly constituted governments, with combat limited—at least in theory—to military personnel, readily identifiable by their uniforms. Terrorism breaks all these rules. It is the warfare of the weak and marginalized, those outside the power structure, who use surprise for strategic advantage. Terrorists also often use irregular weapons, including improvised explosive devices (IEDs) and suicide bombings. But although terrorist attacks are launched without warning, it is still possible to trace the chain of causality that leads to them, and understanding that chain of causality can help explain where so-called Islamic terrorism comes from. For example, the trajectory of warfare and interference with nationalist aspirations that began in mid-twentieth-century Iran led indirectly but nonetheless ineluctably to the rise of the Islamic State in Iraq and Syria (ISIS, also known as the simply "Islamic State").

As we saw above, the 1953 U.S.- and British-orchestrated clandestine operation that overthrew the democratically chosen prime minister of Iran, Mohammed Mosaddegh, led to the increasing empowerment of a deeply unpopular ruler, Shah Mohammed Pahlavi. As the shah's unpopularity increased, so did his intolerance of dissent. Efforts to silence his opposition resulted in the channeling of discontent into the only voice that could not be silenced, that of the clergy. So the clergy became the de facto voice of revolution that led ultimately to the 1979 overthrow of the Shah of Iran.

Because of the West's role in installing the shah and support for him despite his unpopularity, the 1979 Islamic Revolution in Iran was bound to be anti-West. That anti-West stance, in turn, precipitated U.S. support for the Iraqi invasion of Iran in 1980. Because the new government in Iran was opposed not only to the United States but also to its Arab allies, including neighboring Kuwait and Saudi Arabia, those states also supported Iraq's war against Iran. When that long and bloody conflict came to an end in 1988, the Arab powers demanded reimbursement for their support from Iraq. Iraq, devastated by the war, refused to pay. Instead, it invaded Kuwait. That invasion led to the 1991 Gulf War, conducted by the United States to evict Iraqi troops from Kuwait. The 1991 Gulf War was brief, but left U.S. forces stationed in Saudi Arabia, home of Islam's holy cities of Mecca and Medina.

The stationing of U.S. forces in Saudi Arabia was deeply offensive to some religious conservatives, particularly a group led by Saudi Arabia native Osama Bin Laden. Bin Laden had been among the recipients of U.S. training and aid during the 1980s, when the United States supported resistance against Soviet occupation of Afghanistan. By the end of the Gulf War, the Soviet Union no longer existed and Bin Laden offered to replace U.S. troops in Saudi Arabia with his seasoned fighters. The Saudi government rejected Bin Laden's offer and, in fact, revoked Bin Laden's citizenship, sending him and his band of international fighters back to Afghanistan. But with no more Soviet Union to fight, Bin Laden's warriors needed a new cause. They were a diverse lot. Many were from Egypt, where they had grievances against that country's Western-supported autocratic government. Others had grievances against governments in Yemen, Chechnya, or Libya, among others. But all could agree on grievances against the United States for its support of various dictators and of the Israeli government's denial of Palestinian rights. They therefore formed a united "base"—*al-qa'ida* or al-Qaeda—to pursue their collective grievances. Launching terrorist attacks against U.S. targets in 1993, 1998, and 2000, their campaign culminated in the spectacular suicide bombings in New York and Washington, DC, on 9/11. Although no Afghans were involved in the 9/11 attacks, and Afghanistan's ruling Taliban initially agreed to hand over Bin Laden to international authorities, the United States invaded Afghanistan in 2001. Similarly, no Iraqis had been involved in attacks against the United States, nor had its government anything to do with al-Qaeda. Nevertheless, the United States—as part of its ongoing Global War on Terror—initiated a war against that country, as well, in 2003.

The 2003 invasion of Iraq inevitably fractured the fragile bonds that held together that jerry-rigged country. As we saw in Chapter 4, the modern borders of Iraq, like those of many formerly colonized countries, were established by Western powers following World War I. The new country comprised three former Ottoman provinces, two Arab and one with a large Kurdish population. Of the two Arab provinces, Basra was predominantly Shiite, whereas Baghdad had a mixed Sunni and Shiite population, but overall the majority of Arab Iraq's population were Shia Muslims. Britain, which had assumed "mandate" authority over Iraq following World War I, installed a Sunni leader from Arabia as the king of this ethnically diverse and Shiite majority country. The Sunni minority enjoyed privileged status under the Sunni king, leading to resentment among the marginalized Shia majority. For their part, the Kurds, a culturally distinct group, had sought autonomy as early as the 1880s. Following the demise of the Ottoman Empire in World War I, they again pressed their claims for an independent country but without success. Instead of being united in an independent Kurdistan, the majority of Kurds became a minority in Turkey, while others formed minorities in Syria, Iraq, and Iran. Iraq's Kurds, therefore, felt far more in common with Kurds across the borders than with Arab Iraqis and continued to struggle for independence, resulting in a number of armed uprisings. Furthermore, the majority of Iraq's Arabs felt little loyalty toward the British government that supported their ruler. Even after Iraq gained formal independence from Britain in 1932, the royal family continued to rule in compliance with British prerogatives, against the will of enough Iraqis that the Iraqis launched bloody revolutions in 1941 and again in 1958, when the ruling family was finally overthrown. Iraq's military quickly gained control of revolutionary Iraq. In 1979, Saddam Hussein rose to the pinnacle of that power structure.

Iraq's tenuous seams began to fray following the 1991 Gulf War. Northern Iraq's Kurdish region had gained de facto autonomy as the U.S.-led forces imposed sanctions on Arab Iraq and a "no-fly" zone in Iraqi Kurdistan, protecting it from Saddam Hussein's government. There was little chance that Iraq's Kurds would choose to return to the Arab fold, even with the "regime change" effected by the 2003 U.S.-led invasion. What is more, the toppling of Saddam Hussein's Sunni-dominated government in 2003 ended the privilege of the Sunni minority. Democratic elections brought a Shia-dominated government. Sunni tribes predictably led the resistance to foreign intervention in the first place and rebelled against the new Shia-dominated government. Iraq was again three disparate entities, each of which had more in common with people outside Iraqi borders than inside. Sunni attacks on Iraq's Shia thus drew support for the Shia majority from Shiite Iran across the eastern border, and Iraq's Sunnis could evade reprisals by slipping across the porous western border into Sunni-majority Syria.

This is the cauldron in which ISIS evolved. It began in Iraq as a generic anti-U.S. and militantly Sunni al-Qaeda affiliate—al-Qaeda in Iraq (AQI)—intent on establishing an independent Islamic state in the Arab Sunni territories of Iraq. Initially reported to have only a few thousand fighters, AQI launched brutal attacks not only on foreign military and civilian targets but also on Iraqi Shia and Christian civilians. Kidnappings, suicide bombings, and videotaped beheadings became their trademark.

Given the "fog of war," details about ISIS are necessarily speculative. But it appears that their military core is dominated by former members of Saddam Hussein's highly skilled, and Sunni-dominated, military, which was disbanded by U.S. authorities in 2003. Strategizing, if not leading the Sunni rebellion, they were joined by Sunni fighters from across the border in Syria, unhappily ruled by an autocratic representative of a Shia minority. At the height of the Arab Spring in 2011, Syrian opposition demonstrations turned into open antigovernment rebellion, drawing Syrian fighters back from Iraq, along with diverse other mercenaries. Back in Syria, they established al-Nusra Front ([ANF] The Support Front or *Jabhat al-Nusra* [JAN]). With spectacularly destructive attacks in Aleppo, Damascus, and other Syrian cities, ANF/JAN struggled to dominate the multiple militias battling the Syrian government. Many Syrian militias were opposed to Syria's regime because of its authoritarianism and failed economic policies, but ANF/JAN stood out for its radically Sunni orientation; its opposition to the Syrian regime focused on its Shia identity. Because Syria's Shia-dominated government received support from Iran, the revolutionary forces immediately drew massive financial and materiel support from Arab regimes, always in competition with Iran for dominance of the oil rich Persian/ Arabian Gulf. That support attracted more fighters, including "war tourists" from Europe and the United States, thrill-seekers disengaged from their home environments enough to be able to disappear into distant war zones. The increased personnel in turn resulted in more military successes.

By 2013, ANF/JAN was the most successful antigovernment fighting force in Syria, and its Iraqi counterpart, AQI had expanded its self-proclaimed Islamic State in Iraq (ISI) to include Syria. AQI renamed itself the Islamic State in Iraq and the Levant (traditional name for the eastern Mediterranean)—ISIL—and the Islamic State in Iraq and al-Sham (the Arabic name for Syria)—ISIS. The reputed leader of ISIS/ISIL announced a merger of his group with ANF/JAN, a move rejected by ANF/JAN leaders. Central al-Qaeda leaders, headquartered somewhere in Pakistan, attempted unsuccessfully to arbitrate between the two groups, leading to a split between ANF/JAN and ISIS/ISIL. The two groups then fought each other for dominance in the Syrian civil war, with escalating violence and brutality. ISIS/ISIL kidnappings, beheadings, and attacks on religious minorities reached such horrific levels that even al-Qaeda condemned them.

In Iraq, ISIS/ISIL military skill combined with the weakness of the new Iraqi military resulted in stunning successes for the Sunni rebels. Chief among them was the capture of oil-rich Mosul, Iraq's second-largest city, in June 2014. Other cities fell in succession, including Tikrit, home base of Saddam Hussein, and Baiji, home of Iraq's largest oil refinery. These successes brought more wealth, and wealth brought more recruits. By mid-2014 estimates of ISIS/ISIL forces ranged in the tens of thousands. ISIS/ISIL renamed itself and expanded its claims yet again; it became simply the Islamic State (IS), and its leader declared himself caliph, the leader of all people it recognizes as Muslims, meaning all Sunnis worldwide.

This claim is considered not just ludicrous but a political threat to those who consider themselves the real rulers of Muslim states. It forced Arab states that had supported Sunni opposition to the Syrian government to restrategize, attempting to keep their arms shipments and financial support from falling into ISIS/ISIL/IS hands, and supporting strikes against them. The self-proclaimed caliphate was also anathema to the vast majority of Muslims worldwide. In September 2014 more than 120 leading Muslim authorities issued an open "Letter to Baghdadi"—the reputed leader of IS—refuting the terrorist group's claims point-by-point, based on classical

Islamic sources, and specifically condemning the targeting of civilians, religious minorities, journalists, and aid workers; mutilations, including beheadings; the mistreatment of women; taking hostages and abuse of prisoners; and the institution of slavery.[24]

The condemnations of ISIS/ISIL/IS by Muslim religious authorities mirror the condemnations issued after the 9/11 al-Qaeda attacks. They were unanimous and are readily available online. But they do not make headlines, leading to questions about the relationship of Islam to terrorism, such as those mentioned previously. In fact, although some terrorists use Islamic terms of reference, the history of terrorist groups and the condemnations of terrorism by Muslims worldwide demonstrate that Islam is not the source of terrorist violence. Instead, protracted and profound economic and political chaos is the source of their violence. The founders of al-Qaeda and ANF/JAN are long dead. Bin Laden was killed in a U.S. raid in Pakistan in 2011, and ANF/JAN founder Abu Musab al-Zarqawi was assassinated in 2006. Yet as of this writing, ISIS/ISIS/IS, with its capital in Raqqa, Syria, is in control oil rich territories in Syria and Iraq and has a strong presence in Libya, Yemen, and Afghanistan where it has become a part of those countries' civil wars. That is because ISIS/ISIL/IS is, as veteran foreign policy journalist Patrick Cockburn put it, "a child of war."[25] From the 1953 obstruction of Iranian nationalists' aspirations in Operation Ajax, to the 1979 Islamic Revolution, the Iran–Iraq War, and the Gulf War, to the rise of al-Qaeda, the 2001 invasion of Afghanistan and the 2003 invasion of Iraq, the chain of causality of the war that became ISIS/ISIL/IS's incubator is clear.

Some scholars trace the chain of causality ever further back than Operation Ajax—to the 1916 Sykes-Picot Agreement. That agreement may seem like ancient history to people in the West but not to those who suffer its consequences. In June 2014 ISIS/ISIL/IS posted a video titled "The End of Sykes-Picot," explaining—in English with Arabic subtitles—the group's goal: to end the long-term effects of European imperialism in the Middle East (https://www.youtube.com/watch?v=i357G1HuFcI) Thus, Michael Guntner, Till Paasche, and Nahro Zagros conclude:

> The immediate origins of the Isla.mic State in Iraq an Syria (ISIS) lie in the opportunity spaces provided by two bitter civil wars that challenged the existing state system and borders created by the Sykes-Picot Agreement of World War I: (1) The bloody Sunni-Shia civil war in Iraq that followed the U.S. overthrow of Saddam Hussein in 2003, and (2) the even more horrific civil war that has been raging in Syria since 2011.[26]

A similar focus on "opportunity spaces" helps understand the creation of another radical aberration from mainstream Islam, Boko Haram. Like ISIS/ISIL/IS, Boko Haram emerged in a former colony—in this case, the former British colony, Nigeria. Like Iraq, the modern state of Nigeria was created by the British out of religiously, linguistically, and historically distinct regions, in this case, in West Africa, through a series of battles in the late nineteenth and early twentieth centuries. The major ethnic groupings—Hausa/Fulani, Yoruba, and Igbo—had little in common other than a desire for independence from foreign control. Independence was granted in 1960, and the present boundaries were fixed by 1963. Conflicts among regional and national leaders led to the secession of the eastern, mainly Christian region in 1967, which in turn led to vicious reprisals and civil war. When that war ended, with millions dead (estimates range from one to three million), the military took control of the government. With brief exceptions, Nigeria was ruled by military dictators until 1999. Elections in that year, and again in 2003, returned former military ruler Olusegun Obasanjo to the presidency. Since 2010 Goodluck Jonathan, a Christian from the oil-rich Niger Delta region, has been president.

Nigeria, with Africa's largest population (182 million in 2015) is about 50 percent Muslim. Christians make up around 40 percent of the population, and that proportion has been steadily increasing through active missionary work over the past century and a half. Nigeria's economy is also Africa's largest. The country is the eighth-largest exporter of petroleum in the world. It is also rich in gas, gold, tin, and other minerals. Following an oil boom in the 1970s, Nigeria undertook major development programs, including hydropower and telecommunications. However, the agrarian sector—still accounting for over half the country's economy—has been largely bypassed by development. Indeed, living conditions in many rural areas are deplorable. Environmental protections are minimal. The pollution from the petroleum industry in the Niger Delta is epic and has sparked numerous protests. As well, the extensive dam network on the rivers feeding the mighty Niger River resulted in significant displacement of farmers and has been plagued by inefficiency and mismanagement. Further, Nigeria's wealth is highly concentrated among a small elite. The elites include some of Africa's wealthiest individuals with net worth in the multiple billions of dollars, yet the average annual per capita income in the country is under $3000, and more than two-thirds of the population overall live on less than $1.25/day. Primarily rural, this poverty is most characteristic of the largely agrarian north, which happens to be majority Muslim.

Muslims of the Nigeria's north thus suffer disproportionately from the country's extraordinary maldistribution of wealth. This reality contrasts sharply with northern Nigeria's highly successful premodern Sokoto Caliphate (1804–1903), which built on the heritage of earlier sub-Saharan Islamic empires and was destroyed by the British in 1903. Predictably, the source of the Muslim north's widespread suffering was attributed to foreign—non-Muslim—influences, and the cure was seen in a return to the pure Islamic practices of the past. In this context, all things Western, including the Western education that had been imposed by the foreign conquerors and embraced by local elites, came to be considered a major source of corruption. "Boko Haram" means "Western education is religiously forbidden." As Oxford University scholar Daniel Agbiboa puts it, "The extent of relative poverty and inequality in the north has led several analysts and organizations to argue that socio-economic deprivation is the main factor behind Boko Haram's campaign of violence in northern Nigeria."[27]

Muslim activists have been protesting Nigeria's economic disequilibrium and calling for the revival of social strength through religion since the 1940s. The 1979 Islamic Revolution in Iran gave renewed hope that tyranny and marginalization could be overcome through the revival of Islam. Protests in the 1980s were brutally suppressed by the military and some activists associated the repression and brutality with the religion of the colonizers, resulting in sporadic anti-Christian reprisals. When governors in numerous northern Nigerian states attempted to impose Sharia law, some Christian minorities protested, resulting in violence and thousands of deaths. Boko Haram was heir to this poverty-fueled intercommunal hostility.

Boko Haram arose in 2002 under the leadership of Muhammad Yusuf (d. 2009), in the northern Nigerian state of Borno. Yusuf's fundamentalist teachings focused on rejecting anything associated with the imperialist West, including education, and replacing it with premodern Islamic practices. He also led an active uprising against the government and its representatives, all seen as agents of corruption, vice, and oppression. Benefitting from foreign donations for religious instruction, Yusuf established a network of mosques and religious schools in remoter regions of northern Nigeria, with the intention of recreating an independent Islamic state in the region. He attracted unemployed and equally aggrieved youth from across the region, especially those who share the dominant ethnic identities separated by foreign imposed borders between Nigeria, Niger, Cameroon, and Chad. As the movement grew, it began to attract more educated followers in urban centers, as well.

Rejecting the central government and any law except its own version of Islamic law, Boko Haram members actively violated Nigeria's secular laws and armed themselves for confrontation with the police. An altercation in 2009 escalated into reprisals against government installations and churches, resulting in over 700 deaths. Yusuf was arrested and killed under disputed circumstances while in custody. This proved a turning point for the group. Its new leadership established underground cells and conducted an escalating campaign of robberies and abductions, attacks on infrastructure, and more attacks on Christians and government installations. At the same time, it sought and received the attention of foreign terrorist groups, including al-Qaeda, providing volunteers for various regional conflicts, such as those in Mali, Algeria, and Libya. There is credible speculation based on Boko Haram's own claims that they have infiltrated Nigeria's military and security forces, as well, where the group's paramilitary forces can be useful in the pursuit of competing political agendas. Increased violence attributed to Boko Haram during and following the 2011 and 2015 elections supports this hypothesis.

The most notorious of Boko Haram's atrocities is the April 2014 abduction of 276 female students from a government school in Borno state. This and other kidnappings carried out by Boko Haram, like all other terrorist activities committed by self-proclaimed Muslims, have been universally condemned by Muslim authorities worldwide. But although 50 of the girls escaped, the rest have not been found. They remain victims of yet another grotesquely deviant group incubated in postcolonial economic and political chaos, whose members aspire to empowerment through military means, attracting attention by disrupting the lives of communities who would otherwise be oblivious to their existence. Boko Haram, like ISIS/ISIL/IS and other self-styled Islamic terrorist groups, use religious terms of reference. But Islam is not the source of their violence. As renowned Nigerian novelist Chinua Achebe (d. 2013) put it, the context for the rise of Boko Haram is the political instability arising from "economic deprivation and corruption" and "financial and social inequalities."[28]

There are other nonstate groups who self-identify as Islamic and are associated with terrorism, such as Palestinian Islamic Jihad, Hamas, and Hezbollah. But there is an essential distinction between these nationalist groups and transnational groups such as al-Qaeda, ISIS/ISIL/IS, and Boko Haram. Islamic Jihad in Palestine and Hamas are strictly Palestinian groups dedicated to fighting Israeli occupation of Palestinian territories in violation of United Nations Security Council resolutions since 1967. Islamic

Jihad in Palestine was established in 1981 under the influence of Egyptian militants who broke away from the Muslim Brotherhood, convinced that its nonviolent approach to reform was ineffective. Islamic Jihad in Palestine became known for suicide bombings in Israel, including the infamous 1989 Bus 405 attack that resulted in eighteen deaths. Hamas (an acronym for the Islamic Resistance Movement, *harakat al-muqawamah al-islamiyya*) was established in 1987, breaking away from its parent organization, the Palestinian Muslim Brotherhood, again because of the continued failure of peaceful means of conflict resolution. The most popular of Palestine's Islamist groups, Hamas devotes the greater part of its budget to social services for Palestinians living in destitution under Israeli control. But the group also supports a militia known for its rocket and suicide attacks on Israeli targets. Neither Islamic Jihad nor Hamas was the first group to introduce guerrilla tactics into the struggle for Palestinian independence. The secular Palestinian Liberation Organization (PLO), founded in 1964, established a political organization for the stateless Palestinians and sponsored attacks against Israel until 1993 when it agreed to abandon terrorism and join the still unsuccessful "peace process." The Marxist-Leninist Popular Front for the Liberation of Palestine (PFLP) was founded in 1967 by Dr. George Habash, a Christian, with the sole agenda of fighting Israeli occupation through guerrilla tactics, including aircraft hijackings. A Maoist faction broke away from the PFLP in 1969, founding the Democratic Front for the Liberation of Palestine (DFLP). Led by another Christian, Nayef Hawatmeh, the DFLP's most horrific act was the Ma'alot Massacre of 1974, a botched effort to free Palestinian fighters held in Israeli prisons, which resulted in the deaths of nearly thirty people, most of them children. But Islamic Jihad and Hamas are the first Palestinian resistance/terrorist groups that self-identify as Muslim. And although they receive financial support from other Arab states and Iran, their objectives are strictly nationalist; they seek to establish a Palestinian state.

Hezbollah is a Shia group established in Lebanon in 1982 to fight against Israeli occupation of southern Lebanon that began that year. From 1975 to 1990, Lebanon was involved in a complicated civil war that had provided "opportunity space" for Palestinian commandos to launch attacks on Israel in their national liberation struggle. Israel invaded Lebanon in June 1982 to drive Palestinians from that country. In September, a Lebanese Christian militia allied with Israel carried out a massacre in Sabra and Shatila Refugee Camp, leaving thousands of civilians dead. Then Israeli Defense Minister Ariel Sharon was forced to resign when an Israeli commission of inquiry concluded that he bore indirect responsibility. This was the context for the birth of Hezbollah. It was trained, equipped, and supported by the recently triumphant revolutionary Islamic Iran, in cooperation with Syria—itself ruled by a Shia minority allied with Iran, with territorial designs on Lebanon (which had been a part of Syria until the French created it as an independent state in 1943) and a grievance against Israel which maintains occupation of its Golan Heights. When Israel finally withdrew from southern Lebanon in 2000, Hezbollah transformed itself into a political party, competing effectively in Lebanese elections, but it continues to maintain a powerful militia. That militia has been drawn into the Syrian civil war, but its primary agenda is defense of Lebanon's roughly 30 percent Shia minority.

The defining characteristic of groups such as Islamic Jihad, Hamas, and Hezbollah, therefore, is that they are all focused on specific nationalist agendas. Each of them, furthermore, was founded after failures of secularist approaches to conflict resolution. None of them introduced militarism/ terrorism into their respective struggles; they were preceded by militant secular groups that failed to achieve their nationalist goals. It is not their Islamic identity that drives them to terrorism but rather the political and military failure of other approaches. Groups such as al-Qaeda, ISIS/ISIS/IS, and Boko Haram, on the other hand, with their international or transnational agendas and essentially terrorist agendas are recent and anomalous in the history of Islam. As noted previously, mainstream Muslims have universally condemned their atrocious acts, beginning with the 9/11 al-Qaeda attacks on New York and Washington DC. Given Hamas's Palestinian nationalist agenda and the Israel's illegal occupation of Palestine, its authorities justify terrorist acts against Israelis as legitimate resistance. But even they joined with the leaders of the Muslim Brotherhood, Jamaat-i Islami, Tunisia's al-Nahda Party, the Islamic Party of Malaysia (PAS), and forty other major Islamist authorities and political leaders—three days after the 9/11 attacks—issuing the following statement:

> The undersigned, leaders of the Islamic movement, are horrified by the events of Tuesday 11 September 2001 in the United States which resulted in massive killing, destruction and attack on innocent lives. We express our deepest sympathies and sorrow. We condemn, in the strongest terms, the incidents, which are against all human and Islamic norms. This is grounded in the Noble Laws of Islam which forbid all forms of attacks on innocents. God Almighty says in the Holy Qur'an: "No bearer of burdens can bear the burden of another" (Surah al-Isra 17:15).

The same day the leader of Lebanon's Shiite Muslims noted, "Besides the fact that they are forbidden by Islam, these acts do not serve those who carried them out but their victims, who will reap the sympathy of the whole world. ... Islamists who live according to the human values of Islam could not commit such crimes." The next day, the chief religious authority in Saudi Arabia issued a similar statement through the kingdom's U.S. embassy:

> Firstly: the recent developments in the United States including hijacking planes, terrorizing innocent people and shedding blood, constitute a form of injustice that cannot be tolerated by Islam, which views them as gross crimes and sinful acts. Secondly: any Muslim who is aware of the teachings of his religion and who adheres to the directives of the Holy Qur'an and the sunnah (teachings of the Prophet Muhammad) will never involve himself in such acts, because they will invoke the anger of God Almighty and lead to harm and corruption on earth.

Hundreds of such condemnations have been issued since then. In February 2008, in fact, the rector of the conservative Dar ul-Ulum madrasa in Deoband, India, often associated with support for the Taliban, organized an "Anti-Terrorism Convention," issuing the following statement: "We condemn all forms of terrorism ... and in this we make no distinction. Terrorism is completely wrong, no matter who engages in it, and no matter what religion he follows or community he belongs to."[29]

Conclusion: Asking the Right Questions

Returning to the question suggested at the beginning of this chapter, it is clear that Islam is not the source of terrorism and mainstream Islamists are not terrorists. But allegations to the contrary propagated by political leaders who are opposed to the democratic demands of mainstream Islamists are common. As we saw in the case of Tunisia, claiming that Islamists are terrorists can effectively rationalize suppression of Islamists' pro-democracy demands. This has been true in Egypt, as well.

Egypt, home of the ancient pharaohs, was ruled by outsiders for most of its post-pharaoh history: Assyrians, Persians, Greeks, Romans, Arabs, Turks, and the British. As we saw in Chapter 4, it is also the birthplace of the Arab world's oldest and most widespread Islamist movement, the Muslim Brotherhood. The Brotherhood had been active in demanding not only independence from the British since its founding in 1928 but also economic reforms and democracy. These demands led to their suppression and government confiscation of their assets. They also led them to support the movement led by Lt. Col. Gamal Abdel Nasser to overthrow the oppressive, foreign-supported government. On the success of the coup on July 23, 1952 that finally ended British rule in Egypt Muslim Brotherhood leaders publicly reminded Egypt of the Brotherhood's objectives: government-provided social services, education for all Egyptians, male and female; redistribution of land from feudal lords to peasants; protection of labor; and democratic elections for a civilian government. Nasser's government stalled, but the Brotherhood kept up the pressure, leading student demonstrations demanding civilian government. In January of 1954, Nasser's government banned political parties, declared the Brotherhood dissolved, and had Brotherhood leaders arrested. Again, Muslim Brotherhood support for social justice and democracy resulted in its suppression.

The Brotherhood would spend most of the twentieth century as a banned organization. But it maintained its nonviolent stance, even as discontented factions radicalized and split off from the group forming their own militant organizations. As we saw, those militants were responsible for the assassination of Nasser's successor Anwar Sadat in 1981 and increased terrorism in the 1990s. As had happened during Nasser's time, the government painted mainstream nonviolent Islamists with the brush of radicalism and terrorism. Tens of thousands were imprisoned; reports of torture were routine.

Yet the Brotherhood survived. Many members ran successfully as independents in the country's highly controlled elections, and the group continued to provide much-needed social services such as health care and education. When the 2010 Dignity Revolution erupted in Tunisia, successfully toppling that country's longstanding dictatorship, Egyptians were emboldened to start their own popular revolution. The beating death of a young computer programmer in a cybercafé was the trigger; as had happened in Tunisia, a social media campaign sent hundreds of thousands into the streets. Mass protests brought sufficient pressure on the government to force the resignation of the long-time Western-backed rule of Hosni Mubarak. That was in February 2011.

The Egyptian uprising was not led by the Muslim Brotherhood. But during its decades of suppression it had developed an effective organization with deep and widespread networks of popular support. It was therefore well positioned to campaign successfully and get out the vote. The Muslim

Brotherhood's Freedom and Justice Party (FJP) candidates dominated Egypt's first-ever truly democratic elections. But Egypt's military-dominated bureaucracy was still well entrenched. A "Supreme Council of the Armed Forces" (SCAF) had taken immediate control of the government following Hosni Mubarak's resignation. Popular protests demanded elections. A People's Assembly was elected by mid-January 2012, surviving SCAF efforts to disband it. That summer, presidential elections yielded victory—by a slim margin—for Muslim Brotherhood leader Muhammad Morsi. In the following months, the elected government struggled to develop a constitution acceptable to the majority of Egyptians, while Mubarak regime remnants and the military worked relentlessly to undermine the effectiveness of the Brotherhood-led government. Political missteps on the part of Morsi's government, a deepening economic crisis, and sectarian attacks by radicalized elements led to political chaos in Egypt by late 2012.

A generously funded counterrevolutionary group, Tamarrod ("rebellion") came forward in April 2013 demanding new presidential elections. Mass demonstrations and street violence increased and, with them, demands for Morsi to step down. One year after Morsi's election, he was ousted in a military coup. Claiming that the Muslim Brotherhood were terrorists, the military chief Abdel Fattah al-Sisi took control of Egypt's government. Morsi and thousands of other Muslim Brotherhood members and associates were imprisoned; hundreds have been sentenced to death—including Morsi and other Brotherhood leaders—or lengthy prison sentences; others await trial. Pro-democracy and Brotherhood supporters continued to protest, but they were violently suppressed, their participants also accused of terrorism and imprisoned. A new constitution, hurriedly passed in January 2014, returned overwhelming power to the military and security forces in the name of fighting terrorism, and in May 2014 low voter turnout elections gave Gen. Sisi Egypt's presidency.

A cautionary tale indeed. Egyptians suffering the chaos of revolution and counter-revolution—like outside observers familiar only with headline-grabbing jihadists—may be excused for believing claims that the country's first democratically elected government had suddenly become terrorist. But scholars of Islam and Islamist movements know better. As recently as 2007 Washington DC's Center for the National Interest (formerly The Nixon Center) scholars Robert Leiken and Steven Brooke wrote that the Muslim Brotherhood has never been revolutionary. It has consistently called for "gradual and peaceful Islamization," as well as democracy and an independent judiciary. Citing influential Brotherhood leader Hassan al-Hudaybi (d. 1973),

Leiken and Brooke describe the Brotherhood's unequivocal rejection of the radicals' jihadi views. These, the authors note, "emerged under repression," and when denounced by mainstream leaders, the jihadists left the organization and formed their own cells. In fact, the authors claim, "Jihadists loathe the Muslim Brotherhood. ..."[30] So, too, do authoritarian rulers and others disinclined to entrust national governance to the body politic.

We also saw that in fact mainstream Muslims—Islamist and otherwise—condemn terrorism. Not only do Muslims constitute by far the majority of victims of so-called Islamic terrorism, but also, as Muslims' countless public statements condemning terrorism demonstrate, terrorism is in direct violation of both the spirit and letter of Islamic law. Yet Muslims find themselves increasingly judged on the basis of actions they condemn.

Indeed, among the most pressing concerns of Muslims today is how to deal with the Western world's apparent disrespect for Islam. Historical experiences have made Muslims extremely sensitive to ridicule of Islam, the religion, and its prophet, Muhammad. From its earliest history, Islam found itself dismissed as a false religion brought by a false prophet. Many Jews and Christians became Muslims, of course, and many others lived in peace, maintaining their religious identities in pluralist Islamic societies. But there were others outside the Muslim community who utterly rejected the legitimacy of Islam as a religion. As noted in Chapter 3, there is a long heritage of Christian lore extremely demeaning to Islam and Prophet Muhammad. The Crusades were launched to reclaim the Holy Land for Christianity from the Muslims, who were described as infidels—people with no true belief at all, rather than believers in a different religion. Colonial activity in the Muslim world was often accompanied by the work of missionaries and was therefore easily associated with efforts to eradicate Islam. We noted previously that Churchill attributed the ferocity of Afghans' and Sudanis' resistance to colonial rule not to nationalism but to the "retrograde force" of their religion.

More recently, when author Salman Rushdie published *The Satanic Verses* in 1988, a novel that parodied Prophet Muhammad and his family in extremely insulting ways, the book was hailed as a masterpiece in England and the United States. Shortly after the terrorist attacks of 9/11, U.S. Evangelical preacher the Reverend Franklin Graham called Islam "a very evil and wicked religion." Rev. Jerry Vines, past president of the U.S. Southern Baptist Convention, was quoted describing Muhammad as a "demon-possessed pedophile." In an appearance on the television program, *60 Minutes*, popular evangelist Jerry Falwell (d. 2007) described Prophet

Muhammad as "a violent man, a man of war," concluding, "I think Muhammad was a terrorist." Within two weeks, Falwell realized his offense and issued an apology, saying, "I intended no disrespect to any sincere, law-abiding Muslim." Leading Sunni authority Shaykh Tantawi then issued a public statement accepting the apology. Shii scholar Ayatollah Hussein Mousavi Tabrizi agreed, stating that "a person courageous enough to apologize for his errors is worthy of praise. It's humanitarian and good Islamic behavior to accept an apology from a person who admits making a mistake."[31] President George W. Bush spoke out against those who misrepresent Islam as a terrorist religion and who insult Prophet Muhammad. But the damage had been done. Riots broke out in India, resulting in a number of deaths, and anti-American sentiment clearly escalated in Pakistan. Within days after Falwell's statements, another statement was issued in the name of Bin Laden, attempting to convince Muslims not to be fooled; in his view, the West really seeks to destroy Islam. The statement referred to the U.S.-led "crusade against the Islamic world" and urged Muslims to unite to "defend the targeted faith, the violated sanctity, the tarnished honor, the raped land and the robbed riches. … [T]he Americans and the Jews … will not stop infringing upon us except through jihad."[32]

This is the background for radical reactions to insults to Islam, such as the 2005 Danish cartoons, the 2012 YouTube video "Innocence of Muslims," and highly irreverent cartoon characterizations of Muhammad in the French satirical magazine *Charlie Hebdo*. These depictions focused on aberrant sex and violence attributed to Muhammad and Muslims more generally, and all appeared in the context of the Global War on Terror, which has resulted in hundreds of thousands of civilian deaths. In September 2005, the Danish newspaper *Jyllands-Posten* published a series of cartoons ridiculing Prophet Muhammad. When Muslims protested, the cartoons were reprinted in dozens of newspapers and journals around the world, including *Charlie Hebdo*. "The Innocence of Muslims," filmed in the United States, prompted widespread peaceful protests as well as a series of attacks on diplomatic missions worldwide including, allegedly, the attack on the U.S. mission in Benghazi, Libya, that killed Ambassador Christopher Stevens and three other Americans. *Charlie Hebdo*, known for ridiculing all religions, published not only the Danish cartoons but also a series of insulting depictions of Muhammad in subsequent years. In January 2015, two brothers claiming affiliation with al-Qaeda's Yemen branch stormed the journal's Paris offices and opened fire, killing twelve and wounding eleven others.

Muslims worldwide continue to condemn such atrocities. The most popular Sunni authority in the world today, for example, Egyptian Sheikh Yusuf al-Qaradawi, proclaimed, "We, scholars of the Islamic nation, strongly condemn any action that sheds the blood of innocents, spreading corruption on earth, whoever the perpetrators are and whatever their religion."[33] Nevertheless, although Muslims recognize the right of free expression, the negative depictions seem gratuitously insulting and, in the context of war, highly inflammatory.

Steadfast support for Israel despite its violation of United Nations Security Council resolutions concerning the rights of people who happen to be predominantly Muslims, and ongoing military campaigns in Afghanistan, Iraq, and beyond, are easily interpreted by radicals as part of a campaign to destroy Islam. That conviction has resulted in attacks against Christians in some parts of the Muslim world. In Egypt and Pakistan, churches and even Western aid workers have been attacked. These attacks, like those on the United States on 9/11, were committed by people convinced that Islam is under dire threat. Terrorist tracts invariably attempt to inflame emotions and recruit followers by recounting the suffering of Muslims at the hands of those who ridicule and want to destroy the religion. But again, the views of the majority of Muslims are represented in the unequivocal condemnations of terrorism by Islamic authorities around the world.

Although terrorists attempt to exploit stereotyping for their own purposes, the far more common reaction to ongoing conflict and misrepresentations of Islam is increased effort on the part of Muslims to represent Islam in ways they believe are authentic. They deplore the "hijacking" not just of jets, but of Islam itself by terrorists and radicals. They reject the right of fanatics to define Islam. Muslims living in the West particularly feel the responsibility to take the initiative to speak out against radicalism and in favor of Islamic values of peace, tolerance, and commitment to justice. Muslim scholars have been producing works in English and European languages for decades, generally for academic audiences. But since 9/11, the need for discourse among everyday believers has become glaringly apparent, particularly in the United States. At countless interfaith gatherings in communities throughout the country, Muslims have attempted to present their faith to Americans whose only exposure to Islam has been the kind that makes headlines.

Typical of these efforts is a collection published right after 9/11 by concerned Muslims: *Taking Back Islam*.[34] The collection includes essays by Muslims from all walks of life who felt they simply could not allow the

Figure 7 The mosque of Shaykh Lutfallah (1603–1619) in Isfahan.
Source: © Mark Daffey / Getty Images

"moral nihilism" of terrorism to be associated with Islam. Michael Wolfe explains the rationale for publishing the book: "We knew something had to be done or our religion risked being tarnished, even corrupted." He cites the frustration U.S. Muslims feel when "anti-American fanatics quote the Qur'an to justify mass murder, and … anti-Muslim bigots quote it back—both sides using bad translations and phrases out of context. … [W]e have sought to replace them with a truer interpretation: that Islam is a peaceful, progressive, inherently forgiving and compassionate religion. Anyone who believes otherwise misses the core values of Islam."[35]

The great play of Islamic history outlined above—from the formative period, through the medieval flowering of Islamic culture, the decline, colonization, and modern recovery efforts—is fascinating in its drama and breathtaking in its scope. But it scarcely reflects the enduring faith of Muslims in everyday life. Many Muslims, in fact, question the description of contemporary reformism as something new or out of the ordinary. For them, Islam is essentially reformist, encouraging humanity to constantly struggle to prefect itself. As such, it has endured as a daily, lived experience of faith in God's power, benevolence, compassion, and mercy. With that faith, Muslims face the challenges of daily life. The effects of centuries of political conflict and the impression of spectacular criminal acts will no doubt take time to fade. But the efforts of devout Muslims to reflect their faith in daily life continues, guided by revelation—summarized eloquently in the popular Quranic verse cited previously:

> It is not a matter of piety
> that you turn your faces to the East or West.
> Righteous is the one who
> believes in God and the Last Day,
> the angels, Scripture, and the prophets;
> gives wealth, however cherished,
>   to relatives and orphans,
> the needy, travelers, and beggars,
>   and for freeing slaves;
> and prays and gives zakat.
> And those who fulfill their promises
> when they make them, and are patient in
>   misfortune, hardship and peril –
> these are the ones who are sincere;
> these are the righteous ones.

(2:177)

Notes

1. Salon Staff, "Bill Maher: Islam's 'the only religion that acts like the mafia. ...'" *Salon*, October 4, 2014, http://www.salon.com/2014/10/04/bill_maher_islams_the_only_ religion_that_acts_like_the_mafia_that_will_fking_kill_you_if_you_say_the_ wrong_thing/.
2. Michael W. Chapman. "Rev. Franklin Graham: Islam 'Is a Religion of War." *csnnews.com*, December 10, 2014, http://www.cnsnews.com/blog/michael-w-chapman/rev-franklin-graham-islam-religion-war.
3. Nathan Lean, "Richard Dawkins Does It Again: New Atheisms' Islamophobia Problem." *Salon*, August 10, 2013, http://www.salon.com/2013/08/10/richard_ dawkins_does_it_again_new_atheisms_islamophobia_problem/.
4. Winston Churchill, *The Story of the Malakand Field Force: An Episode of Frontier War* (New York: Dover Books, 2012. Republication of 1916 edition published by Thomas Nelson & Sons, Ltd., London, Edinburgh, and New York.)

5. Winston Churchill, *The River War* (London: Longmans, Green & Company, 1899): Vol. II: 248ff.

6. Mohammed Reza Shah, *Mission for My Country* (New York: McGraw-Hill, 1960), 171.

7. Mehran Kamrava, *The Modern Middle East: A Political History Since the First World War*, 3rd ed. (Berkeley: University of California Press, 2013), 145.

8. Quoted in Michael M. J. Fischer, "Imam Khomeini: Four Levels of Understanding" in John L. Esposito, ed., *Voices of Resurgent Islam*, 154, from *Zendigi-Nameh, Imam Khomeini* (Teheran: Fifteenth of Khordad Publishers, n.d.), II:38–43.

9. Imam Khomeini, *Islam and Revolution: Writings and Declarations of Imam Khomeini*. Trans. and annotated by H. Algar (London: KPI, 1985), 187.

10. Khomeini, *Islam and Revolution*, 210–211.

11. Statement by H. E. Seyyed Mohammad Khatami, President of the Islamic Republic of Iran and Chairman of the Eighth Session of the Islamic Summit Conference, Tehran, Dec. 9, 1997; http://www.undp.org/missions/iran/new.html.

12. Mohammad Khatami, *Hope and Challenge: The Iranian President Speaks* (Binghamton, NY: Institute of Global Cultural Studies, Binghamton University, 1997), 77–78.

13. "U.S. Still Believes Iran Not on the Verge of a Nuclear Weapon." *Reuters*, August 9, 2012, http://www.reuters.com/article/2012/08/09/us-israel-iran-usa-idUS BRE8781GS20120809.

14. http://www.hrw.org/sites/default/files/wr2013_web.pdf

15. Zogby Research Services, LLC, "Iranian Attitudes, September 2013." http://www.zogbyresearchservices.com/blog/2013/12/6/zrs-releases-september-2013-iran-poll. Accessed October 23, 2014.

16. Gheissari and Nasr, *Democracy in Iran: History and the Quest for Liberty* (New York: Oxford University Press, 2009), 158. See also Nader Hashemi, "Religious Disputation and Democratic Constitutionalism: The Enduring Legacy of the Constitutional Revolution on the Struggle for Democracy in Iran." *Constellations* 17, no. 1 (2010): 50–60.

17. Hafeez Malik, ed., *Pakistan: Founders' Aspirations and Today's Realities* (Oxford: Oxford University Press, 2001), 5–6.

18. Shibzada Masul-ul-Hassan Khan Sabri, *The constitution of Pakistan, 1973 (with All Amendments up to 1994)* (Lahore: Publishers' Emporium, 1994), 24–25.

19. Patrick Keatley, "The Brown Bomb," Manchester *Guardian*, March 11, 1965.

20. Abul A'la Mawdudi, *Islamic Law and Constitution*, ed. and trans. Khurshid Ahmad (Lahore: Islamic Publications, 1967), 172; 158.

21. http://www.pewglobal.org/2014/08/7/a-less-gloomy-mood-in-pakistan/.

22. See "Most Muslims Want Democracy, Personal Freedoms, and Islam in Political Life," Pew Research Center Global Attitudes & Trends, July 10, 2012.

http://www.pewglobal.org/2012/07/10/most-muslims-want-democracy-personal-freedoms-and-islam-in-political-life/.

23. See Samuel P. Huntington, *The Clash of Civilizations and the Remaking of World Order* (New York: Simon & Schuster, 2011).

24. See http://www.lettertobaghdadi.com/. Various Muslim groups around the globe have spoken out as well, launching, for example, the "Not in My Name" campaign on YouTube, https://www.youtube.com/watch?v=hAxIOC8Zisc.

25. Patrick Cockburn, *The Rise of the Islamic State: ISIS and the New Sunni Revolution* (New York: Verso, 2014), 8.

26. Michael Guntner, Till Paasche, and Nahro Zagros, "Understanding ISIS," *Journal of South Asian and Middle Eastern Studies* 38, no. 2 (Winter 2015): 1.

27. Daniel Agbiboa, "The Ongoing Campaign of Terror in Nigeria: Boko Haram versus the State," *Stability: International Journal of Security & Development* 2 no. 3: 8.

28. Chinua Achebe, *There Was a Country* (New York: Penguin, 2013): 250–251.

29. A collection of anti-terrorism statements may be found at http://www.unc.edu/~kurzman/terror.htm.

30. Robert S. Leiken and Steven Brooke, "The Moderate Muslim Brotherhood," *Foreign Affairs* 86, no. 2 (March/April 2007): 107–121.

31. Alan Cooperman, "Christian Leaders' Remarks Against Islam Spark Backlash; Anti-American Feelings Intensify in Muslim Countries." *Washington Post*. Oct. 15, 2002, A16.

32. "Excerpts of Purported Statement by Bin Laden," *Washington Post*. Oct. 15, 2002, A14.

33. "Muslim Reaction to the Charlie Hebdo Massacre." www.judaism-islam.com/muslim-reaction-to-the-charlie-hebdo-massacre. (January 8, 2015). Accessed July 19, 2015.

34. Michael Wolfe, ed., *Taking Back Islam: American Muslims Reclaim Their Faith* (New York: Rodale, 2002).

35. Wolf, *Taking Back Islam*, xi.

Further Reading

Art and Architecture

Blair, Sheila, and Jonathan Bloom. *The Art and Architecture of Islam, 1250–1800*. New Haven, CT: Yale University Press, 1994.

Ettinghausen, Richard, Oleg Grabar, and Marilyn Jenkins-Madina. *Islamic Art and Architecture 650–1250*, 2nd ed. New Haven, CT: Yale University Press, 2003.

Fathy, Hassan. *Architecture for the Poor: An Experiment in Rural Egypt*. Chicago: University of Chicago Press, 1976.

Hoag, John D. *Islamic Architecture*, 3rd ed. U.S. Ed. London: Phaidon Press/Electra, 2004.

D. Fairchild Ruggles. *Islamic Art and Visual Culture: An Anthology of Sources*. Oxford: Wiley-Blackwell, 2011.

Current Affairs

Bayat, Asef, ed. *Post-Islamism: The Changing Faces of Political Islam*. New York: Oxford University Press, 2013.

Cockburn, Patrick, *The Rise of Islamic State*. New York: Verso, 2015.

Esposito, John L., Tamara Sonn, John O. Voll. *Islam and Democracy After the Arab Spring*. New York: Oxford University Press, 2016.

Islam: History, Religion, and Politics, Third Edition. Tamara Sonn.
© 2016 John Wiley & Sons, Ltd. Published 2016 by John Wiley & Sons, Ltd.

Hashemi, Nader. *Islam, Secularism, and Liberal Democracy*. New York: Oxford University Press, 2012.

Jalal, Ayesha. *The Struggle for Pakistan: A Muslim Homeland and Global Politics*. Cambridge, MA: Belknap Press/Harvard University Press, 2014.

Mandaville, Peter. *Global Political Islam*. London: Routledge, 2007.

Ramadan, Tariq. *Islam and the Arab Awakening*. New York: Oxford University Press, 2012.

Rashid, Ahmed. *Taliban: Militant Islam, Oil and Fundamentalism in Central Asia*. Waterville, ME: Thorndike Press, 2002.

Rubin, Barry. *Political Islam: Critical Concepts in Islamic Studies*. London: Routledge, 2007.

Smith, Jane I. *Islam in America*. New York: Columbia University Press, 1999.

History

Armstrong, Karen, *Islam: A Short History*. New York: Modern Library, 2002.

Esposito, John L. (ed.). *The Oxford History of Islam*. New York: Oxford University Press, 1999.

Hitti, Philip K. *History of the Arabs: From the Earliest Times to the Present*. New York: Palgrave Macmillan, 2002.

Hourani, Albert H. *A History of the Arab Peoples*, Cambridge, MA: Belknap Press/ Harvard University Press, 2002.

Jenkins, Everett. *The Muslim Diaspora: A Comprehensive Reference to the Spread of Islam in Asia, Africa, Europe and the Americas*. Jefferson, NC: McFarland, 1999.

Robinson, Francis. *Cambridge Illustrated History of the Islamic World*. New York: Cambridge University Press, 1996.

Literature

Burton, Richard Francis. *The Arabian Nights: Tales from a Thousand and One Nights*. New York: Modern Library, 2001.

Gibran, Khalil. *The Eye of the Prophet*. Berkeley, CA: Frog, 1995.

Khayyam, Omar. *Rubaiyat of Omar Khayyam*. Broomall, PA: Chelsea House, 2003.

Philosophy

Adamson, Peter, and Richard Taylor (eds.). *The Cambridge Companion to Arabic Philosophy*. Cambridge: Cambridge University Press, 2005.

Campanini, M. *An Introduction to Islamic Philosophy*. Edinburgh: Edinburgh University Press, 2008.

Fakhry, Majid. *A History of Islamic Philosophy*. New York: Columbia University Press, 2004.

Reference

Belt, Don. *World of Islam*. Washington, DC: National Geographic, 2001.

Esposito, John L. (ed.). *The Oxford Dictionary of Islam*. New York: Oxford University Press, 2003.

Esposito, John L. (ed.). *The Oxford Encyclopedia of the Islamic World*. New York: Oxford University Press, 2009.

Glasse, Cyril. *The Concise Encyclopedia of Islam*. San Francisco: Harper & Row, 1989.

Leaman, Oliver (ed.). *The Qur'an: An Encyclopedia*. London: Routledge, 2006.

McAuliffe, Jane Dammen (ed.). *Cambridge Companion to the Qur'an*. Cambridge: Cambridge University Press, 2006.

McAuliffe, Jane Dammen (ed.). *Encyclopedia of the Qur'an*. Leiden: Brill, 2001–2007.

Rippin, Andrew (ed.). *The Blackwell Companion to the Qur'an*, Oxford: Blackwell, 2015.

Religion

Ali, Ahmed. *Al-Quran. A Contemporary Translation*. Princeton, NJ: Princeton University Press, 2001.

Armstrong, Karen. *Muhammad: A Biography of the Prophet*. San Francisco: Harper, 1992.

Mattson, Ingrid. *The Story of the Qur'an: Its History and Place in Muslim Life*. Oxford: Blackwell, 2008.

Nasr, Seyyed Hossein. *The Garden of Truth: The Vision and Promise of Sufism, Islam's Mystical Tradition*. San Francisco: HarperOne, 2007.

Nasr, Vali. *The Shia Revival: How Conflicts within Islam Will Shape the Future*. New York: Norton, 2006.

Neusner, Jacob, and Tamara Sonn. *Comparing Religions through Law: Judaism and Islam*. London: Routledge, 1999.

Sachedina, Abdulaziz, and Joseph Montville. *The Islamic Roots of Democratic Pluralism*. New York: Oxford University Press, 2001.

Rahman, Fazlur. *Major Themes of the Quran*. Minneapolis, MN: Bibliotheca Islamica, 1980.

Ramadan, Tariq. *In the Footsteps of the Prophet: Lessons from the Life of Muhammad*. New York: Oxford University Press, 2009.

Schimmel, Annemarie. *Mystical Dimensions of Islam*. Chapel Hill: University of North Carolina Press, 1975.

Science

Nasr, Seyyed Hossein. *Islamic Science: An Illustrated Study*. London: World of Islam Festival Publishing Company, 1976.

Saliba, George. *Islamic Science and the Making of the European Renaissance*. Cambridge, MA: MIT Press, 2007.

Women

Abu-Lughod, Lila. *Do Muslim Women Need Saving?* Cambridge, MA: Harvard University Press, 2013.

Ahmed, Leila. *Women and Gender in Islam: Historical Roots of a Modern Debate*. New Haven, CT: Yale University Press, 1992.

Stowasser, Barbara Freyer. *Women in the Quran: Traditions and Interpretation*. New York: Oxford University Press, 1994.

Websites

IslamOnline Network: Islamic news, articles, fatwas, and business www.islam online.com.

Oxford Bibliographies Online: Islamic Studies www.oxfordbibliographieson line.com.

Oxford Islamic Studies Online: Reference works, Quranic studies resources, teaching resources www.oxfordislamicstudies.com.

Statements against Terrorism: Compendium of Islamic statements against terror www.unc.edu/~kurzman/Terror.htm.

University of Southern California Muslim Students Association: Quranic studies and other religious sources for Muslim students www.usc.edu/dept/MSA/.

Index

Note: Page numbers in italics refer to Figures.

Islam: History, Religion, and Politics, Third Edition. Tamara Sonn.
© 2016 John Wiley & Sons, Ltd. Published 2016 by John Wiley & Sons, Ltd.

Printed and bound by CPI Group (UK) Ltd, Croydon, CR0 4YY

13/04/2025

14656463-0002